GW00537353

"Ut in omnibus glorificetur Deus"

"In all things may God be glorified"

༄

The Miracles
of
Father Paul of Moll

The Medal
of
Saint Benedict

The Life
of
Saint Benedict

Caritas Publishing

Published in French in 1898 as *Quelques traits de la vie du Très-Révérend Père Paul, de Moll, bénédictin, 1824-1896.*
Translated into English in 1910 as *The Very Rev. Father Paul of Moll.*
Republished August 29, 2017, Feast of the Passion of St. John the Baptist.
Some material has been reorganized.
Footnotes have been updated.
Devotions noted in the text have been added in an Appendix.
A novena in honor of Fr. Paul has been added.

Paperback ISBN: 978-1-945275-43-2

CONTENTS

BOOK ONE

The Miracles of

Father Paul of Moll

EDWARD VAN SPEYBROUCK

Nihil Obstat
FROWINUS
Abbas Neo-Angelo Montanus

Imprimatur
✠ MAURITIUS
Episcopus Sancti Josephi

St. Joseph, Mo., March 4, 1910

The Very Reverend
FATHER PAUL OF MOLL
(Born Francis Luyckx)

Born at Moll, January 15, 1824
Entered the Benedictine Monastery of Termonde, June 25, 1846
Invested with the religious habit, August 24, 1848
Made his vows, September 30, 1849
Ordained Priest at Parma, Italy, November 21, 1858
Intrusted with the re-establishment of the abbey of Afflighcm,
   March 16, 1869
Founded the Monastery of Steenbrugge, September 21, 1874
Died at the Abbey of Termonde, February 24, 1896

MIRACLES OF FATHER PAUL

PRELIMINARY REMARKS

In accordance with the decrees of Pope Urban VIII., in the years 1634 and 1641, we claim for the wonderful facts herein related, no more than human credence. Therefore the author, translator, and publishers, most humbly submit all herein contained to the judgment and approval of holy Mother Church.

These facts were published during the lifetime of the witnesses, and their names and testimony submitted to proper Ecclesiastical Authority.

ᴄᴡᴐ

A Farmer's Wife

living in the neighborhood of Brussels, suffered from a diseased member of her body, which the attending physicians declared incurable. The patient, hearing of the marvelous cures wrought at the monastery of Termonde, sent her sister to Father Paul, who said to her, "You have come to ask for the cure of your sister." "Yes," she replied, astonished at the Father's discernment. "And your sister, treated in vain by the doctors, implores the aid of St. Benedict." "Yes, Father, but how are you aware of that?" "I know it through my holy Father St. Benedict, and he will cure your sister." He gave her some medals and holy water for her sister, who soon after was miraculously cured.

ᴄᴡᴐ

Two Brothers, Engineers,

write from Malines, in the year 1887, as follows:—

"One of our sisters, as a result of a cold, contracted a facial paralysis. Her physician exhausted his medical skill in her behalf; but, despite his efforts, the dread disease spread over the entire left side of her face. Her left eye remained open day and night, she could no longer close her mouth, and her lips became contorted.

"We came to see Father Paul, related her sad condition, and told him that we depended solely on him to obtain her recovery. He seemed much interested in her case, but instead of holding out any hope, he bade us visit a person in the vicinity, and return to him. When we called, it was seven o'clock, and the bell was tolling the evening *Angelus*. He said to us, 'Be quiet, I pray.'

"Such was the tone of Father Paul's voice, that we were assured of his prayers being heard.

"And, indeed, the very moment our sister recited the *Angelus* in Malines, she experienced an extraordinary sensation. Her eye recovered its former activity, the contortion of her mouth disappeared, and she was cured."

ᑐᑌᑐ

An Offical from Thielt

brought to Father Paul his daughter, age seven years, who was suffering from a painful complaint in the nose, which defied all relief. The Father prescribed a novena to St. Benedict, and told him to apply some water, in which he placed a medal of St. Benedict, to the child's nose. In a few days the pain had left her.

This same official also spoke to Father Paul about his little son who was so weak that he was unable to hold himself erect, and it was feared that he would become a hunchback. Father Paul replied saying, the boy would be cured. He prescribed a novena and the use of St. Benedict's medal, and requested the man to tell his wife she ought to wear her scapular, and not leave it hanging on the bedpost.

In fact, the woman did have the careless habit of hanging her scapular on the bedpost. The little boy was cured, and later on entered a military school.

ᑐᑌᑐ

An Afflicted Lady of Bruges

tells how she was cured through the mediation of Father Paul.

"In 1886, I had been confined to my bed for fourteen months by rheumatism. I had lost all control of my lower limbs; the pain was unendurable, and the physician declared that nothing less than a miracle could cure me.

"My husband lifted me into a small wagon, and conveyed me to the monastery, where we were met by Father Paul.

"'You remain,' he said to my husband, 'and look to your wagon, I will attend to your wife.' He then took me by the arm, bade me put my feet on the ground, led me up the four steps to the entrance, and, I found myself quite comfortably seated in the parlor.

"'You are indeed in a serious condition: no blood circulates through your limbs, nothing but water; but you shall be cured after several novenas.'

"Father Paul put on his stole, and for some time prayed fervently, amid intense anguish, his forehead bathed with perspiration. When he put his hands on my head, I felt a sudden shock through my entire body. Suddenly I felt relief; and within a month, I was completely healed. The physician beholding me, thus restored to perfect health, desired to know what wonderful remedy had brought about my cure. When I told him what Father Paul had done he exclamed, 'Ah! did I not tell you, that the physicians of the Most High know these things far better than we do.'"

◌

A Young Lady from Ursel

often brought sick persons to Father Paul from whom they all obtained relief. At each visit he gave her a handful of Benedictine medals, assuring her that the sick persons to whom she would give or send a medal would be cured, provided that they used them with confidence.

On one of her visits, the Rev. Father gave her some leaflets on which were printed the beautiful "Salutation to Mary," which he was so fond of distributing. She was to keep one herself and give the others to the members of her family. Then she asked for another to give to a friend of hers, but Father Paul said, "No, no, that young lady won't recite this prayer."

The girl eventually went astray.

In Zele

there was a boy who was doubly afflicted. He had a hump on his back, caused by the dislocation of a bone; and one of his feet was turned inwards. His two sisters brought him to Termonde. Father Paul pressed the hump with his hand, and applied thereto some holy water. He then took hold of the twisted foot, and straightened it, without any apparent effort. And to their amazement and joy he placed their brother on the floor—completely cured.

Having expressed their gratitude for this sudden cure, one of the sisters told Father Paul, that she desired to enter an institution as a boarder, but did not possess the required sum of money. "I need two thousand francs," she said, "and have but the small share of the inheritance left by my deceased parents."

"Don't you know of any wealthy relative?" asked Father Paul.

"No, I do not know of any."

"Well, then, make inquiries and when you have found one, apply to him; he will give you what you need."

After a long search she found a distant relative, a rich cousin, to whom she made known her desire to enter the institution and her lack of means. She did not mention how much money she needed.

"The last two nights," replied her cousin, "I have had the same dream. Some one came and told me to give nineteen hundred francs to a person in need of it. . . .You must be the person. Here is the money." And, in truth, nineteen hundred francs was the exact amount the girl required.

A Possessed Woman

desiring the assistance of Father Paul to free her from the evil spirits, made the journey on foot to consult him. As she was crossing a certain bridge, she heard an unearthly sound; then an invisible hand seized her and threw her into the water. She succeeded in saving herself. As she entered the monastery, Father Paul thus addressed her: —

"You suffered much at the bridge." "Yes, Rev. Father." "And you were thrown into the water." "Yes," answered the woman, astonished at the Father's insight. "That was the last effort of the devil, the last attack of Satan; you are welcome here, and you will soon be delivered from his assaults."

Father Paul prayed over her, and the happy woman immediately recovered her liberty.

∾

Certain Parents

had lost all their children while still young, except one infant whom the servant, accompanied by its mother, carried to Father Paul that he might bless it. He requested the mother to take the baby in her own arms; and at the same moment, the servant mysteriously disappeared. Father Paul then bade the lady never again permit the servant to enter her house, as she was the cause of all her misfortunes.

∾

To an Acquaintance

from St. Michel, Father Paul said that near the monastery he had met a young girl who was coming to be cured. A few paces away he saw a demon leave the girl and flee, while at the same instant the patient cried aloud, "I am cured!"

∾

Fortunate Recruits.

As the time to enlist for military service drew near, many recruits had recourse to Father Paul that they might draw a lucky number to exempt them from being enrolled as soldiers. Those who complied with his directions were never disappointed.

These were the usual conditions: to make a novena in honor of St. Benedict; to wear a Benedictine medal; and to attach a second medal inside the sleeve, near the wrist of the hand with which they were to draw the number.

Father Paul supplied the medals, and sometimes foretold the number that would fall to their lot.

We here insert a few instances that have come to our knowledge.

∽

A Farmer from Oostcamp

urged his nephew, who was to be drafted, to follow the directions which Father Paul would give him; and the Father foretold a number that favored him.

The farmer gave the same advice to another nephew who was soon to enlist. Father Paul said, "Oh, you will draw the second or third highest number!" and he drew 187, the highest being 189.

Another recruit from Oostcamp who sought counsel from Father Paul declared, "The moment I put my hand into the urn, I felt a number adhere to it, and it was a fortunate number for me."

The same happened to a recruit from St. Michel.

A laborer living in Oostcamp, before drawing for enlistment, made his confession to Father Paul; and he mentioned that he had a great aversion to military service.

The Rev. Father bade him recite five Our Fathers and five Hail Marys every evening for two weeks. He added, "You will draw a good number, 134." And it happened as he had foretold.

∽

An Exceptional Case

has come to our knowledge. A recruit who had commended himself to Father Paul by letters, received the reply, "Count upon me."

The young man contrary to his expectations, drew one of the lowest numbers. He communicated the sad news to Father Paul, who sent him the following answer:

"We must always joyfully submit to the holy will of God; when in fervent prayer, we ask a favor of the Almighty, no matter what may happen, the final result will always be good, as you will realize later."

Let the young man relate his experience: "When I presented myself for medical examination, and was about to remove my clothing, both physicians, who were engaged in writing, without even looking at me, cried out, "Too weak! March on!"

To secure Father Paul's intervention, it was necessary, that a real cause for exemption from military service exist, but no recruit need enter into detail, as Father Paul was as well acquainted with the circumstances as the person interested.

⌒⌣⌒

A Woman of Oostcamp

had a son who was enrolled in the army. A neighbor advised her to seek Father Paul's intercession. "I dare not," she replied. "Well, I am acquainted with Father Paul," said her neighbor, "and we will go together." Father Paul thus questioned the woman: "Is your son well behaved?" "Yes, Rev. Father." "And does he never blaspheme?" "Never." "Then he shall draw a lucky number; and in two years your other son shall likewise draw a good number,"—and it came to pass in both cases, as Father Paul had foretold.

A farmer from the same place said to Father Paul, "I have three cousins who are enrolled for enlistment this year, would you do me the favor to procure a fortunate number for them?" "Yes, but never for the blasphemer." Two drew numbers that exempted them: but the third, who was a blasphemer, failed, because he was addicted to blasphemy.

Father Paul said, "I can never obtain anything for those who are in the habit of cursing and blaspheming."

⌒⌣⌒

A Lady from Bruges

states that her eldest son was to present himself for enlistment, and she had recourse to Father Paul. He told her that her son would draw an unlucky number. "But be not alarmed, your son will not become a soldier." The son drew a number whereby he was exempted.

A second son, actuated by the same motive, also had recourse to Father Paul, who informed him that although he would draw an unfavorable number, he would nevertheless, escape enlistment.

"Your foot is not in a good condition. Is it not so?" "Yes, Rev. Father, it is swollen." "But that is not a sufficient cause; another malady will afflict it, which will render you unfit for military service." The foot became so diseased, that the young man was disqualified for the army.

࿊

A Girl from Antwerp

applied to Father Paul in behalf of her brother who was to be drafted. The Father made no promise, but added that he would pray that God's will might be done in regard to her brother. The young man unfortunately drew a number which forced him to enter the army; and his sister expressed to Father Paul her fears for her brother's future welfare. "Do not worry, your brother will behave himself. I shall pray for that." And indeed, the young soldier's conduct remained irreproachable.

࿊

During His Last Residence

at Termonde, Father Paul informed a friend from Oostcamp, that, whenever he wished to recommend any recruits seeking exemption from enlistment it would suffice to send him their names, with the date of drawing, and fortune would favor them.

A Lady,

accompanied by her servant, asked Father Paul to pray that her son, a student, might pass a good examination. The Rev. Father replied that if the young man would stop blaspheming he would be successful, and moreover, would soon have an opportunity of contracting a very happy marriage. The young man gave up his bad habit, and the predictions of the saintly Benedictine were verified. After the lady had stated her request, the servant with a nudge begged her mistress to intercede also for her.

Father Paul spoke up at once: "Ah, you also wish to ask a favor. You are thinking of getting married. Very well, but don't accept the young man you have in mind. He does not love his mother, and would not make you happy. Wait a little, and a better man will ask your hand." This prediction likewise came true.

⌒↜⌒

A Friend of Father Paul

advised an acquaintance, to seek Father Paul's assistance, as his daughter was cross-eyed, and his son was to draw for enlistment. The Rev. Father sent medals and instructions for their use. The girl's eyes were forthwith adjusted, and the son drew a lucky number.

⌒↜⌒

A Young Physician

writes, "In October 1889, I had to pass an examination, but as I knew but little of the subject matter, I called on Father Paul to ask his advice. He said to me, 'During the few days that still remain, work hard at your studies, then take the examination.'

"However, the dread of the coming ordeal prevented my accomplishing anything. In my despair I wrote to Father Paul stating that I could not possibly succeed. I asked for a reply but no answer came. On October 9th, I presented myself for the examination. Contrary to my expectations, I succeeded.

"Although it was impossible, humanly speaking, for the Rev. Father to know the result of the examination, I received the following letter from him on that very day:—
"Praised be Jesus Christ!"
Sir: There is only one happiness for man, and that is the one which he finds in God. One need not search for it; God gives us sufficient grace to find it. God is good: you shall soon have evident proofs of His goodness.' "
D. Paul, relig.
The same physician writes, "While I was a student at the university, I laid my Benedictine medal which I had received from Father Paul on the table one night before going to bed, the next morning I discovered that it had disappeared. To my great surprise I received a letter from Father Paul the same day, inclosing a medal which he advised me *to wear*."

A Widow

accompanied by her only child, a boy of eight years, paid a visit to Father Paul when he was Prior of the monastery of Steenbrugge. The Rev. Father placed his hand on the head of the little boy and said, "Madam, this child will be your joy, he will be a priest."

While the young man was pursuing his classical studies, Father Paul would write to him before the quarterly examinations and promise to pray for him, that he might secure the first distinctions; and each time he won the highest honors. But when the Rev. Father made no mention of praying for that intention the student was less successful.

When the young man entered the seminary, Father Paul foretold that he would pass his examinations without the least difficulty, a prediction which was verified to the letter.

A Student of Thielt

had failed in his examinations for three successive years, and it was represented to Father Paul that the sole cause of the young man's failure, was the fear of examination. But, after mature deliberation, Father Paul attributed the student's failure to prejudice on the part of the examiners. "I shall pray for him, and next year he will pass without any difficulty." The student passed the examination quite successfully.

A Gentleman of Waloon

informed Father Paul that he desired to go to America to find there a suitable partner, but that his mother did not favor his project. "Do not undertake the journey, you will find your America at home."

This gentleman met at a watering place in his own vicinity, a rich American lady whom he married.

A Rich Young Lady

consulted Father Paul on the subject of her vocation. He spoke to her as follows: "You are called to the religious life, and despite your large fortune, you will not find happiness, but trials, contradictions, and tribulations elsewhere. Your parents will endeavor to dissuade you, but you will persevere in your determination. Your brother is a consumptive, and the physicians have pronounced him incurable. He will be cured before the end of the year, but his recovery will not prove prejudicial to your vocation." Both predictions were realized; the young lady is in a convent and her brother has been restored to perfect health.

At Steenbrugge

Father Paul, on coming out of the sacristy, saw a young girl praying in the church. He went directly to her and said, "You want to enter the convent, don't you?" "Yes, Father, but I have no means, and there is no one from whom I can procure a dowry." "This is not necessary; do not worry about that." Three days after the young lady was received into a convent without a dowry.

A Carmelite Novice

was so delicate that the sisters would not admit her to profession. The Rev. Mother wrote to Father Paul in regard to the matter. He replied that the novice should be permitted to make her profession, and she would then be cured. And it came to pass as he had foretold.

A Nun Writes:

At the age of seventeen, I went to Father Paul to ask him to cure one of our farm horses.

"Think first of yourself," he said, "for you are very sick." I was, in truth, suffering from anemia.

Putting on his stole, he made me kneel down while he recited a prayer over me. Then he said that I would be cured and become a religious.

In a short time I was restored to perfect health, and later on had the happiness of entering the convent. And the horse was also cured.

ᑫᑐ

Two Sisters

sought the advice of Father Paul as to their vocation. The younger, who desired to marry, he declared was called to the conventual life. The elder informed him that she intended to enter the convent, but Father Paul counseled her not to embrace the religious life, as her vocation was for the state of matrimony. But, despite his admonitions, the older girl entered the convent, but left before her novitiate had terminated. The younger married, but was entirely disappointed in her expectations.

ᑫᑐ

A Young Lady of Antwerp

wished to marry, but her father could not be induced to approve her choice. So she went to Termonde to seek advice from Father Paul. When she and her companion arrived at the church of the monastery, they saw Father Paul at a distance, receiving a number of persons. The young lady remarked to her friend, "I do not wish to speak to him in the presence of so many."

Scarcely had she uttered the words, than Father Paul beckoned her to him and said, "You prefer to speak to me in the sacristy?" "Yes, Rev. Father," she answered. After the lady had stated her case, Father Paul informed her that this marriage was the will of God; that it would be a very happy one, and would soon take place. "But you must pray fervently." Her affianced made another equally unsuccessful attempt to secure her father's consent and the young lady was sad at heart. Eight days later her father was taken ill and died. The following month the two betrothed came to Father Paul, who advised them not to delay their marriage any longer. As the Rev. Father had predicted, the marriage was indeed a happy one.

Four children, two sons and two daughters were the joy of the family fireside.

ↄ∾

A Jesuit Father

passing through Termonde by train, wished to indulge his curiosity by seeing Father Paul, of whom he had heard so much. He went directly to the church, and was told that Father Paul was on the choir gallery. He went to the foot of the staircase and called from below, "Are you Father Paul?" And although the Jesuit was attired in secular dress, Father Paul in a similar tone, answered, "Are you a Jesuit?" and left the son of St. Ignatius surprised, somewhat mortified, but edified.

Another priest had charged a certain person to make inquiry of Father Paul concerning the state of the soul of a deceased relative. "She is in purgatory so long," he answered.

"Can that be true?" thought the priest within himself. A long time afterwards he charged another person to put the same question to the Rev. Father, but his only answer was the dry remark, "I know nothing about it." The pastor was not satisfied. "He can't be so renowned, this Father Paul," he thought, by way of consoling himself over his disappointment.

It was useless to call upon Father Paul through curiosity.

ↄ∾

A Poor, Desolate Woman

came to seek help from Father Paul for her sick child which had been given up by the physician. For some time the infant had refused all nourishment and seemed to have but a short time to live. Father Paul told the mother to go home and nurse the little one. "But," said the woman, "my child can no longer take food." "Go and do what I tell you." The mother obeyed and her child was completely cured.

Another mother took her infant, which cried continually, to Father Paul. Hardly had she entered the sacristy, where the Rev.

Father happened to be at the time, when the baby began to laugh heartily. Father Paul said, "See, how powerful St. Benedict is!"

When Father Paul was in Antwerp a woman brought her babe to him, which, although a year old, was so small and delicate that she carried it in a box. The Rev. Father blessed the child and said to the mother, "Come back in three weeks, and the child will be in normal health." After three weeks the woman returned full of joy, carrying the babe in her arms. It had grown to be a beautiful child admired by everyone.

ᐧ

A Little Girl from Antwerp

had been paralyzed for a year. Her parents took her to a house where Father Paul was accustomed to receive the crowd of visitors who came to see him at Antwerp.

"Take courage," he said to the parents, "this child will get well. Make a novena to St. Benedict and at the end of it she herself will come to meet me." After the prayers on the eighth day of the novena, the mother, who held the child on her knees, placed her on the floor to see whether she could stand; and to the great astonishment of the family, the little girl began to walk with perfect ease. On the following day she went to meet Father Paul, as he had foretold.

ᐧ

A Poor Little Cripple

was carried to the monastery church of Steenbrugge; he supported himself painfully with the aid of a crutch. Father Paul, seeing the poor unfortunate boy, said to him, "Go, hang your crutch on the pedestal of the statue of St. Benedict. Then you will be able to walk." The boy did as he was ordered, and was instantly cured. He left the church crying aloud, as if wild with joy.

Another little cripple who used crutches came to church with his mother. Father Paul who was about to celebrate Mass, said to the poor child, "At the moment of consecration, take your crutches and place them on the communion rail." The child did so and was cured.

More than 200 crutches might recently be seen hanging on the walls of the abbey church of Termonde, left there by cripples cured by Father Paul.

❧

One Evening

in 1886, when the pupils of the Franciscan Convent at Steenbrugge were dismissed, the two daughters of a gardener in the neighborhood entered the monastery church, where they saw Father Paul speak to a good-natured old man who supported himself on a cane and walked with great difficulty. The Rev. Father then made the Way of the Cross twice on his knees, again approached the old man, took his cane and placed it upon the pedestal of the statue of St. Benedict.

After this the old man also made the Stations and walked without the least difficulty.

❧

A Priest

writes from Brussels, January 8, 1897: "It is astonishing how people from all parts of the country have recourse to the powerful intercession of Father Paul.

"In 1887, at the castle of . . ., the eldest daughter of the Countess . . . was dangerously ill. She suffered for a long time from a very violent fever. As the Countess could not leave her child, she sent a woman to Father Paul to request him to pray for the recovery of her daughter. Precisely at two o'clock the same day, the fever abated and the patient began to feel better. At that hour it was that the request of the Countess was made known to Father Paul."

❧

An Artist of Ghent

writes: "In 1842, my father, then a young man, went by train to Antwerp, to take part in a festival. The train was wrecked, several persons were killed, and many injured. My father was severely wounded: his nose broken, and a splinter penetrated the bone. In the year 1880 he was taken seriously ill, and suffered from a torturing headache. The physician said that a tumor had formed in his head, and was attacking the brain, and that death was imminent. My father received the sacraments.

"As a last resort, my mother went to see Father Paul, and although she arrived in the morning, she did not succeed in speaking to him until three o'clock in the afternoon, so great was the throng gathered to consult with him. Father Paul simply said to her, 'Let us pray together for his recovery,' which they did for some time. I was in my studio in Ghent, and at half past three—mark well the hour—my door opened, and to my amazement, I beheld my father. His first words were, 'I feel that I am cured, but I am dying of hunger. Give me at once, some coffee, bread and butter.' The physician declared that his sudden recovery was absolutely inexplicable.

ᏣᏍᎣ

Father Paul,

accompanied by Brother Placidus, passed by a lumberyard in Antwerp where twenty men were at work, and noticed a robust young fellow, who had his arm in a sling. The Rev. Father humorously reproached him for his laziness. The poor, young man replied that his wrist was dislocated. Father Paul bade him remove the bandage, touched the affected part with his hand, and immediately after, the young man pushed a heavily loaded barrow with perfect ease.

ᏣᏍᎣ

In 1881, the Pupils

of the Sisters of St. Joseph, in Bruges, were one day out for a walk. At Steenbrugge Avenue they met Father Paul in company with another Benedictine. Father Paul noticed in the ranks a little girl, who wore a very large hat to protect her weak eyes. The Rev. Father took the child by the hand and made her step out from the ranks; then kindly raising the wide rim of her hat, which almost covered her entirely, he said to her, "You have very bad eyes, my little one. You must be cured. Take this medal, wear it around your neck and pray fervently to St. Benedict." Two days afterwards the little girl was cured.

∽

The Number of People

whom the good and saintly Father Paul consoled, healed or converted on his journeys, is incredible. He addressed the unfortunate and consoled them in their miseries. Happy were the third class passengers (Father Paul always travelled third class) who met him on the train; without their expecting it, and sometimes in spite of themselves, Divine Providence showered favors upon them. The people of Steenbrugge tell us, that Father Paul often visited them unexpectedly. He would come in and say, "My friend, how long has it been since you went to confession? It is necessary for you to go now; come to my confessional, you shall have finished in five minutes."

∽

A Woman from Milleghem,

having a very crooked spine, came to the monastery of Termonde. Father Paul straightened her up by taking hold of her shoulders and saying, "Thus should you walk; quite straight." Whereupon the woman found herself relieved of her affliction.

∽

A Young Man from Bruges,

suffering from a felon on his thumb, paid a visit to Father Paul. Pressing his finger upon the felon, the Rev. Father asked, "Do you feel the evil leaving you?" "No," said the young man. "But I do," answered Father Paul. The finger was cured.

Father Paul cured a carbuncle on the neck of a young man from Bruges by simply putting a little saliva on it.

∽

An Old Woman,

living at Aeltre, brought her niece to Termonde in 1892. She was a very beautiful girl, aged twenty years, but suffered from an abscess in her mouth which bled continually, and defied every remedy. Father Paul, having first given her a little lecture on the danger to which many young girls are exposed in the world, and after admonishing her to be prudent, prescribed a novena; then he touched the wound with his finger, and the young girl was cured.

∾

A Farmer from Oostcamp

was carrying a load of chemical fertilizer to Bruges. He took upon his shoulders a sack weighing 150 kilograms. As he did not at once succeed in adjusting this heavy load, a workman tried to help him by pushing the sack with a blow of his hand. Unfortunately it happened that the blow was too powerful; the poor man felt a rending of the tissues within his side, accompanied with such severe pain, that he was forced to drop his burden. The physician to whom he was taken declared the case to be very serious and prescribed a poultice, to be followed by an application of leeches. The farmer, however, had a horror for the latter treatment. Having been acquainted with Father Paul, he went to consult him. The Rev. Father placed his hand on the farmer's side and said, "Do you suffer here?" "Yes," replied the farmer. "Bah! bah! don't put any leeches on, and don't think of it any more." The cure was instantaneous.

∾

Father Paul

was present at the family meal of a woman, who kept a fish store in Antwerp. The Rev. Father left the table for a moment and the salesgirl who had been ill thought that she would ascertain if Father Paul were as powerful as rumor made him. "I am going to sit down on his chair, and if I am instantly cured, I too will believe in his sanctity." Scarcely had she taken Father Paul's place than she exclaimed, "I am cured."

The lady's son, suffering from a sprained foot, was lying on a lounge. Father Paul making the sign of the cross on the sprained limb, said to him, "In two days your foot will be well," and his words were verified.

Another lady who kept a tobacco store in Antwerp, had a paralyzed arm, which the physician entertained no hope of curing. Father Paul listened to her complaints, and passed his hand from the woman's shoulder to her arm, and, at once, she was enabled to use it freely—and it never after caused her any annoyance.

∽

A Woman and Her Sick Daughter

came from Antwerp to the monastery at Termonde. Father Paul said to them, "You are both quite well." "Oh! no," said the mother, "my daughter is sick. Should we not consult a physician?" "Go home, all is well." The lady asking him when he would again come to Antwerp, he answered, "I shall never come again." When the two visitors returned home, the sick daughter was completely cured. And true to his word, Father Paul never again came to Antwerp.

Later on the same lady came back to consult Father Paul in regard to several affairs. She had a severe pain in her shoulder but did not speak of it. To her great astonishment Father Paul gave her a gentle tap on her aching shoulder and the pain ceased.

∽

In 1885, a Workman from Steenbrugge

suffered from a severe attack of heart disease, and the physician prescribed for him a period of absolute rest. "But who will provide food for my thirteen children?" said the laborer to the physician. Father Paul paid a short visit to this poor sufferer and said to him, "You must still work for a long time for your children, I shall cure you." The laborer regained his health, and could continue to support his numerous family.

∽

A Young Lady from Antwerp

having fallen down stairs, was very severely wounded on the ear. The physician having bandaged it, prescribed complete rest. Father Paul, an intimate friend of the family, came unexpectedly on the second day after the accident and said to her parents, "I have come, because I know that not all has been well here since seven o'clock the day before yesterday." The young girl hearing the voice of Father Paul, ran up to him at once, forgetting all about the strict orders of the physician.

"Hello!" said Father Paul to her, "why these bandages about your head? Take them off right away!" The young lady obeyed, and to the great astonishment of all, no trace of the wound was to be seen.

∽

A Farmer's Wife from Moerbrugge

who was ill, begged her brother-in-law to ask the prayers of Father Paul for the recovery of her sick child. The Rev. Father replied, "The little one will be cured, and the mother also." Both patients were cured at once.

∽

A Servant Girl Writes from Roulers:

"My sister's eyes were in a very bad condition. I went to Steenbrugge to tell Father Paul. Without knowing my sister, the Rev. Father replied that she would soon be cured. He prescribed a novena to St. Benedict and gave me a medal to dip into the water with which she was to wash her eyes. From the first day of the novena, a noticeable improvement was observed, and before the end of it my sister's eyes were completely cured.

"When my father died, I called on Father Paul, and told him how deeply I felt my sad bereavement. My father had lived in Ostende, and had never met Father Paul. Yet he said to me, 'Oh, your father was an excellent man; there are few so good as he; he will not have to remain long in purgatory.'"

∽

A Friend,

confiding in Father Paul, told him of fears that some act of his would be reprimanded by the government. "But, if I approve of it."—The friend was never blamed.

This same friend, anticipating trouble from a rash act on his part, spoke of it to his wonderful counselor. Father Paul said, "I put my seal upon it." Instead of censure, his friend was congratulated for his act.

∽

A Certain Lady

whose mother was very sick, had a lawsuit about a piece of land. The lawyers for both parties were prepared to present the case in court, and in the meantime the woman was advised to ask Father Paul's prayers for a just decision. Father Paul answered, "The case will not be brought to court, and your mother will be cured." Her mother was cured, and, contrary to all expectations, the matter was adjusted privately.

Another lady had on several occasions asked Father Paul to pray for the ending of a protracted family lawsuit, but the matter went from bad to worse, until finally she received a letter announcing that there was no hope of a favorable issue. The lady had to make a short journey the same day. Just as she was about to step into the train, she saw Father Paul at the station and hastened to inform him of the discouraging news. But he replied, "Don't tell me another word about it; the case has been settled."

In the evening the lady heard that, at the last moment and contrary to all expectations, she had won her lawsuit, and that the point in question had been decided at the very hour in which Father Paul had told her of it.

∽

A Farmer of Oostcamp,

whom Father Paul frequently visited during his stay in Steenbrugge, relates the following incidents: —

"My sister lost one eye, and was threatened with the loss of the other, which despite all the oculist's care, became worse. Father Paul placed his hand over my sister's eyes, gave her a medal, and prescribed a novena in honor of St. Benedict. The third day her eyes were cured.

On Another Occasion,

I was taken suddenly and seriously ill, just after midnight, and told my brother that I was dying. I desired at once a Benedictine Father. I preferred Father Paul: but as the good monk was old, and perchance could not conveniently come, I told my brother to ask for some other Father. When my brother reached the monastery, much to his surprise and gratification, Father Paul opened the door and was ready to accompany him. The kind Father assured me that I would soon be well again and added, 'It was high time for you to send for me; if I had not come, you would have died tonight.'

∽

As the Monastery

had bought a pig from us, which took sick, Father Paul asked me to come. I did so and he said to me, 'The pig is sick, cure it.' 'What! I? I do not know how. Ah, if I were Father Paul, then . . . .' 'Why certainly, you must cure my beasts, and I shall cure yours.' 'If you wish, I shall try our usual remedies and come back tomorrow.' 'No, no! you cannot leave until the pig is cured,' he said smiling. I took care of the pig until evening, and when I left, it was cured.

"For two years we had ill luck with our pigs; as many of the young died. On being informed of this Father Paul advised me to hang a medal of St. Benedict on the wall of the piggery and dip a medal into the food of the beasts. We did so, and from that time on, we had no more losses."

∽

A Farmer, Living in the Neighborhood

of Steenbrugge, was untiring in the praises of good Father Paul. "How often," said he, "did we have the happiness to receive him into our house. At each of his visits, some unforeseen good fortune was bestowed upon us. He was truly goodness personified, a true father to us, obtaining for us all the favors we asked, and even anticipating our secret wishes. His departure from Steenbrugge was regretted by everyone." This farmer tells the following wonderful stories:—

His eldest daughter had been injured by brambles; her hand was badly swollen and caused her intolerable suffering. Father Paul came, took a medal of St. Benedict, dipped it into water and let some drops fall from his fingers upon the injured hand. The pains ceased immediately and soon after the Rev. Father's departure, the swelling disappeared.

A farmer had in his stable a calf that was at the point of dying. Father Paul leaned over the beast, stretched on the ground and barely breathing, and pressing his hand upon its head, said to the farmer, "Truly, one might say that it is no longer sick; just look! it appears to be cured." The farmer placed a pail near the calf. With a sudden bound, it was on its feet, and greedily consumed the contents of the pail. There was no further doubt about its entire recovery. —

A Man from Ghent

affected with cancer of the stomach, heard people talk of a Benedictine monk at the monastery of Steenbrugge, who performed miracles with the aid of St. Benedict's medal. Desirous of verifying these rumors, he took the train to said place and there met an acquaintance, who asked him whither he was bound. "I am going to see the Father with the medals," he said laughing. "It seems his medals cure all kinds of evils."

Having arrived at his destination, and before he was able to open his mouth, Father Paul said to him, "You have come to see the Father with the medals; go home and purify your conscience; then after nine days return, and I shall cure you." Struck by the Father's insight, the man did as he was told, and was cured.

In 1886, at Steenbrugge

Father Paul said to the wife of a tradesman: "Don't allow your children to go out, for there is a mad dog in your neighbor's field. I have deprived him for an hour of all power of movement. I shall tell the gardener to kill him."

❦

A Young Lady of Brussels

writes: "My sister's child was reduced almost to a skeleton, and could not digest even a spoonful of milk. The physician's prescriptions were of no avail. The child's nurse received a visit from her mother, who urged the parents to have a trustworthy person make a pilgrimage to the monastery of Termonde, and see Father Paul. The parents selected the children's governess, a very devout person, who started, with hopes of arriving in time for Mass the following day that she might receive Holy Communion. By some mistake she got off at the wrong station. As she would be obliged to wait several hours for the next train, she determined to continue her journey on foot. At the church of the Benedictines, Father Paul met her and said, 'Madam, you made a mistake as to the station, you must be very tired; and then you have eaten nothing since yesterday.' The Rev. Father bade the astonished governess, 'Go to a restaurant for some nourishment, and come back.'

"When she had returned, and made known to Father Paul the object of her visit, he informed her that the child was incurable, and had defied the efforts of the most celebrated physicians to afford relief. 'Let both you and the nurse perform a novena; I shall also make one. Pray with confidence, and I hope that child will be cured.' The last day of the novena the boy recovered completely, and is now a young man enjoying excellent health.

❦

An Invalid of Thielt

writes that for eight years he was a victim of the falling sickness. In the year 1891, he called upon Father Paul, who gave him every assurance of a speedy recovery. On wearing the Benedictine medal, and completing a novena in honor of St. Benedict, he was restored to perfect health.

Four years later, the same man had a severe attack of throat trouble. Father Paul blessed his throat, and his cure was instantaneous.

∽

A Woman of Steenbrugge

suffered for a year from nervousness and rheumatism. Four physicians had treated her without success. Finally she applied to Father Paul, and he assured her that she would be well in a few days. A little powder of the miraculous roses of St. Benedict and a novena restored her health.

The son of this woman was infected with a horrible eczema, which defied all medical skill. Father Paul prescribed a novena in honor of St. Benedict, and the washing of the sores with water touched by a medal of St. Benedict. He gave assurance of a prompt cure.

Nine days later, the woman brought her boy to the monastery in the same sad condition. "You have not followed my directions," said Father Paul.

"I did not use the water."

"Go home and do what I told you." The woman obeyed, and obtained the cure of her son.

A cousin of the same woman, a consumptive, given up by the physicians, was perfectly cured by Father Paul, and later on entered a convent in Merckem.

∽

A Man of Caneghem,

from a decayed tooth, contracted a most painful disease of the tongue. He wrote to Father Paul requesting a cure. The Father replied, "You may be cured, if you cease to blaspheme: you have cancer of the tongue in punishment for your blasphemies." So long as the man abstained from swearing, his condition daily improved: but he unfortunately resumed his former evil habit, his malady increased, and death followed.

Another man, with a cancer on his lower lip, went to Father Paul and asked him to cure it. The Rev. Father pressed the lip between his thumb and index finger, and said that he had taken away the cancer. It had disappeared.

❧

A Devout Woman, Aged Sixty-six Years,

an inmate of the great Beguine Convent of Ghent, had a cancer on her breast. In 1888 she came to Termonde and told Father Paul that the physician had decided to perform an operation for the removal of the cancer.

"No operation," replied the Rev. Father, "I shall pray for that."

The cancer disappeared by degrees, and at the end of six months, the lady was entirely free from it. The lady, who herself told the story in 1897, appeared in fact, to be in perfect health, and spoke of Father Paul with the greatest reverence and gratitude.

❧

The Old Housekeeper of a Pastor in Ghent,

reports the following facts: —

"Twenty-five years ago I had a cancer on my back. As the physicians were not able to cure it, I had recourse to a country-woman, a nature-healer, reputed to heal those afflicted with cancer. Finally, not being able to continue in my service, I was on the point of returning to my native village, when some one spoke to me of Father Paul. I went to consult him. Seeing me he said, 'I ought to have gone away this morning, but knowing that you would come, I stayed at home. Yes, yes, I shall help you; for I know how to cure cancer. The good woman who treated you with caustics, will die soon; but don't tell her.'

"The Father gave me some medals and prescribed novenas. After a few weeks, the cancer with all its ramifications dropped out. But at the same time, a growth appeared on my forehead, the nature of which could not at first be determined. I suffered for six months, and then a new cancer was detected. Again I had recourse to Father Paul. He gave me a little powder of the miraculous roses of St. Benedict to apply to the cancer, and at the end of eight days I was cured. Since then, thank God, I have been well."

∽

A Maiden from Ghent

told me that she had asked Father Paul to cure her aged father. The Rev. Father replied, "Your father will not be cured. Your sister will be ill and receive the last sacraments. But do not fear, she will recover." All this happened as foretold.

∽

A Rich Man

of our village was opposed to the marriage of his daughter, in consequence of which she took sick. The young lady went to Termonde, accompanied by my sister. Father Paul said to her, "You are sick, but you will be cured if you marry; if not, you will die. Tell this to your father." The latter paid no attention to the warning, and his daughter died.

∽

Four Years Ago

a Beguine religious from Ghent went with my sister to Termonde. The Sister told her that Father Paul had spoken to her as one knowing her most secret thoughts. She suffered very much from toothache and, although she made no mention of it, Father Paul placed his hand for an instant over her mouth, whereupon the toothache stopped.

After this the religious and my sister went to the church where Father Paul made them kiss a relic of St. Benedict. Seeing a woman seated in a pew, the Rev. Father beckoned her from afar also to come and kiss the holy relic. The woman tried to rise but could not. Father Paul then went up to her, and to their great astonishment, removed from the woman's head a large, vicious beetle, which he threw on the floor and stamped with his foot. Then the woman was able to rise and kiss the holy relic.

∽

A Young Lady from Malines

writes, April 17, 1897: "Once only I had the honor of seeing Father Paul. That was at Steenbrugge about ten years ago. I went there to ask his advice with regard to a growth that appeared on my breast and caused uneasiness to my family and two physicians. They were afraid it might develop into cancer. I spoke of it to Father Paul without telling him on which side the tumor was. But the Rev. Father put his thumb right on the sore spot and kept it there for some moments; then he told me it was nothing but a gland which would disappear, and that I must not apply any salve to it or allow it to be lanced. I followed his counsel and the gland disappeared.

"My sister, who accompanied me, was deaf in her right ear in consequence of an abscess that had perforated the ear drum. I told the Rev. Father that my sister desired to consult him regarding her affliction. 'She will never be cured of it,' he replied, 'because the tympanum is perforated, and that never heals.'

"What struck us most was the great humility of this saintly man; one would have taken him for a lay-brother rather than a priest."

∽

A Young Man

hearing reports of the wonders wrought by Father Paul by means of the medal of St. Benedict, induced a friend to accompany him on a visit to the "medal man," as, he derisively called him. After a long delay, Father Paul entered the parlor and thus rebuked his two skeptical visitors, "The medal man will not receive you."

∽

A Young Lady from Antwerp writes:

"In 1886, I suffered intensely from a bad tooth, and my gums and cheek were very much inflamed. The dentist to whom I went to have the tooth extracted, declared that an operation would now be dangerous, and that I should wait. Having learned that Father Paul was in Antwerp at the time, I went and asked his advice. 'Have you confidence in St. Benedict?' he asked. I answered, 'Yes.'

" 'Well take this medal and dip it into all you drink, also hold it for a moment in your mouth on the side of the bad tooth and say, "St. Benedict, help me and pray for me!" Do not have the tooth pulled; it will fall out of itself.'

"My toothache disappeared and the bad tooth came out shortly afterwards. Since that time I have not suffered from my teeth.

"Later on I suffered greatly from stomach trouble, and as no remedy gave me any relief, I went to Termonde to see Father Paul. After the first word I spoke to him the affliction left me.

"My aunt, living in Hal, one night discovered a burglar in her house. She became so frightened that she was seized with a severe nervous disorder which made her speechless and produced symptoms of epilepsy. After she had received the last sacraments. I wrote to Father Paul, and he answered that my aunt would recover. In a short time she was cured."

∽

The Aged Father of a Rev. Benedictine

was very ill, and Father Paul had been asked to go to see him. Returning to the monastery he said to his confrére, "Your father will not be cured, but you mother will live fourteen years longer." The mother died after fourteen years.

∽

Two Brothers

afflicted with the same malady, had recourse to Father Paul. To the first youth he said, "I shall cure you, because of your great confidence, but comply strictly with my directions." Father Paul gave similar instructions to his brother, but failed to add, "I will cure you." The younger brother, who was inspired with confidence, rapidly improved; while the disease of the latter daily increased.

He returned to the monastery and said to Father Paul, "My brother and I followed your counsel exactly; he is entirely cured, but I am worse than before." "I am in no wise astonished, my friend," answered Father Paul. "Your brother's great faith combined with the efficacy of the medal restored him to health. When you came here with your brother, you said within yourself, 'This simple Father can do no more than I; it is not here that I shall obtain a cure!' Now indulge your fancy, I can do nothing for you."

❧

A Priest from Brussels

says that two of his cousins, suffering from asthma consulted Father Paul The Rev. Father gave each a medal and prescribed some prayers. Both recovered.

❧

A Child,

aged five years, the son of an inhabitant of Lokeren, was subject to frequent convulsions. His father brought him to the monastery, and Father Paul said to him, "Your child is cured and will remain so," which was in reality the case.

❧

A Canon Relates:

"My sister having been given up by the physicians, was at the point of death when she asked me to write to Termonde. Father Paul replied that no matter what the physicians said, he guaranteed that my sister would recover. He ordered the patient to dip the medal into all beverages and make a novena with him in honor of St. Benedict.

"Contrary to all expectations my sister recovered and has been well ever since."

A Redemptorist Father says that his sister had, below her knee, a very troublesome tumor the size of a pigeon egg. She absolutely refused to have recourse to a physician, but at last came to Father Paul for help. "Make a novena," he said to her, "and the tumor will disappear."

"Now on the seventh day of the novena the tumor loosened itself without my sister noticing it, and fell to the ground. Not even a trace of it remained."

The Prior

of a Trappist monastery, who had met Father Paul but once, went to consult him concerning several matters. Before the Prior had time to state the object of his visit, Father Paul briefly answered all the questions he intended to propose: and the results were as Father Paul had predicted.

Father Paul

told me that a boy, who had cancer of the tongue, asked him to be cured. The boy went away buoyant with hope. While he was on his way, the cancer fell to the ground.

A Young Lady from Holland,

who had been subject to asthma from her childhood, came in 1885 with her mother to Steenbrugge. She complained piteously of her sufferings.

"Do you wish to be cured?" asked Father Paul.

"Indeed, I do."

"Well, don't you feel that you are cured?"

Her cure was instantaneous, and there has been no relapse.

An Old Druggist from Bruges,

a friend of Father Paul, being hopelessly ill, requested a mutual friend to ask the prayers of that saintly religious. Father Paul replied, "This druggist will not die yet; he has done so much good." The patient recovered and lived a few more years.

A Priest from Bruges,

at present curate in Hainaut, writes (June 26, 1908) as follows: "During my Easter vacation in 1882, I went to see Father Paul in

Steenbrugge in order to consult him about an important personal affair. If I remember correctly, I had not made myself known to him. After I had submitted my case to him, I saw him lower his head; afterwards he asked me, 'Have you not been a religious?'

" 'Yes, Father,' I answered.

" 'Why did you leave the monastery?'

I gave him a satisfactory answer, whereupon he advised me with regard to my difficulties, and the outcome proved the wisdom of his direction.

"At first I said to myself, 'This monk is too simple, I have yielded to an illusion.' But when he accompanied me to the door he spoke a few words in Flemish on the love of Jesus Christ, with such marks of enthusiasm that I turned around to look at him (for he had made me walk ahead of him) . . . . He was no longer the same man: he was transfigured; his physiognomy, ordinarily so simple, not to say more, had something of the inspired, the ecstatic in it; his speech, so slow and colorless, was now lively, overflowing, impetuous, exuberant. He was, as it were, carried off by a *mentis excessus*. 'Truly,' said I to myself, 'here is a man who changes easily and rapidly, more so than we find in the stories of "A Thousand and One Nights." This occurrence remained deeply engraven upon my mind.

"I have not the necessary learning or discernment to pass judgment upon the supernatural character of the works and deeds of Father Paul; but I must candidly admit that this sudden change and apparent transformation of his person has always puzzled me."

ᐕ

The Wife of the Steward of a Castle

had suffered severely for a long time. She came to see Father Paul at Steenbrugge and asked to be cured.

"But you are not sick!" he replied.

"Not sick? I can endure my suffering no longer, I have been treated by several physicians, but the more medicine I take, the worse I feel."

"I tell you that you are not sick at all!" Then touching the woman's breast with his finger, Father Paul said, "There is the cause of your sufferings. Take this medal and dip it in all your beverage, whilst making a novena, and your malady will disappear." On the eighth day of her novena the woman obtained complete relief.

The same woman came to Father Paul with the following complaint, "My husband is happy in his position, he attends to his business well, and his master is satisfied with him; but he displeases the master's notary, who is doing everything in his power to have him discharged."

"Yes, and the superintendent of the forest is also displeased with him, is he not?" "Yes." "Well, the best thing you can do is to look for another place."

∽

A Young Lady from Antwerp

had grown very thin from illness. Fearing consumption, she induced a friend to go to Steenbrugge and ask the prayers of Father Paul. This was the answer she received, "The patient will not take consumption. She will be cured and will need to have her clothes made larger at three different times." The lady was cured and the predictions of Father Paul were verified.

∽

A Young Lady

of Knesselaere sprained her arm, and purchased a small bottle of liniment to be applied thereto. Some time after she paid a visit to Father Paul, who thus addressed her, "For what are those bandages on your arm?" "Oh! I am suffering so much pain from it." Whereupon Father Paul touched the injured arm, and the young lady was at once able to move it freely. Then Father Paul, in a jocose manner, said to her, "A physician would certainly have charged you at least a franc for such a cure. You have paid fifteen cents for that bottle of liniment; give it to me as my fee." When the young woman was about to leave, Father Paul asked her, "Do you want a little present?" "With pleasure, you are really too kind." "Very well, here is the bottle. It will help you cure poor people, who suffer from sprains or dislocations. But the bottle must be my property." All to whom the young lady applied the liniment received relief; and, when after the death of Father Paul, she had the bottle refilled, she used it with the same unfailing success.

One day when Father Paul had entrusted to her charge an important and difficult affair, he said, "Proceed with it: my prayer will give power and success to all your words." The result was simply wonderful.

The same young lady was troubled with three bad teeth in her lower jaw, so that the gum was beginning to decay. Having complained about it to Father Paul he replied, "You will retain these teeth, I shall stop the pain. You have suffered enough from them." And her sufferings really ceased that very day.

"Truly," Father Paul added, "when I am sad and you are sick, you console me, for you come to me at once with as great a confidence as though I knew how to cure everything."

In 1886, she suffered from her throat so that she had lost her appetite and voice. For several days she had been under a strict diet, and had a heavy muffler around her neck. Father Paul having gone to Knesselaere (the only time he went there) visited the sick girl who greeted him with a low, raucous voice. Father Paul said jokingly:

"Is it possible? The first time I come to see you, you talk to me in such a manner, and receive me in such an unconventional make up! Take that muffler off." After that he made a little cross on the sore spot with his thumb. The pain stopped at once, the patient's voice became clear and strong, and her appetite made itself so sensibly felt, that she went to the kitchen and ate two large rolls. The priest's servant girl was witness of this wonderful cure.

Father Paul told us that a certain sick person, on his way to Steenbrugge to be cured, recovered his health before reaching the monastery, owing to his great confidence.

∽

Cured in Two Minutes.

The 24th of August, 1894, the day on which the Very Rev. Prior Dom Maurus was blessed as Abbot of Termonde, the same young lady suffered from a severe inflammation of the cheek. She met

Father Paul in the church. He touched the inflamed cheek with his finger, and two minutes after, the cheek was restored to its natural state.

⌒⌣⌒

In the Year 1882,

a woman engaged in business in Malines, was by the advice of her physician to undergo an operation, to which she was bitterly opposed. As she was acquainted with Father Paul, she decided to go to Steenbrugge and beseech his aid. Contrary to her expectations, Father Paul encouraged her to submit to the painful ordeal; but she replied that death was preferable. He exhorted the lady saying, "You have never disobeyed me. Have confidence in me, and resign yourself with docility to the judgment of the surgeon." And Father Paul promised her that within two days, she would enjoy the happiest hour of her life.

She accordingly presented herself to the surgeon and said, "Here I am, do with me whatever you may deem necessary and may God aid you." The surgeon again examined her, and in bewilderment exclaimed, "The malady has disappeared: not a trace of it remains: it is impossible to account for it! Truly, indeed, this is a miracle!"

⌒⌣⌒

A Lady of Liege

had written to Father Paul asking the cure of her infant. She received the answer while watching the little one in its cradle. Hardly had she opened the envelope when she found that the child was cured.

⌒⌣⌒

A Child of Nine Years,

the daughter of a farmer in Austruweel near Antwerp, suffered from a polyp. The surgeon cauterized the growth three times a week; but as it grew worse, they brought the poor girl to Termonde. Father Paul prescribed a novena to St. Benedict, and foretold that the child would be cured. In order to dispel the child's sadness the

Rev. Father spoke to her in a cheerful tone and said, "Now, my little one, you will have to put on nice clothes and have pretty feathers in your hat!" The polyp disappeared on the sixth day of the novena, to the great astonishment of the physician.

CWO

In 1885, a Lady

had a cancer on her breast. Three doctors had decided that an operation was necessary; but following an inspiration, she had recourse to Father Paul who told her to wash the sore spot three times a day, with water into which a medal of St. Benedict had been dipped. The Rev. Father added this caution, "Don't be curious, and do not look at the spot until you feel that you have been cured." The cancer disappeared in fifteen days.

CWO

A Woman from Bruges,

who for some time felt indisposed, requested prayers from Father Paul. The Rev. Father sent her some powder of the miraculous roses of St. Benedict, and promised to pay her a visit the following Friday (every Friday Father Paul came to Bruges in order to venerate the relic of the precious blood*) adding that she would be well by that time. And so it was.

CWO

A Physician

of Bruges prescribed a poisonous medicine for a nun. The druggist, by mistake prepared an overdose; and the patient consequently suffered from the torturing effects of the poison. The physician was recalled at once, and knowing that there was no hope of recovery, ordered that a priest be sent for immediately to administer the last sacraments.

---

* The pilgrimage to the Precious Blood, of Bruges, enjoys a European reputation that runs back through seven centuries. In 1900 a booklet was published in Bruges, in which the history of the venerable relic is given, as also an account of the numerous miracles and prodigies obtained by the faithful since the year 1150.

The nearest church was that at which Father Paul was stationed. He came without delay, but would not administer the last rites. He said, "The sister is recovering: in a short time, she will be cured. How, then, can you ask me to give her the last sacraments?" After having blessed the patient, he calmly left the room, and scarcely had he departed, when she arose from her bed in perfect health.

☙

In the Church at Steenbrugge,

a woman from Oostcamp asked Father Paul to cure her husband. "Wait," he said, "I shall say a prayer before the statue of St. Benedict." Going back to the woman, he said to her, "The sickness of your husband is too far advanced; this evening you will be separated." The man died that evening.

☙

A Lady of Steenbrugge

was hopelessly ill. The physicians had finally concluded that it was time to administer the last sacraments. They sent at once to the monastery calling for a priest, but at the time, none of the Benedictine Fathers were at home. Towards noon Father Paul returned and was informed of the urgent sick call. "Hasten, Father, God knows if it is not already too late."

"No, no," he replied, "we shall take our dinner first." After dinner Father Paul went to the sick person, and a few days afterwards the lady was restored to health.

☙

A Lady from Antwerp Writes to Us:

"In 1889 I was in a very serious condition on account of a tumor that had formed in my bowels. The physicians declared that I had to undergo a dangerous operation. As their decision caused me great fear, I went to consult Father Paul, but he also advised an operation and assured me that it would be successful. The Rev. Father was so certain of the outcome, that he did not find it necessary for me to receive the sacraments before the operation, which took place under the most favorable circumstances and without causing me the least pain or fever. The cyst which adhered to the spine was taken out; it weighed no less than ten and a half pounds."

∽

A Sick Woman

had charged a friend of hers to ask a cure of Father Paul. The Rev. Father inquired whether the woman had heart trouble. The answer was that she knew absolutely nothing about it. "Well," he said, "if she suffers from heart trouble, let her rub the affected part with a little water into which a medal of St. Benedict has been dipped." The woman really did suffer from heart disease and was cured by following the counsel of Father Paul.

Another lady asked Father Paul to cure her, and received the following answer: "You cannot be cured, because you are opposed to the vocation of your daughter, who desires to go to the convent."

∽

A Woman from St. Georges Says:

"For a long time I suffered much from severe pains in my head, and the physician failed to give relief. Paying a visit to Father Paul in Steenbrugge, he put his finger to different parts of my head, saying each time, 'Now the pain is here.' And actually I felt the pain move about and stay where the Rev. Father had placed his finger. Finally he said, 'Make the sign of the cross and say, In the name of St. Benedict!' While doing so, the pain disappeared as if by magic."

∽

A Young Girl from Knesselaere

who suffered from a disease of the spinal marrow, asked Father Paul to obtain her cure. "If you are resigned to the holy will of God and ready to die should He wish it, you will be so happy in heaven," replied the Rev. Father; "but if you prefer to be cured, I shall pray for that; however, in this case you will have to undergo great trials. What is your choice?"

"If that is the case, I prefer to die." And she died soon afterwards.

The Four Children of a Boatman

in Antwerp being sick, the latter went to Father Paul. "You did not go to confession in seven years," said Father Paul, "and your wife not in six: this is the cause of your children's illness. Let both of you go to confession in Antwerp, and your children will recover their health."

CRD

In 1874, a Woman of Antwerp

paid a visit to Father Paul at Termonde. Daily the Rev. Father received a crowd of people in the church, and afterwards the woman related some incidents which came to her knowledge that day. She said:—

"A young lady having asked to be cured, received the following answer from Father Paul: 'First be converted, for I am ashamed to see you.'

"Another girl demanded the cure of her mother. This was the reply she received from the Rev. Father: 'Do not any longer prevent your servant from going to church in the morning, and do not ill-treat her. She is a good girl and prays for the cure of your mother, and she will obtain that favor.'

"A married couple came and complained that all their children had died. Answer: 'You yourselves are the cause of your misfortune.' Addressing the woman, Father Paul said, 'You ought to have given a good example, and yet you have not been to confession in twelve years. And you,' he said to the husband, 'have not been to confession in twenty years. What blessings can you expect under these circumstances? Enter into yourselves, be converted, then return and I shall receive you with a generous heart!'

"A girl who returned to Antwerp with me told me that her jaw-bone had been dislocated. Father Paul having said a prayer over her, the jaw-bone adjusted itself in the course of the interview."

CRD

A Girl of Sixteen Years

was attacked by a mysterious sickness which defied all treatment. One might believe her possessed by the devil from her howling and unceasing utterance of the most horrible blasphemies. She grasped all who came within her reach, and foaming at the mouth, bit those who came too near. Her parents having begged Father Paul to come to their aid, he delivered the unfortunate girl from her obsession in the following manner: taking hold of her hand he placed therein a medal of St. Benedict, and put his own hand on the head of the poor creature. The young girl at once became quiet, and humbly said to her deliverer, "I beg your pardon, my Father, I shall not do it anymore!"

༺

A Widow

of Wyngene had a daughter twelve years of age so severely afflicted with a nervous disease that she did not enjoy a moment of repose. The malady became so aggravated that she lost the power of speech, and food had to be administered to her as to an infant. Two doctors had treated her; several novenas were undertaken; a pilgrimage to Thielt made in her behalf, but all to no avail.

The Little Sisters of the Poor from the convent of Bruges, who were soliciting alms in the village, remained with us over night, but they were unable to sleep on account of the cries of the suffering child. The good sisters, grieved at the affliction of the disconsolate widow, said to her, "For the love of God, Madame, go, see Father Paul, and ask him to cure your child."

The servant-girl was sent to the monastery at Steenbrugge, and said to the Rev. Father, "My employer, a widow of Wyngene, has sent me to obtain the cure of her daughter." Father Paul replied, "That child is in a deplorable condition, and cannot live more than two days. However, we shall see what can be done through the aid of St. Benedict."

He then gave the servant-girl two medals. "Place one around her neck, though you will experience great difficulty in so doing. The other you will dip into whatever she may drink, and also into the water wherewith you bathe her suffering limbs. Give her no medicine, only a small powder of the miraculous roses of St. Benedict and make fervent novenas in honor of St. Benedict. You left home at seven o'clock this morning so return at once, for these poor people are, indeed, sorely afflicted."

As soon as the servant had returned, Father Paul's instructions were faithfully carried out. When an attempt was made to fasten the medal around the weak child's neck, she became suddenly enraged; and they succeeded only after giving her a few drops of water into which they had placed the medal.

At the termination of a second novena the child having worn the medal gave evidences of improvement, but she was still unable to speak or eat and her arms remained paralyzed. Then the mother, accompanied by the servant, brought the daughter to Father Paul who received them most cordially. He placed a medal on the table, and asked the girl, "Do you not know how to speak? Take that medal." The girl tried, but in vain. "Try again, it will be easy." All the efforts of the poor child were useless, yet Father Paul insisted that she should take it from the table. At length she lifted her arm and took the medal exclaiming, "I have it." From that moment her arms regained their freedom, and she fully recovered the use of her speech. When about to take leave of Father Paul the child's mother inquired of him what compensation she should offer him, the Father answered, "Nothing."

He then asked the servant-girl, "Do you intend to remain long in this lady's service?" "Oh," replied her mistress, "She is an orphan, where can she go? We are her sole support. And why should she leave us?" "Yes," said Father Paul, "remain for some days."

Shortly after, the servant lost the medal which Father Paul had given her. When she returned to the monastery to obtain another, Father Paul said to her, "Don't worry, you have no longer any need of that medal, God knows where it is."

A few days later she took ill and the physician declared that she suffered from an acute attack of intestinal inflammation. This information caused the good lady great grief, as the servant was much loved by the family. The priest and the physician pitied her but insisted that the sickness must take its course. The intense pain, however, ceased after the lady had given the patient a few drops of water, in which she had dipped the medal of St. Benedict. Shortly after the servant peacefully expired, perfectly resigned to the will of God. Father Paul's prediction was fulfilled, and the next time the lady conversed with him, he assured her that the devout orphan whom she loved so dearly was in heaven.

The lady writes: "Since my daughter's cure, hundreds of people have visited us to inquire regarding Father Paul, and many from here and the surrounding country have had recourse to him.

ᏜᏏ

We Also Had Misfortune

with our property. There was continual sickness in our stable, and one loss followed another. The matter being referred to Father Paul, he sent us some medals to be hung upon the wall of the stable. This proved a powerful remedy, for all sickness ceased, never to reappear.

"The Rev. Father urged my husband to quit the farm we had rented, insisting that if he remained on it he would be persecuted for three years, and in the end be ruined. But my husband who had hitherto had the utmost confidence in Father Paul, would not believe it, persuading himself that the Rev. Father must be mistaken this time, since the events predicted seemed so improbable. Consequently he stayed on the farm.

"And yet events proved the accuracy of Father Paul's words; everything happened as he had foretold. Our life became one series of trials; we were cheated, robbed and calumniated by the very persons of whom the Rev. Father had spoken. This spell of adversity lasted exactly three years, at the end of which the creditor sold at auction all that remained of our goods. Two days before the sale I took away the three medals of St. Benedict which were hanging on the walls of the stable for the protection of the cattle. Now the very next morning several head of cattle were found lying on the ground, suffering horribly, and on the point of perishing.

"Being compelled to leave the farm we established ourselves where jealousy and envy did not follow us. Soon we recovered our fortune, my husband regained the esteem which he had formerly enjoyed, and died regretted by all his fellow citizens.

"I visited Father Paul one day with my daughter whom he had cured, and he asked her for her rosary, saying it was not blessed. That was true, and the Rev. Father blessed the rosary and gave it back to her."

ᏉᏉ

The Wife of a Grocer

in Antwerp was attacked, twenty-two years ago, by a malignant tumor in her lower limb, which baffled the skill of two physicians who pronounced it incurable. The grocer, utterly dejected, was advised to procure the aid of Father Paul. He spoke of his intention to his wife who enthusiastically cried out, "Oh! go then to see this celebrated Benedictine." "Very well," he replied, "but I cannot leave the store." "Pshaw," answered the wife, "is your store dearer to you than I am? Father Paul is my only hope, he can cure me and I am sure he will do so for my children's sake."

The same day the grocer left for Termonde, and saw Father Paul. The Rev. Father told him his wife would be cured because of her great faith, and her desire to be spared to her children. "But," he added, "It will require a long time."

From that day on the progress of the tumor was arrested, and on the following day the physicians decided that the operation might be delayed, while the patient was so encouraged that she declared, "Amputation will not be necessary, I shall be cured for the sake of my children." She was confined to her bed nine months; finally the tumor disappeared, and she insisted on visiting Father Paul to thank him.

Accompanied by her eldest son, and suffering great pain, she went to Termonde, where she saw Father Paul enter the church. He bade her follow him to the sacristy, and requested her son to await her. She expressed to her generous benefactor her gratitude and joy, that he had prevented the operation by his prayers.

"But," interrupted Father Paul, "is that your son outside?" "Yes, Rev. Father,—but oh, my limb still pains me." Again he asked, "Is that your son?" "Yes, Rev. Father.—I am so grateful for what you have already done for me." When he asked the same question a third time, the mother understood that Father Paul wished to teach her the necessity of concern for her children, for whose sake she was so anxious to be cured. She then beckoned him to come in. "This boy does not learn well, although he studies diligently." "That is so," said his mother, "and I leave nothing undone to help him." "His mind," answered Father Paul, "is not yet fully developed; but he is good and wise. Take care of him and occupy him with manual labor." The following year, her boy entered college, and succeeded admirably in his studies.

Now Father Paul directed his attention to the lady. "How do you feel?" "Very well; I am now relieved of that dreadful tumor." "Do not thank me, but St. Benedict. Yet you are not entirely cured, and I am surprised that you were able to journey so far."

"The physician says that I will die if the wound closes." "And yet, you say that you wish to be spared to your family." "Oh, yes, Rev. Father." "In that case the wound must disappear. Follow my directions carefully: dip this medal into everything you drink, saying, 'St. Benedict, obtain for me the grace to be cured.' Recite daily nine Our Fathers, Hail Marys, and Glory be to the Father, together with your household. Finally, from the powder of the miraculous roses of St. Benedict, make seven portions, put a little in your drink, and at intervals during the month, apply it to the wound of your limb." And Father Paul promised her that at the end of a month, she would be cured through the intercession of St. Benedict. The last day of the month, his promise was fulfilled.

∽

A Married Woman from Oostcamp

had lost several children in their infancy. In 1881 her last born child, only five weeks old, all at once became very peevish. The mother not being able to nurse him anymore, brought him to the monastery in Steenbrugge. Sitting down in a pew of the church, she held the baby on her knees. Father Paul knelt down before the child and held his hand, and for the first time the little one began to laugh while looking at Father Paul.

"Don't worry," he said, your child will be cured: but you have in your house baby clothes that came from a strange woman; burn them as soon as possible. When you have done so, the child will be well. Make a novena in honor of St. Benedict; I shall pray also; if the trouble shall continue, come back."

Having returned home, the mother remembered that she had in possession some clothes that her sister had given her after the death of her children, and that her sister had received the things from a woman of doubtful character living in the neighborhood. In accordance with the Rev. Father's advice, these clothes were burned. A few days later, the child seemed to be cured, but on the last day of the novena, it began to cry again as it had done before. The mother made a second visit to Steenbrugge.

"You did not burn everything in your house which came from that strange woman. Go home and seek everywhere, and on the way home, conceal your child and do not show him to anyone."

The woman left the monastery. Hardly had she proceeded a few hundred paces, when an old woman accosted her and said, "Hold on! you went to show your baby to Father Paul; let me see it also!"— "I have no time," the mother replied. As soon as she reached home, she searched every nook and corner of the house. Under a piece of furniture, she found an old pair of infant's shoes which she threw into the fire. From that moment, the child was quieted, and his health was excellent; he became a fine, strong boy.

∽

The Wife of a Laborer in Oostcamp,

a penitent of Father Paul, and mother of seventeen children, had the misfortune of seeing one of her sons, a boy of fourteen years, experience a terrible accident. As he fell under a wagon loaded with lumber, his limb was caught between one of the large wheels of the wagon and a heavy beam hanging from the chains. Although no bone was broken, the flesh of the entire leg was torn and crushed.

The poor boy was carried to the hospital of St. John where the physicians declared that the leg must be amputated.

It happened that the mother came to the church of the Benedictines in Steenbrugge, and there met Father Paul who spoke to her in a severe tone, "Your son has had an accident; why did you not come at once and tell me? Go to the hospital and tell the sisters not to allow an amputation; your son will be completely healed." But at the hospital the sisters told the mother that it was absolutely necessary to amputate the leg. "It would have been better," they said, "if the leg had been fractured in ten places; the boy is young and would have recovered. But now there is no hope."—"Yet, Father Paul said that my son would be healed," replied the mother. And so it happened. The leg was not cut off, the flesh was restored to its former health, and not so much as a trace of the accident remained.

Father Paul also told this woman, that all her children would marry, and like herself have large families.

ᏫᏬ

During a Call

which Father Paul was making to a widow at Bruges, he suddenly interrupted his conversation and said, "I must go at once to a certain convent to see a nun who must undergo an operation of the eyes." In fact, a sister had to undergo such an operation, but humanly speaking, Father Paul could not have been aware of it. He went accordingly and told the sister not to be afraid as the success of the operation was assured. The result was excellent.

Before leaving the lady, Father Paul said to the servant, "Give me the rosary you have in your pocket; it has come apart; I shall fix it for you." The servant much astonished, handed him the broken rosary all the more willingly, as she thereby obtained for herself a precious souvenir of the saintly Benedictine.

ᏫᏬ

The Lady of a Manor at Zevenbergen

in Holland, once brought Father Paul a closed package containing three gross of medals of Our Lady of the Sacred Heart and asked him to bless them. "With pleasure," replied the Rev. Father, "I shall bless them all except one which is a medal of the Precious Blood, and for that I shall say a little prayer." When the lady returned home and looked over her medals, she found among them the one of the Precious Blood of which Father Paul had spoken.

ᑯᕐᓗ

At St. Gilles Near Termonde,

Father Paul visited a sick lady, who was nursed by a consumptive servant. He said to the patient, "Your servant is in a worse state of health than you are. Tell her to come and ask to be restored to health by St. Benedict." A few days later the servant proceeded to the monastery and Father Paul told her to wear a medal, to make a novena and . . . here he suddenly stopped, then continued, "No, don't do it; it is no longer necessary; you are on the way to recovery." At that very moment the servant experienced a strange sensation passing through her from head to foot; she was cured.

Some years later the same servant was living at Steenbrugge where Father Paul was prior at the time. "One morning at four o'clock," she says, "in a dream I saw Father Paul come to me and say, 'I am going on a journey this morning and shall say Mass at five o'clock; rise and attend my Mass, for no one else will be in the church.' I awoke immediately and went to Mass; I was the only one in the church. After Mass Father Paul said to me smiling, 'Aha! who made you come so early?' 'Why, you, Father,' I answered.

" 'I asked our Lord that there might be at least one person in church to hear my Mass.' "

ᑯᕐᓗ

A Former Penitent of Father Paul

relates the following story: "Once I was praying before the statue of St. Benedict in the church at Steenbrugge. It was during a thunder storm. A heavy clap of thunder was heard and at the same time I felt myself lifted from my place and put down some five steps further off. Then I saw that the lightning had struck and broken one of the windows, and the pieces had fallen on the very spot from which I had been lifted. When afterwards I saw Father Paul at the monastery he said to me laughing, 'You had a scare a little while ago; is it not so?' 'Yes, and I was carried off a few steps.' 'If you had been put down a little further off you would have been still more secure from danger.'

"When I entered the monastery, the wall of which had been recently painted, I rubbed my cloak against it. Brother Hilduard was annoyed when he saw the paint taken off the wall, and pointing to my cloak stained with paint, said to Father Paul, 'How shall we remove these spots?' 'That's nothing,' he said, 'come here.' Then he rubbed the stains with his hands and they came off; while the paint on the wall was restored at the same time."

∽

In a House of Antwerp

they tell the following story: "While the family were seated at table, a young girl had the misfortune of overturning her glass of red wine for which she was severely rebuked. But the good Father Paul interfered. Placing his hand over the large, red spot he said, 'Oh, that's nothing!' And the stain disappeared at once.

∽

A Young Lady Writes:

"At Antwerp Father Paul often received a number of visitors at our house. One winter, during very snowy weather, he came twice within three weeks. I told him the house would be pretty dirty from such a crowd of visitors, to which he replied that it would not. 'Well, if it is,' I said jestingly, 'you will have to clean it.' 'Yes, yes, I shall do so,' he said.

"The first day brought from sixty to seventy visitors, and the second about eighty. On both occasions the house resembled a real pool of mud and water. But no sooner had Father Paul, on his departure, crossed the threshold, than our house suddenly assumed its former cleanliness, as though no visitor had entered it. My father (now deceased), my brothers and I were indeed, very much astonished.

Very Often Father Paul

gave me answers to questions which I had intended to ask him, but neglected for want of time; for as soon as the consultations were finished, he was asked to visit the sick that were unable to come to him. One day I intended to consult him on a certain subject, but being preoccupied, forgot all about it. As he was on the point of leaving us, Father Paul gave me the information I desired. As I did not at first understand the meaning of his words, he remarked with a smile, 'It is the reply to the question you intended to ask me.'

The Rev. Mother Superior

of the convent of the Sacred Heart, opposite our house, sent for Father Paul on behalf of one sister whose back was so afflicted that she could not perform her duties. I accompanied him to the convent. As soon as he came into the presence of the sick sister, he gave her his blessing, and she was cured instantaneously.

"The Mother Superior requested Father Paul to say Mass at the convent the next morning at half past five; he promised to do so. Then Father Paul said to me, 'You shall come to my Mass tomorrow.'

" 'No,' I replied, 'I am tired and half past five is too early; I am not such an early riser.'

" 'But you shall come nevertheless,' the Rev. Father said laughing.'

" 'No, I will not come.' With these words I left Father Paul and went home, while he returned to the family where he lodged, some distance from our house. I slept well all night, but towards five o'clock I was awakened by a voice which I recognized as that of Father Paul, and which said distinctly, 'Louise, arise, it is time to come to my Mass.' Fancying that it was all a dream I tried to sleep again; but I heard the voice a second and a third time, and each time it sounded more determined.

" 'As I did not dare to remain in bed any longer, I arose, dressed hastily and went to Mass. After Mass Father Paul came to our house for breakfast and said to me with a laugh, 'Well, I had to call you three times this morning. I told you yesterday that you would come to my Mass.'

" 'How were you able to call me,' I said, 'You were not at our house?'

" 'The good God,' he replied 'permitted me to make you hear my voice without my being with you.'

～

Many a Time

my father spoke to Father Paul of his fear of dying suddenly, because the physician had told him that he would have a sudden end, but the Rev. Father always assured him that it would not be so; however, when he became ill, his anxiety increased, and he requested me to write to Termonde. Father Paul replied, 'Let your father banish all anxiety: he will not die suddenly, but he has only three months more to live, and he will die a holy death.'

"A few days before his death, my father expressed a wish to see his friend once more. On the very day of his death Father Paul came to console him; his sufferings were so intense that he longed to die. 'I would like to die,' said my father, 'for I cannot endure my sufferings any longer.' Father Paul replied, 'I shall go and pray.'

"After an hour's absence he returned and said to the patient, 'Very well, you can die this evening at ten o'clock; you will not suffer during the six hours you still have to live and your purgatory will be short: you will not suffer there.' My father died at ten o'clock that night, cheerfully resigned to the will of God, nor did he suffer any more the last six hours of his life.

～

Father Paul Being Obliged

to accompany a congregation from Bruges to Oostacker, engaged me to go there the same day. On the road of St. Amand, which leads to the celebrated pilgrimage, I saw the Rev. Father passing in a coach. I ran forward to stop the driver, but fell so heavily that I had great difficulty in rising. My knees and left hand were injured. I stepped into the convent of the Sisters of St. Amand where I rested for some time; then I painfully proceeded to the grotto of our Lady of Lourdes. There I saw Father Paul in a crowd of people and told him of my accident. He took my injured hand, made a little cross on it and prayed for a moment. The pain stopped at once. I then said with great confidence: 'and now my knees?' The Rev. Father made the sign of the cross three times, then he touched my knees with his hands and said, 'That is settled; you are cured,' and from that moment the pain was gone."

∽

A Sick Woman

came and asked Father Paul to cure her. She had brought a friend with her. The Rev. Father prescribed a novena and gave her the assurance of a cure. Then turning to the other woman, he asked her if she were not ill. "No," she said, "I come only to accompany my friend."

"Nevertheless, you are very sick," said Father Paul. "I am not," insisted the woman; "I feel quite well."

"It is your soul that is sick," said Father Paul, "it is as black as soot." "Why?"

"Did you not drown your child?"

"Oh, no! I never did such a thing!"

"Certainly you did so, eleven years ago, at such a place (indicating the exact spot) and you never confessed your crime." The unnatural mother burst into tears and made her confession to Father Paul.

∽

Every Sunday

a farmer from Oostcamp would drive to Steenbrugge to attend the eight o'clock Mass. One day arriving at the bridge near the monastery, he saw an old woman making grimaces; his horse shied, and it required an effort to make him cross the bridge. On his return, as well as on several succeeding Sundays, he encountered the same difficulty. He informed Father Paul, who gave him a medal with instructions to fasten it to the halter of the horse. From that time, the animal passed over the bridge without showing the least fear.

Father Paul,

accompanied by the Very Rev. Dom Joseph, prior of the monastery, paid a visit to a friend, a merchant, and he inquired of him if all were well with himself and family. The gentleman answering affirmatively, Father Paul, with manifest excitement, said to him: "Go to your store immediately, your presence is required." On his arrival, he found one of his servants in the act of stealing a considerable amount.

In Stuivenberg a Child was Sick;

as the illness increased, the mother proposed to her husband that they apply to Father Paul, but he opposed the project. The next day she renewed her efforts, but was again refused. On the third day her continued entreaties brought her husband into a rage and he began to blaspheme. Finally he gave his consent and accompanied his wife and child to Steenbrugge. As soon as they were admitted into Father Paul's presence, the latter at once addressed the man saying: "So at the third invitation you decided to come, but even then not without blaspheming!" Then, having given the man a severe rebuke, he cured his child.

A Child

of thirteen was, according to the physician's certificate, the victim of serious nervous attacks; and as the physician entertained no hope of benefiting the child, he advised the mother to seek the assistance of Father Paul. The mother, accompanied by a friend lost no time in visiting the Father. Perceiving the anxiety in the woman's face, he said to her, "Be of good cheer your child will get well for you are a good mother." He then prescribed the usual devotions in honor of St. Benedict. At the end of a novena the child was somewhat improved, but not entirely cured. She visited Father Paul a second time. He was much pleased with the result, as the lady was able to bring the child with her. He requested her to make another novena which restored the child to perfect health.

⌒⌒

An Unnatural Mother,

as she advanced in years, having become blind, begged Father Paul to restore her sight. The Rev. Father held a small mirror before the woman's eyes and asked her, "Do you see now?" "Oh yes," she replied, "and oh! what a beautiful little angel." "Is it not the child which you killed when you were young? You must bear your misfortune in expiation of your crime."

And she again became blind for Father Paul invariably refused to intercede in behalf of those whose affliction was the effect of sin.

⌒⌒

A Nun

happened to be in the Benedictine church of the abbey, and saw a woman lamenting and entreating Father Paul to come to her assistance; but he abruptly turned away from her.

The sister greatly affected followed Father Paul, and ventured to ask why he acted so strangely. He made answer, "It is indeed, too sad, but, in her youth she destroyed her child, she is now suffering the penalty of her crime, and I cannot help her."

⌒⌒

A Poor Girl of Antwerp

who had become blind, desired to obtain her recovery through Father Paul; but having no funds for the journey to Termonde, she applied to a young lady of Antwerp who was well known for her works of charity. The lady was kind enough to accompany the girl to Termonde.

Great, however, was her astonishment, when she heard Father Paul say to the blind girl, "Suffer your affliction in expiation of your crime; you put your new-born infant to death."

The wife of a boatman of the same place complained to Father Paul that she had lost six children immediately after their birth. The

Rev. Father said to her, "Before your marriage you suffocated your newly-born child, and the process lasted seven minutes. The seventh child to which you will give birth will die also, but you will save the eighth."

∾

At Antwerp

Father Paul often received his numerous visitors at the house of a friend, a merchant. One of this man's workmen had his face covered with blotches, and as various remedies had been used in vain, he had recourse to Father Paul. "The eruptions which torment you," he replied, "are caused by the state of your soul which is saturated with evil; go to confession and Holy Communion, and they will disappear." The workman followed this advice and was cured instantaneously.

The merchant prepared a feast in honor of his daughter, who had received her first Holy Communion, and Father Paul was invited to the banquet.

A young lady friend of the family, troubled with sore eyes, and continually haunted by a vision of a crown of thorns, was prevented by her malady from attending. In the meantime, however, she availed herself of Father Paul's presence and asked him to cure her, "You heal so many who are sick, please cure me."

"No," said Father Paul, "for you is reserved the cross which you must carry, for such is the will of God." "But I would like so much to attend the feast." "Very well; be it so, I shall cure your eyes for this day." The young lady joyfully assisted at the feast, but at the close of day, her eyes again pained her, and the crown of thorns still pursued her vision.

A countryman arrived in a buggy at the merchant's house. He was a stout man, but so stooped that his chin almost touched his knees. He was led into the room where Father Paul received his visitors. A few minuter later the man walked out straight as a pole. With one bound he jumped into his buggy, took the reins and drove away in the direction of his house.

The merchant's daughter was suffering from an attack of pleurisy when Father Paul came unexpectedly and said, "I know there is trouble here." "Yes," said the merchant, "my daughter is suffering." The Rev. Father gently passed his hand over that part of the chest where the pain was, and as his hand advanced, the girl experienced a sensation, she said, as if a troop of little animals were trotting away.

When Father Paul withdrew his hand, the patient was cured.

ↄﻪↄ

A Boy of Six Years

the son of a cattle-dealer in Borgerhout, was unable to stand on account of the extreme weakness of his legs. His father hoping to find a better remedy with Father Paul, than with the physician he had already consulted, went to Termonde. He had followed a good inspiration, for the Rev. Father said to him, "I shall be in Antwerp on such a day and at such a place. Bring your boy to me, he will be able to go there on foot." On the appointed day the child, cured, accompanied his father who, full of joy, came to thank the saintly Benedictine.

ↄﻪↄ

A Young Lady of Berchem

relates that accompanied by two friends, she called upon Father Paul, who presented each with a medal of St. Benedict. Then he handed one to her remarking, "You will not wear it." The young lady naturally was annoyed by what Father Paul had said. A month later she visited relatives, where she found the father of the family suffering intense agony, as by mistake, he had swallowed muriatic acid. After treating the patient for nine days, the physician declared that he could not afford the sick man any relief, as he was unable to take even a drop of water. The young lady asked the patient if he had heard of Father Paul, to which he answered in the negative. It was then that she was forcibly reminded of Father Paul's remark concerning the medal, "You will not wear it." For it was in her pocket when she wished to give it to the sick man. He dipped the medal into a glass of water, which he was able to drink, and at the end of six weeks he was restored to perfect health.

In gratitude for his recovery, he treasured the medal religiously, and wore it with the greatest respect and confidence. But a Jesuit Father, hearing of the wonderful cure, came to see him, and begged of him to let him have the medal for a poor woman whom he believed to be possessed by the devil. The man obstinately refused to part with his medal; and it was only after the most urgent entreaties that the Jesuit Father succeeded in procuring it. He went the next morning to his cabinet shop, but in ill humor, because of the persistency of the Jesuit. To his utter astonishment he beheld on the workbench a beautiful, new medal of St. Benedict, which could in no wise be accounted for.

"I once called on the Rev. Father, accompanied by a lady from Antwerp. This lady told him that the physicians had pronounced her incurable, on account of a lesion of the stomach. 'Has the physician seen it himself?' asked Father Paul, 'No, that is impossible.' 'Of course he could see it by performing an operation. . . .but there is nothing the matter with your stomach; your sickness comes from a great vexation. You will be cured in a short time.' The lady was perfectly well in eight days.

"I went to see Father Paul and spoke to him about a woman of Brechem who was confined to her bed by illness. 'The woman will soon be cured,' he said, 'and she will come to meet you upon your return.' When I got back I saw the woman on the threshold of our house. She had come to ask me all about my interview with Father Paul.

༄

I Drew Rent

from a house in which an old woman lived. As the value of the property began to decline, my notary advised me to sell it. I did not wish to cause pain to the poor, old woman, and therefore asked Father Paul what I should do. He replied, 'Do nothing about the matter and don't worry; better conditions will prevail.' Seven years later the woman died and the sale of the property brought more than enough to repay me.

ᨆ

One Day I Called

on Father Paul and asked him for the conversion of a certain man with whom I was acquainted. His reply was that the man would be converted only near the end of his life. Four years later that person was taken sick and refused all the consolations of religion. I returned to the monastery and informed Father Paul of the matter. 'Be quiet,' he said, 'this person will be converted; he will suffer such severe pains that he will end by calling upon God. This will happen after a while, for it cost me a deal to obtain for him that grace.' All came to pass as foretold by Father Paul."

Once a young person of Antwerp suffered from an affliction which hindered her breathing through her nose. Father Paul touched her forehead with his thumb and she was immediately cured.

ᨆ

A Merchant

of Eecloo relates the following occurrence: "A woman living in Ursel brought her sick child, which had been given up by the doctors, to Father Paul to obtain its cure. The Rev. Father raising a corner of the wraps with which the baby was covered said, 'Oh, that child will learn well, it has such intelligent eyes!' Then he spoke at some length with the friends who had accompanied the mother. She, on her part, renewed her request for the child's cure. Father Paul again looked at the child and said, 'Oh, this child will learn so well, look at those intelligent eyes!'

"The mother tried in vain to obtain a more reassuring answer; every time the Rev. Father repeated the same words, and she had to depart without obtaining anything further. The future, however, proved that the Rev. Father had said enough to fulfill the desires of the poor mother; for the child soon recovered, and Father Paul's prediction came true. At school the child distinguished himself by his cleverness and precocious intelligence."

61

A Certain Person in Ghent

had a very bad neighbor. As she saw him pass one day she said to Father Paul, "I wish that man would leave our neighborhood." The Rev. Father looked closely at the neighbor for a few seconds and replied, "Don't say that, for that man may become one of your best neighbors." Soon after the man was converted.

A Little Girl of Antwerp

was thought to be possessed by an evil spirit: she dragged herself about on her hands and knees, unable to raise herself. Her parents brought her to Termonde where Father Paul hung a medal around her neck and said a prayer. All at once the girl arose crying out, "I am saved!" She threw her arms around the neck of her deliverer, and it was quite a task to make her loosen her hold.

The Wile of an Official

in Steenbrugge endured very great sufferings from a cancer on the breast. As the physicians declared that the poor woman had to suffer three more months, she went to Termonde. Father Paul consoled her and exhorted her to resign herself to the holy will of God. Returning to Steenbrugge, the sick woman went to bed without suffering any longer, and died full of joy at the end of ten days.

A Person from Malines

reports a few facts that came to her knowledge:—

"A young girl from Brecht, eighteen years old, stayed in the hospital. Her little sister, aged six years, was sick and there was no hope for her recovery. The girl obtained permission from her mother to take the little one to Father Paul. Looking at the child, the Rev. Father said to the young girl, 'Your little sister is in a very serious condition. Your father is dead and your mother is leading a bad life, tell her to be converted. She must go to confession and make a novena to St. Benedict; the child will get well. But if she does not do so the child will die.' The young girl asked if she herself might not make the novena. 'No, your mother must make it. As to yourself, follow the inspiration which you have had as to your vocation, for your happiness depends thereon.'

"The sick child died in the course of a year, and the girl is now in the convent.

"A servant girl suffering from a disease of the eyes, besought Father Paul to do something to alleviate the pain. He answered, 'First restore the three bottles of wine that you stole from your employer; then make a novena to St. Benedict, and you will be cured.' The girl certifies that she returned the wine, and during the novena, her eyes were healed.

"A young lady, contrary to the advice of her confessor, fasted until she became very ill, and applied to Father Paul for the restoration of her health. This was his reply, 'You have disobeyed your confessor. Now, wander about, like a little bird, and await God's good pleasure to restore your health.' "

∽

A Lady from Deurne Writes:

"My mother had been deaf since childhood. Accompanied by my sister she came to consult Father Paul. The Rev. Father said to her, 'You have lost one ear completely, but I will take care of the other one which will get well.' Then he said to my sister 'Do as your mother does and you will be happy, for she prays all the time.' My mother's ear was soon cured.

"I often consulted Father Paul in difficult matters, and whenever I followed his advice, everything went well. I always felt quieted and reassured when leaving him.

"A young lady from Antwerp, who suffered from her eyes came to see Father Paul. For a moment he applied his fingers to her ailing eyes, and said to the girl, 'Your eyes will not hurt you any more; here is a prayer which I do not give to everybody; recite it.' The young lady's eyes were cured.

"A widow who kept a hotel in Deurne, fearing for the future of her three daughters, wished to give up her place. Nevertheless, before doing so, she went to consult Father Paul in Termonde. 'You cannot leave your hotel,' he replied, 'you are honest and watchful, and your daughters are in no danger.'

"In spite of his advice the widow gave up the hotel and went into other business, but had no success. Remembering Father Paul's advice, she bought back her hotel, and from that time on prosperity returned.

"At the death of her parents, the daughter of a farmer abandoned her farm and intended to enter a convent. Father Paul advised her not to do so, and told her to open a little store in the village. 'It will be needless to advertise your wares,' he added, 'for you will have plenty of customers.' From the very beginning her business prospered."

⌒〜⌒

A Lady of Borgerhout Writes:

"Three of our children died within five weeks. The oldest was taken sick and died at the end of fifteen days, after having made her first Holy Communion on her death-bed. Then a little boy of ten years died without the blessing of the priest, and finally I lost a baby only six weeks old. There was no one to console me; my sadness was so much the greater because I imagined that two of my children were still suffering in purgatory. At last I had recourse to the Rev. Father Paul, and had the happiness of finding in him that consolation which I had sought in vain elsewhere. He said to me, 'If I had been with your children, they would not have died. You would have preferred to keep them, but they are happier now, for all three are in heaven.'

"My older sister lived in our house and suffered great pains in her stomach. Father Paul said to her, 'You will not die of this trouble, tell your mother.' Now the thought that this sickness might cause

64

the death of my sister, had been worrying my mother for a long time. Several years later my sister died of apoplexy.

"My sister Mary was very devout, but had little confidence in Father Paul; yet one day she went to him for advice. The Rev. Father said to her, 'If you have no confidence in me, why do you come?' These words greatly astonished her, and from that day on, Mary showed the most perfect confidence in the Rev. Father."

∽

One of Our Children,

four years old, was very delicate and sickly; her sufferings were continual, and the frequent convulsions that sometimes lasted several hours, made her a little martyr. Often after these attacks, the poor child lost her speech, and an arm or a leg was paralyzed. The doctor declared that only a miracle could save her. I spoke to Father Paul about her, and he said, 'If I had been with you, I would have put my hand on the child's head and the convulsions would have ceased; but console yourselves, this affliction will have no serious consequences. When the girl reaches the age of six or seven years she will be completely cured, and no trace of her sickness will remain; but pray much.' As the child grew up, the convulsions became less frequent. She has now reached her eighth year and is in perfect health.

"And yet how often she met with accidents! I mention but two. One day the restless child fell from the window to a platform, a distance of eight feet, without being hurt in the least. 'I have my scapular on,' she said calmly rising. A few months ago while taking a walk with her older sister who held her by the hand, she tore herself loose and rolled under the legs of a horse that was drawing a wagon. The horse touched her slightly with its foot and one of the wheels of the wagon passed over her leg. A druggist of Antwerp, who witnessed the accident, was sure that her limb was broken, but upon examination it was found intact; only a slight, bluish mark showed where the wheel had passed.

"We often visited Father Paul, and in all our affairs he was our best counselor."

⌒↭⌒

A Lady of Bruges Says:

In 1884, the doctor who was called to visit my sick child, twenty months old, declared that he had meningitis and was incurable. The nurse thought he had typhus and would die in a few hours. Having heard about Father Paul, I entreated my husband to go to Steenbrugge. He drove there at once, entered the church and was told that Father Paul was in his confessional. The Rev. Father, as if he had been called, came out of the confessional and said to my husband that he was ready to accompany him. A few minutes later, I had the happiness of receiving him into our house.

About the same time the nurse and an assistant priest of the Notre Dame parish entered, and in their presence Father Paul put his hand on the forehead of the child and prayed. Having finished his prayer, the Rev. Father said, "The sickness is not in his head."

Then he put his hand on the breast of the dying child, and after praying for some time, said, "It is here. The child is in a very desperate condition; but do not worry, he will soon be cured. Do exactly what the doctor tells you." That very evening a decided improvement was noticeable, and after a few days my child was cured.

⌒↭⌒

At Oostcamp There Lived

a little boy, three years old, who was covered from head to foot with an eczema which caused him intolerable pain. His mother and uncle brought him to Termonde in 1895. "Tell me all the quarters in which you have already sought relief," said Father Paul to the mother; to which she replied that she had been to several doctors, to a druggist, to such a convent, and to such and such a saint's shrine. "After that," continued Father Paul, "you proposed to come here, and from that moment the child began to get better; but noticing the improvement you abandoned your project, seeing that the child began to get worse again, you have come here at last." "All this is true!" exclaimed the astonished mother. Father Paul continued, "It is useless for you to apply elsewhere; this is the work of St. Benedict; he will cure your child, or nobody will."

He then took the boy by the hand for a walk through the garden, accompanied by the mother and the uncle. The little fellow who till then had been a prey to profound sadness became at once very lively, displaying a remarkable precocity, so that Father Paul remarked, "This child is quite intelligent, he must be cured. This summer he will go to school."

The Rev. Father prescribed a novena, gave a little powder of the miraculous roses of St. Benedict for him to take, and a medal which he was to wear. From that time the child did not feel the least irritation and was completely cured on the last day of the novena.

∽

A Young Lady

of Antwerp thus writes: "I saw Father Paul for the first time in the year 1887, at the monastery of Termonde. For several months I had suffered from nervousness and stomach trouble, caused by my grief at the death of my mother.

"Before I had uttered a word, Father Paul upbraided me for sorrowing so much for her who is now so happy in heaven. He said to me, 'Your mother loved peace. She was very much devoted to the Blessed Virgin, hence, she died on Saturday, which she so much desired. Imitate her example, thus will you also be very happy. As to your sickness, St. Benedict will assist you, and another saint's intercession will completely cure you.' Two years later, after many prayers and a pilgrimage to Lourdes, I was cured through St. Anthony of Padua.

"In 1879 my father offered one of his houses for sale or for rent. A tenant presented himself, but this person not having a good reputation, my father refused to deal with him. The man flew into a rage, cursing my father and wishing him every evil. During three months from that time, we received no new offer. I spoke of it to Father Paul one day when he honored us by a visit. He said, 'All the evil which that man has wished you will fall back upon himself, and will do you no harm. I shall pray and make a novena to St. Benedict, and before the end of the novena, persons will come ready to buy; but it is not certain that they will come to a definite agreement. However, if you do not sell the house, you will surely find a good tenant.'

"Hereupon, Father Paul left us. Half an hour later, my father who had been away during Father Paul's visit, came home and I repeated to him the encouraging words of the Rev. Father. At the same time two ladies came and inquired about the price of the property, saying that the house, which they had inspected pleased them. But the ladies never returned. Three days later we rented the house to an excellent person who after the death of my father bought the property, and is still living there."

∽

Father Benedict,

a young priest of the monastery of Steenbrugge, being consumptive, expressed a desire of going to Lourdes to be cured; but Father Paul, who was his prior, would not give his consent. Thereupon Father Benedict appealed to the Rt. Rev. Abbot of Afflighem who gave him the necessary permission. Upon his departure Father Paul declared that the patient would not be cured, and his words proved only too true; for Father Benedict died in the church of Lourdes during the time when Father Paul said Mass in Steenbrugge. Immediately after his Mass Father Paul declared that during the consecration he had seen the body of the deceased being carried to the sacristy of the basilica at Lourdes.

∽

The Daughter of a Village Mayor

being at the last extremity, one of her friends who was acquainted with Father Paul proposed to her father to have her carried to the grotto of Our Lady of Lourdes at Oostacker; but the father would not give his consent, because the doctor had declared that the patient would die on the way. As a last resource the friend wrote to Father Paul for advice. He strongly recommended her to urge the father to allow his daughter to be brought by train to Oostacker, assuring her that the patient would be cured at the grotto

Yielding to these entreaties the mayor at last gave his consent; there being no hope otherwise of saving his daughter. The journey was made, but not without great pain and difficulty. When the grotto had been reached, and the invalid placed in an arm-chair before the statue of our Lady, her friends began to recite the rosary aloud. When the third decade of the rosary had been recited, the invalid raised herself up, to the great astonishment of those present; her complexion, hitherto of an ashy paleness, began to assume its natural color and a new breath of life animated her exhausted body. The recitation of the rosary was continued and soon the young lady to her great delight, was able to walk around the grotto. She was cured.

∾

A Woman of Sixty Years

who lived in Steenbrugge, suffered for a long time from rheumatism which deprived her of all power of movement. Ceaselessly she wept and complained. Upon the request of her husband Father Paul paid her a visit and touched her head and feet with his hand. At the same instant the woman was able to get up; she was cured.

In 1886 a woman of seventy-one years, living also at Steenbrugge, was afflicted with rheumatism to such a degree as to be unable to make a step, and the doctor could do nothing for her. Father Paul went to her house and said to her, "Oh, you will be able to walk very well!" The following year the woman began to go out on crutches, and after a few days she could walk with ease. And now at the age of eighty, she is as spry as ever.

∾

A Woman of Beveren,

who suffered from a deep wound in the leg, had been unsuccessfully treated by her physician and a professor from Louvain. Then she commissioned a friend of hers to consult Father Paul, and he, without knowing the patient, said, "The woman who sent you, has a cancer below the knee, and part of the bone is already exposed. I can do nothing for her; but let her make a daily visit for a month to

Our Lady of Gaverland: the Blessed Virgin can obtain everything from her Divine Son. The wound will be healed in the course of this month." The patient followed the advice of the Rev. Father and was cured.

❧

In 1890, a Man of Antwerp

was dying of consumption. His wife realizing that medical science was powerless, came to Termonde for help. Father Paul listened to her with great kindness and inquired if all the other members of the family were well. "Alas!" she replied sadly, "my youngest boy cannot walk without crutches." "Very well, pray with me: your husband will be spared to you, and your son will not need his crutches much longer."

The husband was cured, and the same year, during a pilgrimage to Our Lady of Montaign, the paralyzed boy left his crutches there.

❧

A Lady of Twenty-eight Years,

who lived in Knesselaere, had her left side paralyzed, and besides was suffering from a disease of the spinal marrow. As there was no longer any hope for her, a friend induced her to have recourse to Father Paul, and was kind enough to write to the Rev. Father herself. Father Paul sent her a medal to wear and prescribed a novena to St. Benedict. On the third day of the novena the invalid began to walk, and on the ninth day, to the great amazement of the physician, her recovery was complete.

❧

A Countryman from Moll-Genebuiten

tells the following story: "For a long time I suffered so much in my abdomen that I feared I would have to die. Instead of curing me, the physicians were not even able to diagnose the nature of my sickness. I went to see Father Paul in Termonde and described to him my painful condition. The Rev. Father gave me a strong blow with his hand on the abdomen, and from that time I felt the pain no more."

⌒⋌つ

At Steenbrugge,

a young girl who was consumptive had already lost one lung. The help of Father Paul having been invoked in her behalf, he simply replied, "She will be cured tomorrow." And so it happened. Since then she has been married more than once, and to judge by her healthy appearance, no one would ever suspect that she has but one lung.

The woman in charge of the pews of the church, seeing that the physician had no hope for her, implored Father Paul to pray for her. The Rev. Father blessed a bottle filled with water and put a medal of St. Benedict into it; then he directed the patient to take daily three small glasses of the water. "But," they told him, "the physician said if she takes even as much as a drop of water she will die." "Not at all," replied Father Paul, "let her do what I have told you: she will be cured when she has finished the bottle." And so it was.

⌒⋌つ

A Master-mason

of Antwerp seriously injured his arm while working at a sewer. He was taken to the hospital where he remained for seven months. The arm grew so bad that the physicians decided to amputate it; but the mason refused to give his consent because in the meantime he had heard of Father Paul, and was determined to have recourse to him. The Rev. Father sent him word that an operation was not necessary; he recommended him to make a novena with great confidence to St. Benedict, assuring him that he would be cured. On the last day of the novena the arm was completely restored.

A leader of the nation at Antwerp suffered great pains in his stomach for thirteen years. Having followed without benefit the treatment of several physicians, he betook himself to Father Paul and was cured instantaneously.

A Working Woman of Thielt,

hearing of the sad condition of a gentleman who suffered from spinal disease, advised him to have recourse to Father Paul and kindly offered to accompany him. Receiving the visitors, the Rev. Father said to the woman, "How did you dare to make such a journey? You are in a worse state of health than you imagine; you might have dropped dead on the way." "You frighten me, Rev. Father," she replied; "but please help me. For some time I have suffered cruelly in my throat;. I have great pain when I swallow and each time I feel as though something rises up in my throat threatening to strangle me. Rather than go to the physician I wished to see you, the more so as the gentleman here offered to defray the expenses of my journey."

"Yes, yes, you might have died on the way but I shall cure you." Thereupon Father Paul with his hand strongly squeezed the woman's neck and said, "Do you feel that strange body disappear?" "Yes, and I am greatly relieved." "Very well, go into the next room, while I occupy myself with this gentleman. But you will soon come back, for your affliction will return." Father Paul listened to the complaints of his new visitor, advised several novenas and promised a cure. The prediction was verified; the patient recovered completely and was married in Febuary 1901.

In the meantime the woman reappeared. "Ah! are you again attacked?" "Alas!" Then the Rev. Father put his right hand upon the throat and his left hand around the neck of the patient, and applied a strong pressure for about two minutes at the end of which he said, "The affliction has now left you for good." And so it was. At the same moment, when Father Paul made a few steps, the woman heard a noise as if somebody had struck the floor several times with a hammer.

"What's the matter now?" he said smiling. "You, walk, perhaps the noise will be repeated." The woman obeyed, but there was no noise. As soon as Father Paul had made a few steps, the same knocks were heard. "Oh!" he said laughing, "It is the devil."

A Wealthy Gentleman

of Antwerp suffered in the last stages of dropsy, and the physician believing that he could not survive more than two days longer, recommended that he receive the last sacraments. In the meantime, the son-in-law of the dying man, being acquainted with Father Paul, called upon him, and obtained a medal of St. Benedict, and some powder of the miraculous roses. Father Paul said to him, "Pray fervently for the patient, and I will help you; and your father-in-law will soon be cured." The following day, at the appointed hour several physicians met in consultation; but to their great surprise they found the patient, who the day before was dying, sitting up and smiling. He was completely restored to health.

❦

On a Farm in Oostcamp

a valuable hog had died. The farmer complained of his loss to Father Paul and received the following reply:

"It is your own fault: you did not pray." At the moment, the farmer's memory was deficient, and therefore he maintained that he had prayed well according to his usual custom.

"No," the Rev. Father replied, "you did not pray: you did not even recite the half of the Our Father. The farmer thereupon remembered that, being too tired, he really had neglected his prayers on that evening.

❦

Strange Things Occurred

in a farmer's stable at Oostcamp. Every now and then some accident befell the live-stock; their least movement produced a sprain, a twist of the legs or partial paralysis. Cases of limping and lameness were of daily occurrence. In this despair the man had recourse to Father Paul. He prescribed a novena and gave a medal to fasten to the door of the stable. From that time all trouble ceased. The farmer said that without Father Paul's intervention his ruin would have been inevitable.

To another farmer who complained that he was losing all his young pigs, Father Paul said, "God has sent you here, there is still time for help; we shall drive the evil into the water from which it will go into the sea where it will no longer molest anybody. Otherwise it would continue its work and attack the cows, then the horses and at last the people." From that time everything went well on the farm.

༄

An Old Farmer of St. Michel,

near Bruges, whose wife was sick, had begged Father Paul to accompany him to his home, for he trusted to the intervention of the saintly Benedictine who cured so many sick persons. The Rev. Father placed his hand on the breast of the old lady and asked her if she still felt the pain. She answered that she did not feel any better. Father Paul again put the same question and received the same answer: but after repeating the question a third time, the patient cheerfully answered, that she no longer felt any pain: she was cured.

The same farmer had trouble in his stable: three very fine pigs had been attacked by an infectious disease, and in accordance with the law they were to be killed. The farmer having complained of his bad luck, the Rev. Father assured him that the pigs would get well. "But," said the farmer, "will there be no danger in eating their meat?" "Not at all," Father Paul replied, "on the contrary it will be delicious." Without any other remedy the pigs soon got well.

Then the farmer showed him a large calf that was sick and refused to eat. He asked Father Paul if it were not best to kill it. "But it is cured," the latter replied, "just give it to drink, and you will see." When the water was placed before the calf, it drank eagerly. It was cured.

༄

A Farmer's Wife of Liezele lez-Puers

had found it impossible, for some length of time to make butter. Having complained of it to Father Paul, he gave her a medal to put into the churn during the process of churning. Having followed this advice, she declares that with the greatest ease she obtained butter, superior both in quantity and quality to any she had ever before made.

A similar case occurred on a large farm at Leeuw, a hamlet of Zedeleghem, with the exception in this case, that the churning operations had been going on for a whole year without any result. A veterinarian, having for a long time doctored the cows in the hopes of improving their milk, finally abandoned his efforts as useless. Then the farmer's wife went to Steenbrugge where Father Paul said to her, "A lack of confidence! Why did you not come sooner? Here is a medal and some powder of the miraculous roses of St. Benedict; put them into the churn and you will have butter."

The woman did so and everything went well for a year, when the same trouble occurred again. She visited Father Paul once more and complained to him. He gave her a second medal, and the butter had never failed since.

∽

On a Farm in Oostroosebeke

things were going from bad to worse. Already there had been a long series of misfortunes; the cattle, the crops, nothing escaped the evil influence, even the milk had become unpalatable. The farmers were rapidly drifting towards inevitable ruin. In 1894 these good people had recourse to Father Paul of whose great power they had been informed. His answer was, "The causes of all this evil are the blasphemies and the impurity of those who lived on the farm before you; but take courage and do what I tell you. Pray with great confidence and make use of the medal of St. Benedict."

The farmers followed the recommendations of the Rev. Father, or at least they thought they had; but fifteen days passed without any improvement. Father Paul being informed of this said that they had not observed everything as he had directed, adding that if they would follow his advice to the letter, they would surely be delivered from their misfortunes. They did so, and at the end of four weeks, the farm presented an improved appearance and everything proceeded according to their wishes.

∽

A Contractor in Antwerp

had thirteen horses in the stable, and as if an evil spirit hovered over them, twelve became sick in succession, and died to the great grief of the unhappy owner who could not explain the cause of the disaster. He had recourse to Father Paul, who visited the stable, prayed there and gave a medal to be hung on the wall; he also told the proprietor that he might have the stable calsomined, but that this was not absolutely necessary, and that he might now restock the stable without having anything to fear. The thirteen horses remained well, the stable was filled with other horses, and the disease did not reappear.

༄

A Young Girl of Waloon

who had run away from home, left, at the same time the path of honor and virtue. After many vain endeavors to induce her to return to the bosom of her family, her heart-broken mother betook herself to Steenbrugge and asked the advice of Father Paul. "You have come to consult me," the Rev. Father replied, "but you did wrong in delaying until now, for you were told long ago to take this step. Your daughter obstinately refuses to return. Some priests have made vain attempts to induce her to do so, but I shall make her come home before three months have elapsed. Between now and then a serious event will take place in your family, but do not grieve excessively over it. Have confidence and courage, and pray fervently."

Two months later the woman lost a son, and immediately afterwards the lost sheep returned to the fold.

༄

Some Poor Peasants

owned a little patch of land which they tilled and carefully cultivated. But alas! a severe hail-storm visited the neighborhood, and injured the crops that gave bright promise of a rich harvest. In order to secure themselves against further damage, they had recourse to Father Paul for protection. He advised them to bury four medals of St. Benedict in the four corners of the field, and his instructions were immediately complied with. A few days afterwards, a second and still more violent hail-storm utterly ruined the crops in the vicinity. But the little field protected by St. Benedict escaped untouched, and in due time produced a splendid harvest.

༄

A Field

in which the flax was beginning to come up, was devastated by insects. In his despair the owner went to Father Paul and complained of the misfortune. "Here is a medal," the Rev. Father said, "put it into your field, and the flax will start to grow again." The man did as he was told and reaped a fine harvest.

A country curate cultivated a little field near his house, but in spite of every care, the weeds sprang up in such abundance that it was difficult to raise a crop. He complained of it to Father Paul, who gave him four medals of St. Benedict to be buried in the four corners of his little plot. The weeds disappeared as if by magic.

༄

A Woodcutter

begged Father Paul to cure his sick child. The usual prescriptions were given; to wear a medal of St. Benedict, to dip another into all the drink of the child, and to make a novena in honor of St. Benedict. Ten days later, the woodcutter returned and said to the Rev. Father, "My child is not better . . . ." "Because you prayed only three days!" They made a complete novena and the child was cured.

༄

A Farmer of Assebrouk

complained to Father Paul that he had a succession of misfortunes with his cattle. Thereupon Father Paul reminded him that he had in his employ a one-armed cow-boy to whom all the misfortune might be attributed. "He has secretly in his possession books treating of magic; while in the army, he attempted to commit suicide, but the bullet instead of entering his head, penetrated his arm, which had to be amputated." The farmer then recalled having observed the cow-boy deeply absorbed in reading a book, which he endeavored to conceal. He was at once discharged, and all the farmer's ill-luck ceased.

ᏇᎧ

A Farmer's Wife im Varssenaere

was overwhelmed with misfortunes. There was a succession of sicknesses in her house, which spared neither her children nor her cattle. She spoke to Father Paul about it. "There is an old woman who sometimes comes to your house and to whom you have already done a great deal of good," the Rev. Father replied; "she won't come again, and your troubles will stop. Go home, you will meet the old woman on the road, but don't talk to her." It happened as Father Paul foretold. She met the evil-minded woman, but the latter never again was seen on the farm, and all sickness disappeared.

ᏇᎧ

A Countryman from Meldert

discovered that a large sum of money had been taken out of his trunk. This happened one summer evening at seven o'clock. In despair the man went at once to the abbey of Afflighem and complained of his loss to Father Paul. The Rev. Father promised to look into the matter. That same evening the stolen money was found in the trunk. The daughter of this man, who now (1897) lives in Denderbelle and who told the foregoing story, does not remember the other details connected with the affair. This wonderful case of restitution happened more then twenty-five years ago, when Father Paul was charged with the reestablishment of the old abbey of Afflighem.

Five hundred francs in gold were stolen from a country-woman of Steenbrugge, one Saturday in August 1886. She had the money in a small linen bag in her clothes-press. The theft must have occurred the evening before. The woman carried her complaint to the mayor, but without any effect. On the following Tuesday, towards evening she had recourse to Father Paul. "Go home quietly," he replied, "the money will be returned to you; the thief will be forced to bring back in his own person what he stole from you."

The woman was unable to close her eyes all that night. She rose at four o'clock and explored again all the corners and recesses of her house; at last she came to a door in the rear which had a small opening at the bottom, and there, to her great joy, she found all her beautiful gold pieces scattered over the floor. The thief must have come during the night to make restitution in that novel manner.

∽

A Woman of Steenbrugge,

overwhelmed with sorrow because her son had left her, and no one knew whither he had gone, came to Father Paul for consolation. "Don't worry," said the Rev. Father, "he will return within three days; and he will remain at home to be your support, but do not tell him that you were to see me." Three days later, the young man, who had procured employment as a farm-hand in a distant village, was seated at dinner with his employer, when suddenly he became strangely agitated. To the astonishment of all present, he left the farm, and hastened toward Steenbrugge. Almost breathless and bathed in perspiration, he entered the house of his parents, who were confidently awaiting his arrival.

"What has happened here," he inquired, "that I have been irresistibly forced to return?" "Oh, nothing serious," answered his mother, in a calm tone of voice, "and you see we are all in the best of health, thank God." "Very well, mother, I will never leave you again, and we will all work together."

∽

The Wife of a Farmer

at St. Gilles, near Termonde, relates the following stories: —

"For several days my child was suffering and crying all the time. I went to Termonde and complained to Father Paul. 'Oh, that's nothing,' he replied,—'even now your child does not cry anymore, and by the time you return, it will be cured.' And so it was.

"We had sold our crop of hemp to a merchant; but when he came to make his purchase, he noticed the presence of little worms, and refused to pay the price agreed upon. I then saw Father Paul and complained to him of the failure of our bargain, whereupon he said, 'The insects are on the point of dying.' And sure enough, as soon as I came home we found the insects all dead, strewn about the ground.

"We also had a field of turnips, the leaves of which, unfortunately, were eaten up by the caterpillars. I went again to Father Paul, and complained to him of this new trouble, but he replied, just as he had done in the case of our hemp, 'Don't worry; the caterpillars are dying.' On my return these injurious insects were lying lifeless on the ground."

∞

In a Field of Beets

different kinds of insects caused great damage. The farmer called on Father Paul to tell him of his threatened interests, and asked his advice and assistance. The Rev. Father gave him two Benedictine medals and told him to put each in a corner of the field which was threatened. "Do not put them" he said, "in two adjacent corners, but in the two opposite corners of your plot of ground which is square."

The peasant obeyed and carefully marked the spot where the medals were buried, in order to be able to find them later on and preserve them religiously. In this, however, he did nothing else but what a number of Father Paul's privileged clients were doing.

The field at once assumed a better appearance and, yielding to curiosity, the owner determined to have a look at the medals. What was his surprise when he found each medal surrounded by myriads of withered insects which seemed to have met by appointment near the medals destined to destroy them. The insects were gathered up by the farmer and brought to the Benedictines of Termonde as a convincing proof of the power of the blessed medals.

∞

A Good Merchant of Antwerp,

who had three small children, two boys and a girl, found his affairs going from bad to worse as if some evil genius had brought misfortune to his home. Among those who brought provisions to the store there was a country woman about forty years of age who from time to time delivered her products, such as eggs, butter, milk, fruits, and vegetables.

One day in 1890, this woman gave the older boy a few apples and shortly after, the child was taken so sick, that the physician, who confessed that he was unable to understand the nature of the illness, declared there was no hope of his recovery. Four other physicians arrived at the same conclusion. The parents noticed strange occurrences, that took place with this boy the cause of which they could not explain: when a blessed statuette of St. Joseph or any other blessed object was presented to the child he was afflicted with extreme terror. The boy finally died, and then the same sickness befell his little brother.

In the meantime the country woman continued to bring her provisions to the store. One day these words escaped her: "Is the little one not dead yet?" but it was only later that they were understood.

Following the advice of an acquaintance of Father Paul, the sorrowing father went to Termonde and submitted his sad case to the saintly Benedictine. This is what Father Paul said to him: "It is never well to allow strangers to give children apples, candy, or similar things; your little boy will soon be a beautiful angel in heaven."

The child died soon after and Father Paul came to visit the parents at their home; he offered a prayer and gave a medal of St. Benedict to be attached to the wall of the store, saying that as long as he lived the woman would not again put her foot into their house. So it was and from that day the affairs of this merchant began to prosper. The Rev. Father also told them, if the wicked woman ever returned, they should send her away, but without anger.

Father Paul died the night of February 24, 1896, five minutes to eleven, and the next morning at nine, and before the news of his death had become known, the evil-minded woman, who lived two miles from Antwerp, came to the store, not however, to bring any provisions, but to buy some trifle. "Give me some pieces of soap," she said. "We have no soap," said the merchant impatiently, hardly able to contain himself; and told her to go.

"Well, then," she said give me a broom." The merchant replied that he had none; then she wanted two small candles, but the merchant refused to sell her anything and finally told her to get out of the store. "How everything has changed here!" she exclaimed.

Some time before the death of his two sons the merchant had been visited by two Carmelite Fathers who were his friends. One of them spoke to him of the great power of the medals of St. Benedict and sent him one which afterwards was worn by his little daughter. The merchant ascribes the preservation of his only child to the wearing of that medal.

In the course of another visit Father Paul said to these people, "You do not expect any more children, but you will have one. It will be a boy." The prediction was fulfilled.

To a Notary

who was bitterly disappointed at having no offspring, Father Paul said, "Do not worry, you will have a son, and you will not lose him." These words came true, and Father Paul's memory is kept sacred in that family. The son was given the name of Paul after the saintly religious.

∞

The Doctor of an Important Place

in Flanders writes: "In November 1894, in the course of my visits, I was suddenly seized with a violent chill, so much so that I was hardly able to keep warm by a brisk walk. Having reached home, I had to go to bed. A high fever, accompanied by general indisposition and profuse perspiration, soon broke out, there were sharp pains in the region of the stomach, in a word, there appeared all the symptoms of a serious gastric complaint, aggravated by perityphlitis. I could not make the slightest movement without feeling great pain.

"Seeing that nothing gave me relief, my son, also a doctor, went to Termonde to find Father Paul, who for a long time had been our friend, adviser, and benefactor, and whose sanctity was well known to us. Father Paul told my son that I would be cured. He prescribed a novena to Our Blessed Lady and St. Benedict and promised that he would join in it. He also told me to wear a medal of St. Benedict, to dip it into my drinks, and take some of the powder of the miraculous roses of St. Benedict. We all had full confidence in the words of the Rev. Father, and on the very day of the feast of the Immaculate Conception I was perfectly cured.

"Again in October 1896, as I was coming home, all at once I had a violent hemorrhage in consequence of a congestion of the lungs. My family and I made a novena in honor of St. Benedict and of Father Paul, promising a visit to the tomb of the late lamented Father if I would be cured. Having applied an old letter of the Rev. Father to my chest, the hemorrhage stopped, and at the end of two weeks I was on the way to recovery. Some weeks later, my health was perfectly restored.

"One day as I was speaking to the Rev. Father about a tumor which defied all treatment, I asked him if an operation was not necessary. The saintly man replied that I should not submit to an operation; the tumor would be cured of its own accord. In the course of time it disappeared. I retain the most grateful recollection of the prophetic words of this holy religious."

∽

A Lady of Bruges says:

"Shortly after the birth of my third child, I became sick, and remained ill for seven years. My sister so often spoke to me of Father Paul, that I decided to go to Steenbrugge with my husband. 'You are very sick,' the Rev. Father said to me, 'and the stomach trouble from which you suffer is caused by some vexation or other, which is the greatest scourge of women. There is no reason for your vexation; you blame some member of your family, but what can you do? Nothing. There is no family without troubles. If you stop thinking about it, the vexation will pass away and you will be perfectly restored within two years. And once you are cured, the good God will yet give you two children.' The prediction came true, I was cured after two years, and we were blessed with two more children."

❧

A Young Lady of Bruges

was commissioned by a friend to ask the prayers of Father Paul for the successful issue of a certain affair which she desired to keep secret from the Rev. Father, as well as her name. When the messenger arrived at Steenbrugge Father Paul revealed to her the matter for the success of which she had come to ask his prayers and added, "Tell the person who sent you that this affair will be settled in accordance with her wishes."

❧

Father Paul said to a Young Lady

who came to visit him, "A very heavy cross is in store for you . . . . Are you not afraid of it?" "Oh, well," she replied, "it will probably not be so heavy when it comes." "Ah, but it will, and you will groan under the weight of it. But come afterwards, and I will help you to carry it."

A few weeks later her brother-in-law committed suicide, and all the relatives were overwhelmed with grief. Remembering Father Paul's invitation the young lady returned to the monastery, and the Rev. Father gave her some reassuring information concerning the state of the soul of the deceased, saying, "Your brother-in-law committed suicide in a fit of fever and was not responsible. He was very good to his wife and children and was beloved by them; but all his thoughts were centered on the material things of the world, he never thought of the future of his soul which is now in the depths of purgatory. You must pray a great deal for him." Then Father Paul went over the whole life of the deceased, as if he had followed his career step by step.

❧

A Nun from Ranst (Lierre)

commissioned a servant of the convent to have the cross of her rosary blessed by Father Paul, but should not tell him to whom the cross belonged. Having blessed the cross the Rev. Father said, "Tell that sister that I pray for her; she suffers from heart disease, but that will soon pass away." Then the Rev. Father gave a medal of St. Benedict for the nun, and prescribed a novena.

༄

Receiving a Young Lady from Eecloo

Father Paul pointed his finger at her and said, "You allow yourself to be tortured by scruples. That is bad. The good God is not pleased with scrupulous persons. Tell me what it is." "I dare not," she replied.

"Tell it anyway." "I am ashamed."

"Ah, go on; let us see!"

"No, I am too bashful . . . . you say it yourself!"

Then Father Paul told her in detail what the scruple was and added, "Above all, don't tell it in the confessional for it is ridiculous. And don't be scrupulous any longer."

The young lady also had a fleshy growth on her hand. Father Paul noticing it, asked her what it was, and she replied that she had that eight years. The Rev. Father then took her hand and pressed his thumb with all his force upon the tumor. "Oh! you hurt me," the lady exclaimed. But Father Paul continued the pressure for a while.

The next day at home, she noticed two little boys teasing each other, and one of them struck with some force the hand of his little companion. The young lady reproved him for it saying, "This is not good, for by striking one like that you may cause an injury like the one I have here," showing her hand and at the same time looking severely at the boy.

"Well," the latter asked laughing, "what have you there?" Then the young lady noticed that the fleshy excrescence on her hand had disappeared without leaving the least trace.

༄

A Trappist Brother

was tramping over the country, making dupes of the superiors of religious communities, where he demanded alms for some fictitious good work. In the last place he succeeded in cheating the superior of a charitable institution in Bruges out of ten francs, and from there he went to the monastery of Steenbrugge where the prior, Father Paul, received him, but gave him no chance to detail his lies; on the contrary he was thus severely addressed by the Rev. Father: "You have escaped from your monastery and spend your time in deceiving the people; you are begging for yourself."

"How do you know that?" the stranger asked full of confusion. "Return at once to your monastery where they will again receive you," dryly replied Father Paul and sent the brother on his way.

❧

A Man Leading a Wicked Life

actuated by a spirit of merriment, paid a visit to Father Paul in Antwerp. The Rev. Father spoke to him in a severe, and at the same time sweet tone, these words: "Change your life and do not blaspheme any longer." The visitor was so surprised and touched by the insight of the saintly man that he at once made a sincere confession, and thenceforth, led an edifying life.

❧

A Young Man

in the last stages of consumption, daily expected his death. Two of his friends jokingly suggested that he go to see Father Paul. "You treat the matter sneeringly; very well, I will go," replied the poor invalid. "As we desire to witness a miracle, we will accompany you," said the two friends.

At Antwerp they were received by Father Paul who said to the sick man, "Your condition is most serious, but God will have pity on you; you will be cured." To him who had indulged the most in raillery, the Rev. Father said, "Two months from now you will die; prepare yourself for a good death, for soon you will appear before

God." To the third he said, "Change your manner of life and be converted, for the state of your conscience is deplorable."

These predictions were fulfilled; the sick man was cured and the second died, while the third is now leading an exemplary life. These three young men were inhabitants of Borgerhout.

ↂ

A Peasant from the Suburbs of Ghent

when speaking of Father Paul, had the habit of calling him in mockery, the Father with the medals. But when his daughter took sick, he deemed it well to cease his raillery, and more advisable to have recourse to the good religious in order to obtain the cure of his child. Father Paul told him that his irreligious conduct was the only cause of the great pains which his daughter suffered, and as he gave him a medal for her, he added, "Here you have a medal for your child from the father with the medals."

ↂ

A Young Lady of Antwerp

wishing to make her confession to Father Paul made a long examination of conscience; this time she was going to tell everything, absolutely everything that burdened her, and consequently she had enough material on hand to fill a journal. Quite satisfied with the great collection of faults which she was going to tell, she entered the confessional still preoccupied with the long list of sins which she had carefully arranged and classified in her excellent memory.

Father Paul, however, leaving his penitent no time to speak, said to her, "Let us see, now tell me everything, don't be bashful, tell me everything, absolutely everything."

The lady made an attempt to begin, but could not recall a single point of all those things she had prepared as subject-matter of confession. Father Paul repeatedly encouraged her, saying, "Don't be bashful, tell everything," but the young lady was unable to remember a syllable of all she had so carefully prepared, so that at last she blurted out, "You are a queer confessor, when I come to you I don't know any more what to say." "Indeed," said Father Paul, "keep all your baggage, for it won't be heavy to carry."

∽

A Sister from the Neighborhood of Termonde Says:

"One day I went to the church of the Benedictines of Termonde to go to confession to Father Paul whom as yet I did not know; but I saw that his confessional was vacant. Whilst I was walking away I heard a sound and returning saw Father Paul seated in his confessional. It was he who had called me, although I had not seen anybody enter the church.

"Entering the confessional, I told him that I was somewhat embarrassed, not knowing how to begin. 'Oh, that is nothing,' he replied, 'I myself shall make your confession.' And this he really did, to my great astonishment, going into minute details and in such a manner that I did not need to add a single word."

∽

Father Paul

gave to one of his friends, a farmer of Oostcamp, a number of medals which he was to bury in every one of his fields, in order to prevent the evil one from injuring the crops. And truly, that protection was marvelous as the following example will show:

Another farmer had just cut the grass on a meadow adjoining the farm of Father Paul's friend. The weather was delightful, but suddenly a tornado appeared above the horizon and soon dark clouds were driven rapidly onward by a violent wind in the direction of the fields wherein both farmers just then were superintending their workmen. The path of the storm was marked by a heavy shower of rain which inundated the fields and overthrew the crops. This misfortune befell the farmers of all that vicinity; but as soon as the tornado approached the farm protected by the medals of St. Benedict, it changed its course, and in so doing produced a strange phenomenon. For, while all the country around was obscured by dark clouds, the sun continued to shine brilliantly on the farm in question, and not a drop of rain fell on it.

Owing to excessive rain, the potato crop in 1894 was very poor; yet on the farm before mentioned, the crop of potatoes was abundant. A neighboring farmer who assisted at the digging of the precious tubers, could not explain this exceptional good fortune, and shaking his head he said to the lucky farmer, "This is not natural! I am more and more convinced that you are a sorcerer." "Sorcerer?" the farmer replied, "nothing of the sort, these good results are the effect of the medals and prayers of our great friend Father Paul."

The same farmer was told by Father Paul that the medals of St. Benedict protect the fields from caterpillars, spiders, snails, and other vermin. These things, he added are from the evil one and we have the power to repel them. From the time that the farmer had the good fortune of becoming acquainted with Father Paul, his crops have been preserved from noxious insects.

༄

A Person from Thielt

asked of Father Paul the cure of a niece who lived in Iseghem and whose diseased nose caused her intolerable sufferings. The Rev. Father prescribed for the patient to wash her entire body in water blessed with a medal of St. Benedict and to snuff some of the water into her nose. Two months passed and the nose not being cured, the person returned to the monastery and reported the failure of the cure.

"I believe it," the Rev. Father replied, "your niece did not do what I told you." And so it was, for the patient afterwards confessed that she had soon lost patience continuing the applications as prescribed by Father Paul. When at last she complied with the prescriptions, she was restored to perfect health.

A Servant Girl of Thielt

having heard of Father Paul, told her confessor, a Recollet Father, that she was going to see the saintly Benedictine; but he formally forbade her to do so. Later on this same Recollet Father became ill, whereupon he engaged the servant girl to visit Father Paul and charged her to ask him for a cure. The girl was greatly comforted by her interview with Father Paul. When she was through with her own affairs she demanded the cure of the Recollet Father to which Father Paul replied, "Give him a medal, but he won't be cured." The Father died soon after.

∞

A Youth

now (1897) a religious in the monastery of Courtrai, suffered from fits of epilepsy. In 1882, his aunt brought him to Steenbrugge. Father Paul prescribed a novena to St. Benedict and assured him that he would be delivered from his terrible affliction as long as he wore the medal of St. Benedict. "If you cease to wear it," he said, "the evil will return."

After several years the terrible disease again manifested itself; and the young man's family recalling Father Paul's words, inquired if the medal was still attached to his scapular to which it had been affixed. The recurrence of the affliction was explained, for behold! the medal had fallen off and was lost. Another medal of St. Benedict was soon procured and securely fastened to his scapular, and since then the attacks of epilepsy have not returned.

∞

A Gentleman

desirous of employing his leisure time profitably, told Father Paul that he wished to devote himself to painting. "Very well," the Rev. Father replied, "go to work and I will help you with my prayers, and you will become a celebrated artist." In the course of his studies the artist wrote frequently to his Benedictine master about the paintings he had made; and without having seen the canvasses, Father Paul replied in the language of an expert artist, giving sound advice and predicting the success of the paintings which he approved.

∞

A Young Man

had left the paternal roof to try his fortunes in America. His parents were very anxious about him, for they received no news from him. In 1895 his mother went to confide her trouble to Father Paul.

"Madam," he replied, "your son died on such a day, but he died like a Christian, fortified by the last sacraments." Two weeks later the lady received from the priest who had attended the young man in his last illness, a letter confirming the facts revealed by Father Paul.

∾

Father Paul Foretold

a woman from St. Gilles, near Termonde, that she would be accused of theft. "But I never stole!" the woman exclaimed. "I know that, nor will you ever steal; but all the same they will accuse you of it, but don't be worried." This woman had a hoarder in her house. Now, a few days later this stranger accused the woman of having stolen his pocket money. Afterwards the man declared that the money, without his noticing it, had slipped between the mattress and the side of his bed.

∾

A Young Composer

had been advised to make the acquaintance of the Rev. Father Paul. Having paid him a visit he exclaimed, "What an extraordinary man this Rev. Father is! One might, indeed, believe that he knows everything!" Father Paul had talked music to him like a master.

∾

A Woman of Termonde,

visiting Father Paul, told him of the many misfortunes that assailed her from all sides. "I sympathize with you," he replied. "You are truly to be pitied; I shall help you drink your chalice." From that day the woman was delivered from her troubles.

∾

A Gentleman of Bruges

and friend of Father Paul, feeling somewhat indisposed thought he had an attack of influenza, a disease then prevailing. In a letter to the Rev. Father he declared his fear, but received the following answer: "Your indisposition is but a slight one and will soon disappear; you will not have an attack of influenza, for I shall pray for that." The malady did not touch the ward of Father Paul nor any member of his family.

∽

"Some Years Ago,"

writes a lady of Antwerp, Sept. 5, 1898, "I went to Termonde with my second son who wished to enlist in the navy. The Rev. Father said to me, 'Do not permit your son to cross the ocean, for you shall not see him again.' These words prevented my son from leaving home; but in 1897 he asked for a position in the service of the Congo and obtained it, and I did not succeed in keeping him from it. He left June sixth, and died in Boma the twenty-sixth of July following, after having received the last rites of the church."

∽

A Young Soldier from Oostcamp

returned to his family, after finishing four years of military service. As he had neglected to go to confession during this time, his mother asked him to go to Father Paul which he did. He relates, that having finished his accusation the Rev. Father asked him, if he had nothing else to tell, to which he gave a negative answer. Father Paul insisted that there was something else, but the young man replied that he remembered nothing more.

"Were you not acquainted with a young girl in Brussels and promised to marry her?" "That's true." "And did you leave her under the impression that you came from the Waloon country?" "Yes, Father."

"Well this poor girl is wandering all over the Waloon country in quest of you, begging her bread, with an infant in her arm, and this child is yours. . . . You must marry her." "But I do not know where she is," pleaded the young man. "You have enough money in your pocket; take a train to Brussels and go to the house where you first met her, she will join you there."

The soldier, repentant, took the first train to Brussels and went to the house indicated by Father Paul. The marriage took place, and now the pair are living happily together.

A Merchant of Eecloo

despaired of saving his daughter who had been given up by the physicians. One day he was trying on a new overcoat which he had ordered from his tailor in Ghent, and was astonished to find in one of the pockets a bright new medal of St. Benedict. A few days afterwards the merchant visited one of his customers in Ursel and spoke to her of the sad condition of his child. This person, who knew Father Paul, advised him to have recourse to St. Benedict who, she said, works great wonders through the medium of a certain Father Paul of the monastery in Steenbrugge.

"St. Benedict! St. Benedict!" exclaimed the merchant as if in a dream, "why do you speak to me of St. Benedict?"

"Why this astonishment?"

The merchant then told her how he had found the medal in the pocket of his new overcoat, and saw therein a dispensation of Divine Providence. It was, therefore, an easy matter for the lady to inspire the merchant with great confidence in the powerful intercession of Father Paul. He had recourse to the Rev. Father and thus tells the story of the cure of his child:

"My daughter, fifteen years old, was very ill on account of neglected pleurisy, and through a complication of several other diseases, her case had become desperate. Father Paul arrived, touched for an instant the patient's sides and said, 'Oh! this will be nothing.' The next day my daughter was completely cured.

A Young Lady,

a former penitent of Father Paul, writes as follows: "The Rev. Father said to me one day, 'Oh, what a great treasure is the love of Jesus! Come tomorrow morning, I will pray for you and ask that you may experience even a little drop (een spellekop) of this love of Jesus.'

"I went to Steenbrugge early the next morning, and Father Paul said to me, 'Before approaching the Holy Table you will 1. Make an act of contrition; 2. Ask the Blessed Virgin to give you her maternal blessing in order to obtain through her intercession the grace of receiving her dear Son into your heart with a love as intense as all the love with which Jesus has ever been loved; 3. Pray to St. Joseph, St. Benedict, and St. Scholastica, and all the saints of heaven, and especially your guardian angel to obtain this favor for you through the intercession of Our Blessed Lady.' When the divine office was over, and I was alone in the church, Father Paul came to me and said, 'Repeat once more the acts which I have taught you, as a preparation for Holy Communion.'

"After that I knelt down at the railing while the Rev. Father prepared to give me Holy Communion. Suddenly I perceived a perfume so delicious that I was quite distracted by it. I imagined that one of the lay-brothers must have brought a bouquet of flowers. I raised my eyes and to my great astonishment, I saw Father Paul standing before me in ecstasy, raised a considerable distance above the ground, and holding the sacred host. I cannot tell exactly how long he continued in this attitude, but I think it was at least five minutes. It would be impossible for me to describe how attractive the countenance and attitude of the Rev. Father appeared, and the atmosphere was scented with the most delicious perfume of roses and other flowers, such as I had never before experienced.

"Father Paul then advanced, and placed on my tongue the Bread of angels. My emotion was so great that I found it impossible to formulate any prayer. I was barely able to say, 'Lord Jesus, how admirable Thou art to those who know and love Thee!' After Communion Father Paul invited me to the parlor of the monastery and there he said, 'Well, are you now satisfied to have received our Lord?'

" 'Yes,' I answered, 'and this pleasure is so great that one might lose one's head.'

" 'Certainly,' he continued, 'such a thing is possible, but not for you, who have not advanced that far. St. Mary Magdalen of Pazzi experienced this happiness; one day her heart was so overflowing with love, that she ran around the convent three times, crying out unceasingly, O Love! O Jesus, my Love! Those who saw her said she had gone mad; but her madness consisted in possessing, to a high degree the treasure of love. Would you also like to become a child of love?' 'Is such a thing possible?' I asked. 'Everything is possible,' he replied, 'with good will and the grace of God.' 'But what must I do?' 'In the first place, you must refuse the fortune which has been offered you: secondly, you must avoid being particular as to dress; thirdly, do all your actions for the love Jesus.'

" 'And is that sufficient?' 'Yes,' he replied, 'because when we wish to teach an infant to walk alone, we go about it step by step. When I wish to teach any one the love of Jesus and put him on the road of a perfect life, he must proceed slowly, step by step. If a beginner wishes to abandon himself to a life of excessive penance, he ruins his health; his soul, also, becomes sick, and then he renders himself incapable of doing any good whatever. Therefore, great prudence is needed and little by little one arrives at the top of the mountain of the cross. Such is the school of the interior life which leads to the port of salvation and love. In this school you will *learn to know yourself, to humble yourself, and to exercise yourself in works of charity.* Be prudent, pray much, follow my counsel and your life will be happy.

" 'Yet, understand well that to the children of the love of Jesus, crosses are never wanting, and these crosses sometimes come from those for whom they have done much good, sometimes even from their best friends. But if you have courage and do violence to yourself, Jesus the Well-Beloved will keep near you in order to support you under your crosses. Where there is a good will, grace is never wanting.

" 'I have no time to say more about the subject now. You may come back from time to time to learn how to cultivate in your heart the tree of love. You may take me for your guide. Good-by, my child; have courage. May the blessing of God be with you. Praised be Jesus Christ!' "

∽

During a Visit of Father Paul

to a religious community at Bruges, the sisters declare they noticed that the Rev. Father while passing from one room to another, hardly moved his feet but seemed to glide over the floor rather than step upon it.

◌↤◌

A Person from Ghent

reports that sometimes she saw Father Paul raised above the ground. He would first distract her attention elsewhere, saying for example, "Just look at those beautiful pigeons in the garden!" But when she turned around, after having looked at the pigeons, she would see the Rev. Father raised a few feet above the ground absorbed in an ecstasy which lasted about ten minutes.

A young lady from Ghent paid a visit to Father Paul in 1889. In the course of the conversation he suddenly stopped and exclaimed, "For the love of Jesus!" and as if wrapt in ecstasy, he was raised about three feet above his chair and remained thus eight or ten minutes; then he slowly descended upon his chair and resumed the conversation.

◌↤◌

A Person from Beveren Writes:

"As I one day visited Father Paul at Termonde with my cousin, he spoke to both of us about things that were absolutely secret, and which we had not confided to him. My cousin and myself looked at each other in astonishment.

"Another time, being at the church of the Benedictines in Termonde, and seeing there how the Rev. Father Paul gave to the people a relic to kiss, I saw to my great astonishment, a shining aureole surrounding his head.

◌↤◌

One Day in 1888

Father Paul was dining at the house of a lady in Bruges. As the servant in the middle of the repast, reentered the room she suddenly uttered a cry of astonishment as she looked at the Rev. Father. The hostess, at a loss to understand such unusual conduct, demanded an

96

explanation, saying, "What's the matter with you? Surely it is not the first time you have seen the Rev. Father Paul."

But the servant, confused and speechless, was unable to explain herself. The fact is that she saw Father Paul all rejuvenated, appearing to be not more than about thirty years of age, his head surrounded by a brilliant aureole about a foot in diameter. When Father Paul met the servant after dinner he asked her why she had made such a noise. "Why, because you had a star on your head," replied the servant, who had not yet recovered from her surprise, "Yes, yes, that is all right," Father Paul said nonchalantly, and walked away.

∞

In 1887, Shortly after His Departure

from the monastery of Steenbrugge, Father Paul put up at the house of an old invalid lady at Schaerbeek. At seven o'clock in the evening there was a reunion of the inmates of the house, including besides the old lady, a sister who nursed the patient, a young lady from Ghent, and another lady. The sister, having asked the Rev. Father to say a few words on the great subject of which he loved to treat best of all, namely, the love of God, as soon as he had begun his discourse, all at once saw him transfigured. His face had become white as snow, while a brilliant aureole surrounded his head, and lighted up the room in an astonishing manner. Father Paul appeared to be quite rejuvenated. With an eloquence simple and sublime, he kept his audience spell-bound, communicating to all the burning love which overflowed from his heart.

Fearing that the ecstasy might carry him to the points of death, they requested him three times to take a rest. But as if he had heard nothing, he continued his discourse without intermission, like a bee that gathers honey from roses, going from flower to flower; so he went on without taking a moment's rest, and that lasted until eleven o'clock at night.

∞

In 1891, a Young Lady

residing in Flanders had an attack of influenza, and besought her sister to go to Termonde and solicit Father Paul's prayers in her behalf, as the patient had been acquainted with him for some time. Consulting the time table her sister ascertained that it was impossible to go to Termonde and return the same day, and therefore decided to postpone the journey. The illness, however, assumed so dangerous an aspect, that the patient bade her sister summon at once, the curate of the parish. Her sister set out with all possible speed, but when she had gone half way she distinctly heard the voice of Father Paul saying, "Pray, don't be in such a hurry; be calm."

In her amazement, she stood still, for she positively saw no one. But there was no mistake about it; it was undoubtedly the voice of Father Paul, and she cried aloud, "Father Paul, is it you?" The voice answered, "Yes, it is I; go back: your sister will be cured." She returned immediately to relate this extraordinary occurrence, and soon after, the patient was restored to health.

ᴄᴡᴏ

A Working Woman of Thielt relates:

"Since his residence in Termonde, I have seen Father Paul twice praying in our church in Thielt, and a few moments afterwards he disappeared suddenly. I wrote to the Rev. Father and asked if I had really seen him in the church, and he answered, 'Yes.'

"Since the death of Father Paul, I have seen him three times at prayer in our church. From afar I greeted him, nodding my head, and he responded in the same manner. Some moments afterwards I saw him leave the church and go away. I followed him; but the more I advanced, the more the distance that separated me from him increased, until at last he disappeared from my view.

"Receiving a letter one day from Father Paul in which he replied to several questions, I read also the following lines: 'There is a poor peddler in your street whose children are without bread; they are awaiting their father's return in order to procure the necessary food. This peddler sells needle-cases, buy one from him.' It was a puzzle to me why Father Paul had written these words, but soon a peddler came along and offered me his needle-cases at ten centimes each. Naturally I did not hesitate to buy one.

⁓

A Farmer

with whom I am acquainted, had in his stable a beautiful horse on the point of dying. Being there at the time, I took the medal which I had received from Father Paul and put it around the neck of the horse which immediately became well. I reported this wonderful occurrence to the Rev. Father, and begged him for another medal, but he sent me this sharp reprimand: "What I have blessed for your personal use, you dare not apply to beasts."

⁓

A Sister

from the convent of Belcele, relates the following facts:

"For two years I suffered much from a cancer in my foot. In 1878 I wrote to Father Paul about it, and he told me to make a novena to St. Benedict and to use the medal which he sent me. He moreover told me if the affliction continued, to make another novena. On the fifth day of the second novena my foot was cured.

"In 1886 while working in the country our horse struck his foot forcibly against the plowshare so that the bone was fractured, and the foot hanging down. I wrote at once to Father Paul, and he replied, 'Make a novena to St. Benedict and wash the leg of the animal with water blessed by the medals.'

"After three weeks, to the great surprise of the veterinarian, the foot was healed, nor was the horse sick in the meantime.

⁓

The Nephew

of the Mother Superior of another convent of our Order, at the age of twenty, had been suffering two months from rheumatism in the arm. To seek relief, he went to Father Paul with a companion.

" 'May I speak to you in presence of your companion?' Father Paul asked. 'Oh! yes,' the young fellow replied, 'he is a friend of mine and may listen to everything.'

" 'Well, then, it is with this arm that you one day struck your father, and this is the cause of your sufferings. Are you sorry for it?' 'Yes, Rev. Father.'

" 'Well, go to confession at once and then come back.' After confession Father Paul touched his arm and the rheumatism disappeared.

༄

Our Cows

having been attacked by a contagious disease, I wrote to Father Paul saying that if the cattle were cured, we would place a statue of St. Benedict in our chapel. The Rev. Father replied that we had no right to impose conditions on St. Benedict, and added,

" 'First put up the statue.'

"As soon as the statue was placed in the chapel the disease disappeared from the stable.

༄

Father Paul Came

to our convent at Antwerp for the first time in the year 1894, and asked permission to be shown through it. On entering the convent he met two sisters, and turning to the sister who had admitted him, he remarked, 'These two religious are more advanced than you. . . .' Then accosting a group of nuns, he asked, 'Is there no one here who knows me?' 'We have not the honor,' the nuns replied. As Father Paul was about to leave, a sister asked him who it was to whom she had the honor of speaking. 'Ik ben de liefde van God,' 'I am the love of God,' the Rev. Father replied. Hearing these words, the two sisters about whom Father Paul had made the remark to the sister who had introduced him, and to whom he had a long time before revealed their vocation, cried with joy, 'It is Father Paul, beg of him to remain longer.'

"Soon all the nuns, filled with delight, flocked around the Rev. Father; they showed him the entire convent, not forgetting the infirmary, where there were four patients. The first suffered from a large abscess under the arm and complained much of the pain. The Rev. Father said to her, 'Ah, that is a mere trifle.' 'Oh, no,' replied the sister, 'it pains me intensely.' Father Paul placed his hand over the abscess and instantly her suffering ceased.

"The second patient was the Rev. Mother, who had a sore throat and could not speak. 'A trifle,' Father Paul exclaimed with a certain amusing gesture habitual with him; then he touched the swollen neck, and the patient's voice became clear and strong again.

"The third sister suffered from her foot and had been unable to walk for three weeks. 'A trifle!' repeated Father Paul. He touched the lame foot and said to the sister, 'Walk now, you will see that it was nothing at all.' Whereupon the sister, cured of her complaint, began to walk with great strides, smiling all the while with evident delight.

"The fourth sister had a felon on her finger. Again the same remark from Father Paul, who touched the sister's finger and the whitlow disappeared. At last the good Father departed, bearing away with him the blessing of the community.

∽

A Little Orphan Girl

who was entirely paralyzed, and who, through nervous trouble, had lost the use of speech, was brought by our sisters to Termonde, on the feast of St. Joseph, March 19, 1878. The poor child had been carried to the station, but when they arrived at Termonde, they were at a loss to know how they could reach the monastery as there was no public conveyance, and Father Paul had not been notified of their coming. Much to their surprise, on their arrival at the station of Termonde, a driver approached, raised his hat, and said, 'My carriage is waiting to take you to the monastery, and I shall return for you in the afternoon.' As soon as Father Paul saw the child, he declared she would be cured; and told the sisters to make two novenas, and if necessary, commence a third one. One morning, at the beginning of the third novena, the sick child began to walk and speak. Her cure was permanent.

∽

In the Year 1875,

the Rev. Mother of a convent in Antwerp was suffering from a disease which the physician pronounced incurable. The sisters accordingly had recourse to Father Paul, who replied as follows: 'The Mother Superior will be cured after two novenas, and during the third, she will be restored to perfect health; do not, therefore, call the physician again.' His prediction was fulfilled.

∾

Here Is Another Prodigy,

certified by a parish priest in Antwerp who related the story to us, as follows:—

"A lady of my parish was suffering from a dreadful disease which the physicians declared incurable. One day as death seemed imminent, I proposed that Father Paul be consulted. The lady's husband who was a pronounced 'liberal' and had no religion, scoffed at my proposal, while his unfortunate wife begged him to follow my advice. Finally to please his wife, he gave his consent, and declared that if this cure were obtained, he would be converted. Father Paul replied to the messenger as follows: 'Tell them to make a novena. Here is a medal of St. Benedict to be applied according to my instructions. The lady will be cured. The physicians must no more meddle with the case.' Before the termination of the novena, the lady was restored to health, her husband himself came to thank Father Paul and was converted, to the great joy of his wife and family.

"I am very sorry that I never had the happiness of seeing the Rev. Father Paul, but I have preserved a great number of long letters from him, treating of the love of God, and these letters are admirable. One day he wrote to me, 'Until now you have not received more than a little ray of the love of God, but I am going to inscribe you in the Sacred Heart of Jesus.'"

∾

In 1892, Father Paul

paid a visit to a friend in Antwerp, who, on the same day, was entertaining one of her friends. The unexpected visit of Father Paul suggested the idea of inviting him to make an excursion to Stabroeck to visit Catharine Vingerhoets, a young ecstatic girl, well known to the people of Antwerp. Father Paul accepted the invitation on condition that it should be possible for him to return home the same evening. Stabroeck is about ten miles from Antwerp, and a railway connects the two places. The train, left Antwerp in good condition, but when they got about half-way, it stopped, because the engine was disabled. A dispatch was sent to Antwerp for another engine, and in the meantime the passengers were obliged to take their misfortune as philosophically as possible. A lunch was improvised under the most picturesque circumstances with the help of some little provisions that had been brought along, and thus a considerable time had passed, still no engine came. After the lunch Father Paul said to his companions, "Let us see if the accident which befell the locomotive is as bad as they say. . . ."

They went accordingly and found two mechanics and some passengers standing near the engine. One of the passengers had a cane in his hand. Father Paul asked him for it, whereupon he thrust the end of the cane into one of the pipes of the engine and said with all seriousness to the engineer and tender:

"Why this pipe seems to me choked up! Go and clean it out!"

But they only smiled with an air of pity at this poor old monk, who pretended to know more about their business than they themselves; nevertheless, Father Paul continued to explore the pipe from which, for a good reason, he could extract nothing. The passengers during the time amused themselves at the expense of the poor monk, who seriously undertook to repair the engine with the help of an ordinary walking-stick. At last Father Paul said to the engineer:

"Try now, I think the machine will work all right. It is easy to imagine the derision with which this remark was received. But Father Paul, changing his tone, repeated his request and said in a determined manner, "Start up the engine; it will go all right now, for it is I who tell you." The engineer, in spite of himself, obeyed at once, and the train began to move!

The arrival of Father Paul at the house of Catharine Vingerhoets was a real treat for the ecstatic girl. It was the only time that the

Rev. Father visited her. One of his companions opened a bottle of wine which she had brought along. Father Paul refused to touch it unless Catharine also took some of it; but her sister Mary replied that Catharine never took wine, and that she would get sick if she took any.

But Father Paul said, "No, no! this will do her no harm, on the contrary, it will do her good; for it is my wish that she drink with me." So they filled a glass for Catharine, and Father Paul blessed it. She drank it and felt very well.

∾

The Daughter of a Physician

had been for some time, deaf in one ear and hardly able to hear with the other. Accompanied by her mother and a lady friend, she set out for Termonde to visit Father Paul. During the journey the hearing of the ear which had been the least affected was lost altogether. Admitted to the presence of the Rev. Father, the girl's friend said to him, "Rev. Father, please cure this young girl of her deafness; it is such an affliction to be deaf!" Thereupon Father Paul placed his hands on the ears of the deaf girl, and at the very instant she recovered her hearing so completely that she could understand words spoken in a low tone, at a distance of several paces. The deafness never returned.

Father Paul also said to this young lady, "You will obtain some of the love of Jesus." After that time she has had several experiences in the church, a few of which she describes as follows:—

"August 2, 1894, which was a day of adoration, I had the happiness of seeing, for the first time, in the sacred host in the monstrance, our Lord attached to the cross.

"Holy Thursday, 1896, while making my adoration, I beheld a large host on the veil of the ciborium; shortly afterwards this host was changed into a most amiable face.

"The feast of the Sacred Heart, 1896, I saw on the veil of the ciborium our Lord stretching out His arms; one of His arms was raised higher than the other, and His hands were open. His heart was red, and His face had a very amiable expression.

"At another time I saw the person of our Divine Lord slowly disappearing behind a veil.

"Christmas, 1896, during the elevation of the Mass, I saw our Savior on the cross in the host.

"Several times I have seen the sacred host appear on the veil which covers the ciborium.

"Only once I saw great brightness in the tabernacle."

∽

An Ecstatic

submitted, in writing, the following case to the Rev. Father Paul: "The Blessed Virgin appeared to me, carrying the Divine Child in her arms. The Blessed Mother was resplendent with beauty; a crown adorned her head, her eyes were brown and full of heavenly sweetness. She presented the Divine Infant repeatedly to me, spoke for about twelve minutes, and then blessed me." This she wrote to Father Paul in order to ascertain if he considered the vision divine. The Rev. Father answered that the ecstatic might consider the vision a truly divine one, and added, "But I am grieved that you did not ask this good Mother to give her blessing also to me."

∽

In 1880, Three Sisters

from a convent in Bruges went to Steenbrugge to ask the prayers of Father Paul for the recovery of the Rev. Mother Superior. When the interview was over, Father Paul joined his hands and raising his eyes towards heaven said to one of the sisters, "Five years ago you would have left the convent if St. Teresa had not held you back; and for the last three days you have been staying away from Holy Communion through fear." "But Rev. Father, how do you know that?" the sister cried out in astonishment, "nobody knows it, not even those in the convent!"

"Tell your superioress that you must now communicate nine days in succession."

∽

To a Working Woman,

whom he had cured, Father Paul said, in 1892, "In making the Stations of the Cross, meditate especially on the sixth station where Christ imprinted His adorable face on the veil of St. Veronica. Later on you will see our Lord in person in the Most Blessed Sacrament." She followed the Rev. Father's recommendation and with tears in her eyes she relates what she saw: —

"My emotion almost prevents me telling it, so terrible it was! I beheld in the host the living head of Christ, but so covered with blood and so horribly disfigured that I was benumbed with fear. This vision has been frequently repeated, and Father Paul wrote several letters to me on this subject, and these I communicated to my confessor, a Recollet Father.

"Some time afterwards Father Paul said to me, 'God demands and expects of you especially three things:—

1. Special prayers for sinners and blasphemers.

2. Prayers for the souls in purgatory.

3. Prayers for the soul of your mother, who suffers cruelly in purgatory on your account, because she was opposed to your religious vocation. This is the reason why God gives you the grace to see in the Blessed Sacrament the person of our Divine Lord, His head all covered with blood and crowned with thorns. In this there is a great mystery for you, and a great thing ("eene groote zaak") for myself. Every day make a short meditation on the passion of Jesus. Love humility; Jesus loves souls that are humble, and sends them many trials.

" 'My child, do not have the least doubt as to what you see in the Most Holy Sacrament of the Eucharist; for I myself have asked God that you might see Him. If you begin to doubt the reality of what you see, regarding it as a mere illusion; or if you attribute this vision to the artifices of the devil, you will never enjoy it again. It is an extraordinary grace which God grants you; if you do not believe in it any longer, this grace will be withdrawn from you.

" 'Go on as I have told you; pray to God that it may not be to you a source of vanity; then you will perceive that this grace will increase from day to day.' "

〜

In a Convent

the sisters were a prey to violent obsession. At night they were boxed on the ears by an invisible hand and thrown out of their beds. This state of affairs having lasted for a long time in spite of all the means that were applied in order to stop the trouble, Father Paul was at last asked for his advice.

The Rev. Father replied that a very easy means of getting rid of the enemy is to humble one's self profoundly, and to realize that by ourselves we are nothing and can do nothing. "The devil," he added, "cannot bear humility, it is his great enemy; the very moment he notices it, even partly, he becomes impotent and flees."

The sisters followed the advice of Father Paul and soon everything became quiet in the convent.

〜

A Young Lady from Herenthals Writes:

"I felt a soreness in my right side which became very painful as soon as I took the least food. In 1889 my aunt advised me to have recourse to Father Paul, and I did so. Having questioned me, the Father placed his hand for a moment over my ailing side and told me to make a novena, adding that he would also make one. Then he gave me a medal of St. Benedict with the prescription to dip it into my drinks during the days of the novena, also to dip it into the water with which I washed. Having followed these prescriptions of Father Paul, I was fully restored to health.

"Some time afterwards we received a visit from the Rev. Father, and he assured me that I was completely cured. I did not feel the least pain any more. I never consulted the doctor and do not know the nature of the evil from which I suffered so much. I am now sorry that I did not ask Father Paul what the trouble was.

"At the time of the first visit of Father Paul in our house, I desired very much to consult him on a certain point; but knowing him only slightly, my timidity prevented me doing so. To my great aston-ishment the Rev. Father gave me at once an affirmative answer.

Afterwards he asked me if I had a rosary. I said, 'Yes;' but my rosary was broken into several pieces, each of which I carried in a different pocket.

" 'Show me that rosary,' the Rev. Father said. Having shown him one piece of it after another, Father Paul said with a smile that I was in need of a whole rosary.

"In 1889, Father Paul invited my first cousin to come to the chapel of the Perpetual Adoration in Antwerp, and told her that she would see our Lord in person in the exposed Blessed Sacrament. The Father furthermore told her:—

" 'You must not go there through vain curiosity, but with great faith. One day I told a certain woman to go there also and see, but she saw nothing because she went there through curiosity. If our Lord tells you to demand this or that, you must demand it of Him; but if He does not tell you so, you may ask Him anyway.' When I went to the chapel, I saw our Lord clothed in white as far as the waist, the rest being black. 'When you see Him, you must not break out into exclamations, as another woman did in the chapel; but let it all pass, as if unnoticed. . . '

"My cousin said that she saw our Lord in the sacred host, His eyes were cast down, and His hands joined.

"Some one complained to Father Paul saying, 'My brother who did not lead a good life, and for whose conversion I have prayed so much, fell into the water and was drowned.' The Rev. Father replied, 'The space between the bridge and the water is great; your brother had time to make a good act of contrition.' "

∽

While Giving a Retreat

in a convent, Father Paul gave a conference on confession. During this discourse, one of the sisters present expressed her discontent interiorly, muttering to herself, "Confession again!" At the very moment, Father Paul stopped and spoke to the sister these words: "Yes, yes, Sister Justine, it's about confession once more!" And he then went on with his sermon.

∽

To a Person from Thielt

Father Paul told the following story:—

"I said to a man who often came to see me, 'The Blessed Sacrament is exposed in the church, go there and you shall see something astonishing.' This man, full of fear, obeyed at once and saw our Lord in person in the monstrance, in consequence of which he was filled with great joy. Being unable to conceal his secret, he soon communicated his mysterious experience to several persons. Some believed, others ridiculed him.

$$\sim$$

The Wife of an Innkeeper in Oostacker,

who was acquainted with Father Paul, reports the following: —

"On the 4th of February 1896,* at eleven o'clock in the morning, I suddenly noticed the presence of Father Paul in my inn, without having seen him enter. He seemed to be in excellent health, yet I reproached him for coming on foot, because, as a rule, I provided a carriage for him, free of charge, whenever he came to Oostacker.

" 'Oh! I feel very well.' the Father remarked gaily as he rubbed his hands. I offered him a glass of wine which he declined, saying, 'No, I shall not take anything, for I am in a hurry and have to make other visits, at the Beguinage and at a notary's. You will never see me again; carefully note the day and hour of my visit. I came because you still require this.'

"So saying Father Paul took out from beneath his mantle a scapular of rough wool, about seven inches by five, to which a medal was attached, and this he gave me in exchange for my old one which he threw into the fire. Then he gave me a handful of medals to distribute among those who would make good use of them. Having given me further advice, he strictly forbade me to assist at his funeral because, he said, I would not be able to overcome my emotion. After this short conversation of only ten minutes, he said, 'Go now to the kitchen and put your potatoes on the fire.'

---

* At this date Father Paul had been confined to his room for a long time by dropsy of which he died on the 24th of the same month.

"The potatoes were, as a matter of fact, peeled and ready for boiling. I went to the kitchen and came back to the room after a few minutes, but to my great astonishment, Father Paul had disappeared.

"Was this a case of bilocation? It would seem impossible to have the slightest doubt about it, as may be seen by a remarkable coincidence. On the 4th of February, the day of his mysterious visit, Father Paul sent us his last letter. The envelope is marked Feb. 4, 7 P. M. The writing indicates a very trembling hand, which had not been the case before, and shows that the Rev. Father had lost all vigor.

"Towards the end of December 1896, we went to a notary in Ghent, who was a friend of Father Paul, and asked him if the Rev. Father had paid him a visit on the 4th of February, but the notary was unable to remember.

"Then we inquired at the Beguinage in Ghent for the Beguine whom Father Paul used to visit. At first, this religious could not recall the date or the time of the Rev. Father's last visit; but later she recalled a circumstance which revived her memory. She had bought, about that time, a piece of cloth which she afterwards sent to the abbey of Termonde, and the date of the payment of that invoice furnished her with a proof that Father Paul's last visit must have taken place about the time of which we are speaking. But she could not recall the exact date. So much is sure that Father Paul visited this Beguine and conversed with her for about half an hour. She offered him a glass of wine, but he did not accept it and said to her, 'I shall not return here any more.' 'And why shall you return no more?' asked the religious, but received no answer to this question. Then she asked, 'Are you going to visit other persons at the Beguinage?' to which he replied, 'No, I am going to depart at once.' And with these words he walked off in a hurry.

"December 28, 1896, we wrote to Dr. Planquaert, a homeopath, in Brussels, for details concerning the last sickness of the Rev. Father Paul, his patient.

"He replied as follows: 'Sir, I saw the Rev. Father Paul for the first time June 30, 1895. He was then in a state of health which left much to be desired, as he could walk only with the greatest difficulty, so great was his weakness from a feeling of oppression. His condition, however, improved so much as to permit the Rev. Father to enjoy a few holidays outside his monastery.

" 'During the last weeks of 1895 his condition took a noticeable turn for the worse, and when I went to Termonde January 31, 1896, I found Father Paul in such a state of health as absolutely to preclude the possibility of his leaving the convent on that day, or on the 4th of February following.

" 'February 13th I found the patient considerably weaker than on my previous visit, that is January 31st, and this weakness constantly increased until the day of his death, which took place February 24, 1896.

" 'Such are the details as I find them in my notebook and of which my memory, which is good for dates, has kept until now a faithful remembrance.' "

Dr. Cyr. Planquaert.

∽

The Innkeeper's Wife Relates Also:

"In 1888 Father Paul advised me to join the Flemish pilgrimage to Rome, and gave me a letter to be handed to the Holy Father. I told him that it would be quite difficult for me to discharge this commission. 'How am I to present myself to the Pope, and give him a letter? I would never dare do such a thing!' 'Go along anyhow!' he replied, 'and don't worry about anything, that will be done very easily; the circumstances will be favorable, for I am intimate with the Pope.'

"Among other counsels Father Paul cautioned me not to kiss the Pope's ring. 'His Holiness does not like it,' he said. He also warned me not to visit the catacombs; he assured me that my emotion would hinder me from doing so. Finally he told me to get different objects blessed by the Holy Father, death-bed crosses, medals, and little statues. 'They will be useful to you,' he said, 'as well as to your family.' Being still single (for I was married only in 1892), I replied that I had no family. 'You will have one later on,' he said.

"Accordingly I accompanied the pilgrims to Rome. Being admitted into the presence of the Holy Father (we were two thousand), I found myself beside a Flemish prelate, who stood near the pontifical throne and to whom I presented the letter of Father Paul; the prelate at once delivered it to the Pope.

"Five days afterwards a messenger from the Vatican came to the hotel and brought me the answer of His Holiness. On my return, Father Paul came to me at Oostacker for this answer, just as he had previously told me he would when charging me with the commission.

"In Rome I did not pay any attention to Father Paul's advice with regard to visiting the catacombs. I entered along with the other pilgrims; but all at once an indescribable emotion came over me; I was on the point of fainting and was obliged to retire."

∽

A Friend of Father Paul

being anxious to consult him on a weighty matter, proceeded towards noon to the monastery of Steenbrugge. The brother in charge of the door told him that Father Paul had left by the first train and would not return till late. But at that very moment the Rev. Father showed himself a few steps away in the garden, to the unutterable amazement of the brother who could not understand the mystery. Was it another case of bilocation?

∽

The Daughter of a Blacksmith

at Vieux Dieu, five years ago, suffered from influenza but had recovered; of late, however, she had a relapse, and owing to other complications, there was little hope of recovery. The physicians met for consultation and considered an operation necessary. Her parents, however, having heard of Father Paul, decided to have recourse to him and went to the monastery of Termonde. Father Paul, who had never seen these people before, said to them, "Yesterday I was in Antwerp and expected you there. Poor artisans, you go to such an expense to consult physicians! Here is a medal, have your daughter wear it, also dip it into her drinks during a novena, which you will make together in honor of St. Benedict. Your daughter will be cured." The girl was cured on Christmas day, during the novena.

⌒⌇⌐

The Wife of a Blacksmith in Antwerp

was on the point of delivery, but it was a difficult case, and the physician declared her delivery impossible without an operation. The husband, full of anxiety went to find Father Paul. "The operation is not necessary," the Rev. Father said, "return home, the children will come of their own accord."

Feeling reassured, the blacksmith went home, repeating to himself the words of Father Paul, without being able to explain them, for the Father did not say, "The child will come of itself," but "The children will come of their own accord." When he arrived at his house, he found newly-born twins; the mother had been delivered in the absence of the physician.

⌒⌇⌐

As a Young Lady

was about to take leave of Father Paul in order to set out for the station at Steenbrugge, she noticed that the hour for the departure of the train had already arrived, at which discovery she manifested great uneasiness.

"Be calm," said Father Paul, "the train will be good enough and wait a little for you. Go on and finish what you were telling me." Having done so, the Rev. Father bade her go to the station without hurrying; arrived there she found that the train was twenty minutes late, having been delayed on the way.

⌒⌇⌐

A Benedictine Father from Downside Abbey,

England, relates as follows: "One day I found myself with several other travelers in the waiting room of the station in Bruges; we were all seated and silent. Another traveler, who attracted the attention of all, arrived. He was a religious who held in his hand his closed breviary. His originally black habit had already turned greenish while his hat was old and his shoes worn out. As he walked slowly from one end of the room to the other, a priest whispered into my ears, 'Don't you know that Father? It is Father Paul of Steenbrugge.' I was happy to see the good Father of whom I had already heard so much. Then a poor old woman entered, walked up to him and said, 'Father, I would like so much to speak to you! When may I find you at the monastery?'

" 'Well, tell me now!' he replied. 'No, it would take too long and the train will soon arrive.' 'Oh! the train will be twenty minutes late, just take your time and tell me your trouble.'

"The telegraph operator having overheard these last words, walked off laughing aloud. Nevertheless the conversation between the religious and the old woman began and lasted a long while. Finally, the porter announced the arrival of the train. . . it was exactly twenty minutes late!"

∽

A Person from Bruges

meeting Father Paul on the evening of the elections of 1881, and having asked his prayers to obtain a good result, the Rev. Father replied with a smile, "We shall pray that the Catholics win a decisive victory."

The next day there was a complete victory; all the Catholic candidates won by a majority of more than 130 votes. Later on, elections for the legislature were to be held and everybody expected that the Catholics would carry off the victory; but Father Paul foretold that the liberals would be victorious.

"The country," he said, "must still be severely punished; it is the Catholics who vote for the candidates of the Masonic lodges who are the cause of the misfortunes that weigh heavily upon the country. The liberals are the devil's sorcerers; they will cut a ridiculous figure when they arrive one day in the other world."

∽

A Young Lady of Thielt

begged Father Paul to cure her sister who had become demented. The Rev. Father gave her a medal, but said that as soon as it would be handed to the crazy girl she would instantly throw it away. "Try it, if you wish," he said, "it will be necessary to sew the medal on to her dress without her knowledge; and many novenas will have to be made in order to obtain her cure."

The young lady paid a visit to her sister the following morning. "Look here," she said, "what a beautiful medal has been given me for you!" "Oh, yes!" said the crazy girl with joy, "give it to me!" But hardly had she taken it into her hand when she threw it far away with great violence. She was cured, however, at the end of two years.

∽

A Franciscan Sister

went to Steenbrugge with the intention of making a general confession to Father Paul; but the Rev. Father told her it was not necessary, and he himself described the whole life of the sister. She admitted that Father Paul showed himself better acquainted with all the details of her life than she herself.

∽

In 1893, a Friend of Father Paul,

who lived in Ghent was made the possessor of a polychrome group representing Christ dead on the knees of His Blessed Mother, a so-called Pieta. Father Paul blessed the group and immediately, as he himself related, tears flowed abundantly from the eyes of the Blessed Virgin. This prodigy has been repeated very often, and in the presence of several witnesses.

On Thursday Sept. 20, 1894 for the space of two hours we were witness of this marvellous flow of tears in the presence of the Rev. Father Paul, who then gathered for us two or three of these tears in a little glass tube and told us afterwards to fill it up with water, in order to prevent the tears from drying.

Polychrome Group, blessed by Father Paul, in 1893,
whereupon tears flowed from the eyes of the Blessed Virgin

The author of this book is now the happy possessor of this Pieta the
height of which is only thirty-three centimeters (about 13 inches).

ᴄᴠͻ

A Young Sister,

very sick and without any hope of recovery, had an excessive fear
of death. The most encouraging words of the other sisters had no
effect on her. As Father Paul came to visit the Rev. Mother Superior,
she introduced him to the sick sister. A few words from the Rev.
Father soon changed the great fear of the poor sister into a most
intense desire to die as soon as possible; without a stop she repeated
(it was the eighteenth of March), "What a pity that I cannot die
now, so that I might be in heaven tomorrow, on the feast of St.
Joseph!" The sister died full of joy the day after, the eve of the feast
of St. Benedict.

ᴄᴠͻ

The Rev. Mother Superior

of a convent in Bruges was at the last extremity, so that her death was expected every moment. The sisters who had the greatest veneration for their superioress were disconsolate at the thought of soon being deprived of her prudent direction. Each of two physicians whom they consulted, recommended a different remedy. In this perplexity, the sisters resolved to send to Father Paul for advice. Before the messenger however had time to tell him the names of the two physicians and each one's prescriptions, the Rev. Father said, "Tell the sisters to follow the prescriptions of the second physician they consulted. I shall pray much for the Rev. Mother, and everything will go well."

From that time there was a marked improvement in the health of the venerable patient, and after eight days her recovery was complete.

∾

A Married Couple from Antwerp

were cast into deepest sorrow on account of the loss of their only child; they gave themselves up to continual grief. Following the advice of a friend, they had recourse to Father Paul. "As long as you give yourselves up, without restraint, to such great sadness, no other child will be born to you; but if you resign yourselves to the will of God, another child will be given you."

The parents followed this wise counsel and a second son brought back joy to their disconsolate home.

∾

A Lady Had the Misfortune

of losing her husband, and the physician attributed his death to cancer of the stomach. The disconsolate widow went to Termonde to communicate her grief to the Rev. Father Paul. This is what he told her: "Your husband did not have cancer, but he swallowed a little piece of glass, and since then he felt those internal pains; for that piece of glass cut into his intestines." The lady then remembered that eight years before her husband having taken a small glass of liquor cried out, "I think I have swallowed a little piece of glass."

Father Paul continued, "Your husband suffered his purgatory here, he went straight to heaven and is praying for you. You fear for the future of your children and yourself; have no anxiety; your children will be your consolation. One of your sons will become a priest, and one of your daughters a nun; but do not urge them on to their vocation, leave the good God do the work. Your business will prosper; moreover, an excellent means to make things flourish is to set aside a certain portion of the income or the profits, say two per cent, for the relief of the souls in purgatory; you may spend this money for Masses or good works for the suffering souls who can obtain everything for their benefactors." The lady followed the good advice and had reason to congratulate herself on the happy results.

Father Paul told the same lady that she would see Our Lord in person in the Most Holy Sacrament, and she asserts that she has often seen Him.

∽

A Gentleman Living in Ghent,

a great benefactor of the monastery of Steenbrugge, at the time Father Paul was prior, suffered from sciatica; the pain was so intense that he could no longer keep himself in an upright position, and was hardly able to take a few steps with the help of a cane. He asked his friend, Father Paul, for prayers to obtain relief, but the latter sent him this answer: —

"No, no, I shall not pray for that; it is a trial that Divine Providence has sent him; let him bear it patiently. This disease will leave no bad effect, later on he will be able to walk as well as before."

∽

A Little Boy from Thielt,

eight years old and deaf in one ear, had undergone an operation in Courtrai, but without any results. His mother thereupon met Father Paul in Termonde, and he advised her to dip a medal of St.

Benedict into water and pour a few drops of it into the ear of the child. As soon as she came home, the mother did as she had been told, and when the first drop of water was poured into the ear, the infirmity disappeared.

༄

An Amateur at Works of Ancient Art,

a friend of Father Paul, often consulted him with regard to pictures which he wished to acquire. The Rev. Father always proved himself well-informed, although anything but an expert in such matters. Besides the art collector lived in another town and did not have the opportunity of submitting work of that kind to the Rev. Father's inspection; he therefore, asked his advice by letter, and Father Paul replied in a few words, but clearly enough to remove all doubt. For example, if the painting was of doubtful value, he would reply, "Don't burn your fingers," or "The seller is a rogue, don't trust him," or "Such a price is exorbitant;" in the case of an authentic work of art he would reply, "I think it is genuine."

Once the amateur discovered a beautiful painting, though covered with the rust of time, offered for a very small sum. Having consulted Father Paul he said, "It is a fine picture; you can buy it at that price, provided the seller is not in needy circumstances." It was a good advice and doubly valuable, because accompanied by a very appropriate lesson in charity.

On another occasion the amateur, trusting to himself, had a worthless production imposed on him. Quite proud of his supposed bargain he wrote about it to Father Paul. The latter replied, "The seller has probably a good laugh at your expense." After a close inspection it was detected, as a matter of fact, that the painting was of no value at all.

༄

A Woman in Antwerp

who sold liberal papers, being threatened with total blindness, went to Termonde to ask Father Paul to cure her. He replied, "You cannot be cured, because you sell bad papers."

∽

The Aunt of a Benedictine Brother

was afflicted with gangrene in one of her legs to such a degree that the physicians had resolved to amputate the limb. But when Father Paul was consulted in the matter, he opposed the amputation and assured a cure, saying, "I shall make a novena of Masses, and you make a novena of prayers and wash the limb several times a day with water blessed with the medal." On the last day of the novena the gangrenous leg was cured.

∽

A Discalced Carmelite Friar

received orders from his superiors to change his residence at which he was very much grieved. A friend promised that he would ask the prayers of the Rev. Father Paul, in order that the command might be revoked. "No, no!" replied Father Paul, "I shall not pray for such a thing. Tell the Friar that he should submit with good grace to the will of God." At his new residence the Carmelite was happier than ever before.

∽

A Young Lady from Bruges Declares:

"A young girl in my service was tortured with great fears on account of a slight attack of chicken-pox. Having heard of the wonderful cures wrought by Father Paul, she begged me to go and recommend her to the Rev. Father. When I came to Steenbrugge—it was winter, some Sundays after Christmas—I saw Father Paul alone in the church and spoke to him of the sick girl. He gave me a medal for her and said, 'Oh! there will be no difficulty, this girl will be cured and all fear will leave her. . . . It is not so very long since your mother died, is it?' 'No, Rev. Father!' I replied astonished. 'She is in purgatory and you must still pray a great deal for her. . . . Now, there is only your old father with you; take good care of him.' Father Paul told me many other things, as if he were perfectly acquainted with everything that happened at my home. I was very much astonished.

"The brother of the girl mentioned before, happened to break his leg. I also spoke of this to Father Paul, but to my repeated questions he only shrugged his shoulders. At last he said, 'There is yet another thing that is not right with this young man. You may give him a medal, but he won't be cured.' This brother was addicted to drink, and died a year after. The young girl was promptly cured, nor did the disease leave the slightest mark.

"Having told the story of my interview with Father Paul to one of my lady friends, she asked me to take her son to Steenbrugge, a child of three years, who had the falling sickness. Father Paul looked at the child and said, 'I have power to arrest the affliction for nine days, but no longer for the present.' Then he gave him his blessing. The poor child was free from attack the next nine days, but after that it came back within a short time. Several times Father Paul stopped the attacks, but each time only for nine days. The Rev. Father told me one day that the child could not be cured completely unless the parents themselves did penance; but I had not the courage to tell them this."

ༀ

Whenever a Certain Friend

of Father Paul desired information regarding any subject, he thought the best thing to do was to go to Father Paul. His reply came directly and with as much exactness, as if the Rev. Father could read the heart of every one as an open book. "Truly," said a certain person who often had recourse to him, "I believe this Father possesses a mysterious mirror in which he sees everything. If there were a number of Father Pauls in the world, many people would be preserved from deception."

ༀ

One Day a House in Oostcamp

without any apparent cause was invaded by vermin. The inmates having asked the prayers of Father Paul, the pest immediately disappeared. But at the same time innumerable mice infested a neighbor's house, the more that were caught, the more came; it was a literal assault. The people living in this house also had recourse to the prayers of the saintly Benedictine. Father Paul asked them if among these mice they had not observed one much larger than the others.

"Yes," they said, "we saw an enormous one with whiskers; but we did not succeed in catching him." "Very well, you will soon be delivered from this plague." And from that time the house was free from mice.

∽

A Pastor of Hennegau Says:

"For three years strange things had happened in my rectory. Doors that were locked made a noise as though they were being opened. Strange sounds were heard from the furniture and the windows. Very often during the night we were roused from sleep by a tumult as though burglars had broken in.

"One day while at table with my aged mother and sister, the latter noticed that a large crucifix, that was adorned with a particle of the true cross, slowly slid down upon a piece of furniture as though carried by an unsteady hand.

" 'What does this mean?' she said. 'The crucifix is moving and seems ready to fall.'

"And in fact, it did fall, and was damaged. But what seemed very strange was that the upper part of the crucifix first touched the floor, although its massive base was a great deal heavier.

"On the occasion of a confirmation trip, the Rt. Rev. Bishop of Tournai paid us a visit. I begged his Lordship to exorcise the evil spirits in our dwelling. He complied with my request, but the annoying and mysterious noise in the house continued as before.

"Later on a Dominican Father was our guest. He, too, noticed the same strange occurrences, although we had not mentioned a word to him about it. This religious advised me to write to Father Paul. I immediately did so. It was in 1892, and I am glad to this day that I wrote to him. Father Paul sent his reply from Termonde, saying, that such things frequently occur, and encouraged us to have no further fear about the matter. Twenty-four hours after we received the letter we were no longer troubled.

"The above mentioned Dominican Father told me that similar things were experienced in a house at Tirlemont where he had lived. Father Paul, whose advice was asked, said, that it was caused by poor souls from purgatory who desired prayers. As a proof, a white handkerchief was placed on some piece of furniture. The next day the imprint of a burning hand and the five fingers could be seen scorched upon the cloth."

∞

A Young Priest

had fallen seriously ill, and his sickness baffled all medical science. One of his friends went to Father Paul and begged him to help the priest. Father Paul, however, seemed not to heed the petition. After much and earnest entreaty, the friend finally succeeded in obtaining a little powder of the miraculous roses of St. Benedict, on condition that he was not to give the powder to the priest if the latter should entertain the least doubts as to its efficacy.

The priest had often on previous occasions been requested to recommend himself to Father Paul, but he always intimated that he had no faith in these remedies. But when his friend mentioned to him the condition that Father Paul made, he recognized the sagacity of the holy man. With firm confidence he made use of the supernatural remedy and was soon restored to health.

∞

A Young Lady of Mariaburg Writes:

"My sick uncle went to see Father Paul.—'You have a natural sickness,' said the Rev. Father, and quickly pulling out his watch, added: 'Go to the depot at once; but hurry, hurry! You will catch the train yet. Step into the first coach, there you will hear tell of a physician who will cure you.'

"And really, my uncle did hear tell in that coach of a physician. . . He immediately went to him, and the physician said, 'You have heart disease, but in two weeks you will have no more attacks, you will be cured.' And my uncle is now well.

"My mother was afflicted with a serious malady of the liver. Father Paul pressed a medal of St. Benedict against her side and said, 'Madam, say three times: St. Benedict, heal me!' She did so, and felt at once that she was cured. Father Paul also cured the brother of a forester of consumption."

~~

Among the Numerous Friends

upon whom Father Paul used to call during his frequent visits to Antwerp, was an invalid lady and her servant Theresa. In 1887 the Rev. Father told Theresa that henceforth she would be informed beforehand of his approaching visits, adding that God delights to manifest His goodness to simple people. At his next visit Father Paul asked her, "Well have the little birds announced my coming?"

As a matter of fact, on the eve of Father Paul's visits to the lady, beautiful little birds, varying in number from two to twelve at a time, began to make their appearance in the garden, singing a joyful air which was always the same. They would also perch on the window-sill of the drawing room which looked out upon the garden, and tap upon the window-panes. Although the tune of the mysterious songsters never varied, they had at each successive visit a different plumage. The lady and her nurse, the sister who attended her, also saw these charming little birds, but could not tell where they came from any more than Theresa could. Were they birds from the tropics? But in that case these delicate little creatures would hardly have ventured into our climate in all seasons, for they came in winter, when it was snowing and very cold, as well as in summer. The sister nurse tried repeatedly to catch one of the birds, but in vain. She spoke of it to Father Paul and he replied, "Oh! they won't let themselves be caught!"

"But what, then, are these beautiful little birds?" they asked, to which the Rev. Father replied with a smile, "Dat is correspondencie," "They are messengers."

Father Paul also told Theresa not to speak of these birds to any one except to an intimate friend of hers. "If during my life," he said, "you spread the news abroad the birds will never come again."

On the eve of Father Paul's death the birds appeared again, but they were quite dejected, and, with drooping wings, sang a melancholy note which foretold some sorrow or misfortune to the inmates of the house. This presentiment, alas! proved but too true. Henceforth the "hemelsche vogeltjes" (the heavenly little birds), as Theresa called them, disappeared. But six months later she heard that Father Paul's photograph was for sale in Bruges; she procured a copy and hung it in the lady's drawing room. That very day the wonderful birds returned and sang their joyful melody, and they still continue to make their appearance from time to time.

The following is the description Theresa gives of the birds as they appeared on Wednesday, Sept. 30, 1897: "Today, at ten minutes to eleven, two little birds of incomparable beauty arrived; their plumage was blue, green and purple, their breasts and heads white, but the latter with stripes of deep purple in the form of a garland."

༄

Vault in which Father Paul is buried.

It seems that Theresa now understands what these birds come to announce; for with their assistance she often reveals events and foretells things which afterwards come to pass. Truly, this sounds like some pious legend of the "good old times."

༄

A Woman of Antwerp

declares as follows: "For years my son Anthony, nine years old, had his face, neck and shoulders covered with an eruption that gave him an appearance of a monster; and my baby, a few weeks old, was in a similar condition. The doctors could do nothing in the case. When Father Paul came to the house and looked at my little Anthony, he said to me in a pleasant tone, 'Anthony!. . . to bear the name of so great a saint, and be in such a state! Such a thing must not be! Make a novena and wash both children with water containing the medal of St. Benedict, they will be cured.' 'But the physician forbade me to wash them in water,' I said. 'I tell you, wash them twelve times a day for nine days!'

"My two children were perfectly cured during the novena."

The same woman says, "I have visited the grave of Father Paul three times, and on each occasion a beautiful little bird came and sang over the tomb, as long as I prayed there. The bird did not fly away, until the moment I left."

∽

A Lady from Antwerp

who had much to complain about a nephew of hers—he had threatened to do her bodily harm—went to Father Paul for help. The Rev. Father reassured the lady, and foretold that she would soon be delivered out of his hands. Scarcely had three months elapsed, when the latter had a stroke of apoplexy which resulted in complete paralysis and mental derangement. Happening to meet Father Paul some time afterwards, she told him about it and the Rev. Father predicted that her nephew would recover the use of reason in order that he might be converted. Having endured terrible sufferings for a whole year, the unhappy fellow recovered and was converted; yet, health was restored to him but for a short time; soon after he succumbed to a second stroke of apoplexy.

∽

One of Father Paul's Acquaintances from Ghent,

being desirous of possessing a relic of the venerable Benedictine, asked him repeatedly for a lock of his hair, but in vain. His constant answer was that his hair was too short. One day, however, at Termonde, she was bold enough to cut off a lock of his hair, at a moment when his attention was drawn elsewhere. As soon as the theft had been committed the lock disappeared in the depths of the visitor's pocket. Father Paul was indignant beyond measure and said, "If you ever again commit the slightest impropriety, I shall forbid you to come here again. You will not keep very long the lock of hair which you have just taken.

These words were spoken in such a severe tone that the person was very much confused; she knelt down and asked pardon but kept the lock of hair of which no further mention was made. As soon as she returned to Ghent, her first thought was to lock up carefully in a drawer the precious relic, having first tied a ribbon around the lock of hair and placed it in a piece of paper.

About four o'clock the next morning, being in bed, she heard an unusual noise in the house; she got up, went down stairs to investigate, and found the hall-door half open. She cast a glance out into the street but saw no one except the night watchman who was making his rounds as usual. Addressing him she asked, "Why did you not ring the bell when you saw my door open?" He replied, "I thought you had left it open on purpose." "That is a poor excuse; I shall bring a complaint against you." "Please don't do that, or I shall be punished!" "Very well; but tell me how long my door has been open? And did you see anybody enter or leave the house?" "Your door has been open for two hours, and I have not seen anybody enter or leave your house."

The lady then went upstairs and looked around to see if anything had been stolen. She opened the drawer in which, the evening before, she had put the lock of hair, and was surprised to find that it had disappeared. The next time she saw Father Paul, he asked her, "Do you still have the lock of hair?"

"No," she said, "I did not find it again."

"Oh, well! I will give you one later on."

A year passed by when, according to his promise, Father Paul gave her a lock of hair which, to her amazement, she recognized at once, being tied with the same ribbon with which she had fastened it.

"Now", Father Paul said to her, "you need no longer reproach yourself with having stolen it; for I myself give it to you."

∽

Visiting a Family

in the neighborhood of the monastery in Steenbrugge, Father Paul made the following remark about their little daughter who was three years old: "This child is so good! She will have a great love for the poor, and will become the happiness of your home."

From the age of six years this girl studied how to procure the means for giving alms to the poor, and she is the joy of her family.

∽

In 1894, Father Paul Being at Ghent

drove out to the residence of one of his friends. While in the act of leaving the carriage he felt himself seized, as he himself said, by an invisible hand, and violently thrown on the pavement where he fell at full length. His friend and several passers-by hastened to help him up; they found that the skin was torn off one of his hands and blood flowed from the wound. They wanted to bandage his hand, but he would not allow them. "Never mind!" he said, "it is nothing." Then he spat on his wounds, rubbed them a little with the other hand and said with an air of real or assumed astonishment, "Hello! What has become of those wounds? I don't see them any more!" And really not the slightest trace of the accident was to be seen on his hand.

∽

We Have Been Informed

from various sources of several cases where children, apparently dead, were revived by Father Paul; but in spite of our investigations we did not succeed in obtaining accurate knowledge of the facts. There are a number of people who absolutely refuse to make known for publication the favors obtained through the intervention of Father Paul.

We shall, however, mention the following hearsay reports:

At Antwerp the body of a child lay stretched on the funeral couch. Father Paul entered and witnessed the despair of the parents. "But are you quite sure that your child is dead?" the Rev. Father asked. "Perhaps he is only sleeping!"

"Oh, no!" the parents answered, "it is only a corpse."

"Let us see!" the Father replied, and giving the child a slight slap on the cheek he continued, "Come on, my child! Do not cause any more pain to papa and mama! Wake up!"

The child revived, opened his eyes and smiled at his parents who were overflowing with joy.

In another case where the child was already dead, Father Paul said to the parents, "I am going to see him; leave me alone!" A few moments afterwards, the child came to life again.

A poor mother of Antwerp told the following story at the house of the ecstatic, Catherine Vingerhoets, in Stabroeck (Catherine forgot to ask the woman's name and address): "As I was carrying my sick baby, I perceived all of a sudden that it had ceased to live and I was wild with grief. At that moment a religious whom I recognized passed by; it was the Rev. Father Paul. I cried out to him, 'O my Father! you who cure so many people, cure also my poor child!' Father Paul drew near and having uncovered the child's breast a little, he said to me, 'Return home, the child will get well!' At that very moment my child opened his eyes."

༄

The Only Son of Rich Parents

had reached the age of seven years but had always been speechless. In 1892 the servant girl brought the child to Termonde where Father Paul said to her, "That child will be able to speak very well if his parents make a novena." "I shall also pray," said the servant. Thereupon Father Paul addressed the child with these words: "Now say together with me, Jesus, Mary, Joseph!" and slowly the child repeated the words, Jesus, Mary, Joseph.

༄

An Innkeeper from Steenbrugge

relates the following story: "My sister-in-law died in giving birth to a child that was very delicate, and likewise died a few days later. While we were getting ready to dress the little corpse, Father Paul entered and said, 'Stop your preparations, for that child is not yet quite dead; I shall take care of him, and he will become a fine, chubby, young fellow.'

"The poor little creature revived; he was soon cured and became a fine, healthy, young man."

ᴄᴡ᎐

During Father Paul's Stay

at Steenbrugge, the report of his death was one day spread at Bruges. A friend hastened to the abbey for information. He was received by Father Paul himself who said with a smile, "But I certainly would have come to warn you of my death!"

About the same time, having recovered from an illness, he went to visit a friend of his, a farmer at Oostcamp. The latter congratulated him on his recovery and said familiary, "You have entered on a new lease, it seems."

"What is the usual term of a lease?" Father Paul asked.

"Nine years."

"Well, my lease is for nine and a half years," Father Paul replied, and he died four days after the term foretold.

ᴄᴡ᎐

During His Last Sickness,

up to the time of his death, Father Paul wore upon his breast an old letter from the Rev. Father Damian, the martyr of the lepers. Shall we one day know the intimate relations that existed between the illustrious martyr and the celebrated Father Paul of Moll, who was the guide of so many souls?

EXHUMATION OF THE BODY OF THE
REV. FATHER PAUL OF MOLL

For two days after his death, in fact, up to the moment of interment, the body of Father Paul in no wise presented the appearance of a corpse; he looked just like a man who had gone to sleep. His complexion had not visibly altered, and no odor was perceptible: the symptoms of dropsy, of which he had died, disappeared, and what is more extraordinary, *the limbs preserved their flexibility and the body its natural heat.* In fact, a visitor asked if it were certain that he was dead; but there was no doubt about it, as the physician had confirmed his death.

In the first edition of this work (1898) the author hinted at the possibility of the body being preserved incorrupt in the tomb, and remarked that it would be very easy to ascertain if such were the case, as the body was buried in the vault of the Benedictine Fathers in the cemetery of Appels which is near Termonde and easy of access. Since then the verification has taken place, and the result was as remarkable as it was gratifying to the admirers of Father Paul.

The mortal remains of the saintly monk had been placed in a zinc coffin, which had been incased in one of wood. But in order to insure the better preservation of the body, some members of his family asked the local authorities for permission to exhume it, in order to replace the zinc coffin by one of lead. The necessary authorization having been accorded by the proper authorities, the body was exhumed Monday, July 24, 1899, at ten o'clock in the morning, in the presence of members of the family of the deceased and about thirty other witnesses.

Having lifted the body out of the vault, they found that the wooden covering was no more suitable to receive the new coffin of lead; it was, therefore, decided to postpone the transfer. However, in order to inform themselves as to the state of the body, they proceeded to open the zinc coffin, and found the body in a state of perfect preservation.

This was a source of great joy to those present who were nearly all friends of Father Paul, and it was truly a touching spectacle to see them all at once fall upon their knees and join in prayer around the beloved remains. Rosaries and other objects of devotion were applied to the body, and each one was eager to carry away, as a relic, a piece of the zinc* coffin, which was afterwards closed up by means of a leaden-plate† and replaced in the vault.

The witnesses of the exhumation signed the following document:—

"We, the undersigned, having been present at the exhumation of the body of Rev. Father Paul (Francis Luyckx) in the cemetry of Appels, Termonde, this Monday July 24, 1899, at ten o'clock in the morning, do hereby certify, that we saw the body through an opening in the zinc coffin, fifty centimeters by twenty-five, that is, about twenty inches by ten, and declare that it was in a state of perfect preservation; the skin of the face was hardened and a bister, that is, brownish color, the hands very white. His monastic habit was clean, and the body had preserved its original position notwithstanding the fact that the coffin had been dragged up almost perpendicularly from the tomb, from a depth of four meters" (about four and one-half yards).

Mr. Pierre Cools-Vermeulen, Bell-Gheel.

Mr. Joseph Cools, Seminarian, Bell-Gheel.

Miss Regina Cools, Bell-Gheel.

Miss Rosalie Cools, Bell-Gheel.‡

Mr. Camille D'Hoore, farmer, Oostcamp.

Mr. Julien van Speybrouck, Bruges.

Mr. Edward van Speybrouck, Bruges.

Miss Marie van Speybrouck, Bruges.

Mr. Emile Willaert, engineer, Waelhem-Malines.

Mr. Louis Willaert, engineer, Waelhem-Malines.

Miss Josephine van den Brande, Malines.

Miss Helene Middelaer, Antwerp.

---

* The zinc did not show the slightest trace of oxidation in the inside of the coffin, contrary to what always takes place in similar cases.

† This plate of lead can be seen in the picture of the exhumation on the lower part of the coffin.

‡ These four are relations of Father Paul.

Mrs. Auguste Mansion, Brussels.

Mr. Edw. Steenackers-van Brusselen, Antwerp.

Mr. A. Vandesmet, Lille.

Mrs. A. Vandesmet, Lille.

Miss Marie Vandesmet, Lille.

Mrs. Beenckens-Ridts, Herenthals.

Mrs. Em. van Velsen, Malines.

Miss Marie van Velsen, Malines.

Miss Irma van Velsen, Malines.

Mr. L. Nauwelaers, Waelhem-Malines.

Miss Marie Siongers, Waelhem-Malines.

Mr. Aug. Cam bier, Termonde.

Mrs. Gorsele, Termonde.

Mrs. Glyssens, Termonde.

Miss Justine Roggheman, Termonde.

Mr. Alf. Heessens, Termonde.

Mr. R. De Munck, Termonde.

Mr. O. Henderickx, Termonde.

Mr. A. De Pets, Termonde.

Mr. P. van Gucht, Termonde.

Mr. C. De Corte, Termonde.

Exhumation of the body of the Rev. Father Paul of Moll.
Found in a state of perfect preservation.

A Strange Thing

took place at the exhumation. The opening in the zinc coffin, as before mentioned, was only about 20 x 10 inches. Among the witnesses, there was present a farmer, who was one of the best friends of Father Paul. This witness was ready to affirm on oath that the *whole* upper portion of the zinc coffin had been removed and that he *saw*, and saw with his *own eyes* the whole body uncovered. He described all the details, the position of the feet, the black stockings, the ends of the stole, etc. All these details are exact, yet the witness was not present when the body was laid in the coffin for burial.

"On my return from the exhumation," he added, "I related what I saw to the Rev. Benedictine Fathers and other acquaintances. At the cemetery I left the coffin twice in order to converse with some of the other witnesses that stood a few steps farther off, and thus I saw the whole body three times; it could not have been an illusion! Or was I the only one that saw this?"

Says The Author:

"We think we have said enough to make better known *the goodness, wisdom, virtues and powerful intervention* of our great and never-to-be-forgotten friend.

"Can there be any doubt that if the Church accords him the honor of beatification and a place on our altars, the good Father Paul of Moll will be invoked by the Catholic world in all its needs? For indeed during his lifetime people had recourse to him not merely in one certain kind of cases, but, as the facts which we have recorded show, the Rev. Father Paul interested himself, as it were, in all the miseries of mankind, and obtained for everyone substantial relief.

"Moreover, we feel confident (and have been informed to that effect) that a number of persons will soon furnish new material for building a monument that will spread more and more the memory of the celebrated *Benedictine Monk;* nevertheless we are proud to have been the first to publish something that will contribute to the glory of him who, during his life, deigned to be our friend and counselor, and who, we firmly hope, will continue to extend to his numerous friends here below his powerful and benign protection.

"Trustworthy persons from everywhere report favors obtained since the death of Father Paul, by having recourse to him with confidence, as to a very powerful saint."

We shall confine ourselves to mentioning the following favors obtained through the powerful intercession of Father Paul after his death: —

In 1879 a Young Servant Girl

on a farm in Oostcamp was on the point of becoming blind. As the remedies which were applied had no effect, she determined to consult an oculist; but the farmer who was a friend of Father Paul proposed that she should first make a novena in honor of the Rev. Father lately deceased.

From the sixth day of the novena the young girl's eyes were radically cured, and the cure has been permanent.

ᐯᐱᐳ

The Superioress of a Convent

writes us as follows: In January 1900 the little daughter of a poor farmer at Waas had a fall which inflicted a frightful wound on her head; the blood flowed so profusely that she fainted. The physician who was summoned at once recognized the seriousness of the case and declared the wound fatal. After great efforts they had succeeded in restoring the unfortunate little girl to consciousness, but she was not able to speak more than a few incoherent words, and continually cried on account of the pain. It was pitiable to witness the despair of the parents; at the bedside of their beloved child they did not cease to weep and lament.

"You see," said the wife to her husband who had given up the practice of his religious duties, "it is God who has punished us!" At this reproach the husband only bowed his head and sobbed. In the meantime a good girl of the neighborhood came in and handed the unhappy mother a small piece of Father Paul's scapular, saying, "Apply by means of a bandage, this little relic of the forehead of your child, and let us then pray of Father Paul." They followed this advice with the result that the little girl became quiet and silent for a quarter of an hour. Then she awoke with a start and cried out:

"Mama! mama! call papa at once, I am cured! A holy religious came and cured me! I don't feel any more pain." The farmer came to the bedside of his child who said to him, "Father, will you now go to church and to confession? A holy religious came to cure me." The father, full of emotion and weeping for joy, replied, "Yes, my child, I shall go to confession." "Very well, father dear, then we will go to church together and thank the good God."

On the following Saturday the farmer, his wife, and their little daughter, who was now quite well, went together to church, to the great astonishment and edification of the people of the village.

∽

In 1896, a Lady from St. Michael

who was very sick sent her servant on a pilgrimage to the tomb of Father Paul in order to obtain the recovery of her health. Upon her return the servant told the lady that while praying before the tomb, she had also asked Father Paul how long her mistress would yet live; and that she had then heard a voice replying to her, "Eleven more years." But she added that she had seen no one, as she was all alone in the cemetery. The sick woman much pleased to hear this, told the story herself to several persons. She died in 1907.

∽

In Moerbrugge

a consumptive infant six months of age, the child of a farmer, was cured at the end of a novena in honor of the late Rev. Father Paul. During the novena a little piece of the Rev. Father's habit was attached to the baby's dress.

∽

A Farmer at Heyst

had a fine black horse taken so sick that the veterinary surgeon declared it incurable. His wife's cousin, however, recommended that the horse be put under the protection of Father Paul.

"I have no relic of Father Paul," she said, "except this memorial card; attach it to the wall of the stable, and let us pray." On the morning of the following day the horse was cured.

∽

At Steenbrugge

a child ten years old, the son of a storekeeper, had been afflicted with several serious maladies since his third year. He was almost deaf, the glands of his neck were badly swollen, his eyes, irritated by a succession of pimples, were moist all the time, and behind his ears there were large wounds that continually discharged an offensive pus. The unfortunate child had already undergone a painful operation, but without relief.

In October 1896 the mother, in conversation with some persons about Father Paul, whom they had known in life, said, "If Father Paul cures my poor child, I promise that I will go to Termonde and thank him at his grave." Indeed, eight days afterwards, as certified by the mother and several witnesses, the boy was completely cured. His hearing was completely restored, his eyes became bright and clear, the wounds back of his ears had disappeared; in a word, the child was cured. The mother, in company with several persons, made the pilgrimage June 28, 1897, on the feast of Sts. Peter and Paul.

This woman never tires of praising the good Father Paul who during his residence in Steenbrugge had been the benefactor of her family, and tells many wonderful things of him.

∽

A Farmer from Oostcamp,

a friend of Father Paul, had cause to complain of a farm-hand, but delayed his dismissal, fearing his revenge. At last he began to pray to Father Paul to find him a good way of getting rid of the undesirable person without danger to himself. The next morning the farmhand, very much agitated and with a haggard countenance, came and told the farmer that he did not wish to remain a minute longer. "I go," he said, "for last night I think I saw all the devils of hell."

A Young Lady

of twenty-two years, living in Oedelem, suffered from epilepsy for nine years, and during this time the affliction grew worse from year to year. The last six years violent fits occurred from six to nine times a day. It was a continual martyrdom; the girl had become an idiot, unable to speak and incapable of taking nourishment herself. She meanwhile had become very thin and emaciated, and involuntarily she struck at persons that came near her, not even sparing her own mother.

In April 1896 a shred of Father Paul's habit was sewed on the girl's scapular and since that time she does not suffer any further attacks except in September, and at long intervals, when the former disease returns, but the attacks are very slight and of short duration. The young lady's health is improving from day to day; her reason has returned, also her speech; and there is no longer any sign of emaciation.

"For Thirty Seven Years,"

an unmarried lady living in Termonde relates, "I enjoyed a small life annuity. In 1897 on account of unforeseen expenses, I found myself short of money. Full of confidence in the protection of the Rev. Father Paul whom I had known in life, I put his portrait in my empty safe and said, "Father Paul, I am in need, you must help me!"

Two days later I opened the safe and to my great astonishment I saw lying next to his portrait more money than I had ever had at my disposal.

A Young Lady from Thielt,

who had the jaundice, went to the Benedictine Abbey of Termonde in the year 1897, where she was advised to make a pilgrimage to the tomb of Father Paul. She did so and commenced a novena at the same time. To the great astonishment of her doctor, the patient found herself on the way to recovery from the third day of the novena. The doctor even thought it necessary to give her medicine to retard so rapid a cure; "For," said he, "in such a case a sudden restoration to health is abnormal and would have serious consequences." But in spite of all, the patient was completely cured before the end of the novena.

❧

In July 1899

an old man who was blind recovered his eyesight before he left the tomb of Father Paul where he had gone on a pilgrimage.

❧

In December 1899 the Baby Girl,

fifteen months old, of a lady in Bruges suffered from a disease of the eyes that caused the greatest apprehension. In spite of the physician's efforts, her eyes could not be opened. It was feared she would become blind. In this emergency the mother had recourse to Father Paul whom she had on a former occasion, consulted in Steenbrugge. She said to him: —

"Good Father, if you were still living on earth, I would quickly go to see you; but you can understand me up there in heaven. Obtain for me. I beseech you, the cure of my baby. I promise that I shall make known this favor, but I want you to do it in an extraordinary manner so that there may be no mistake that the favor is due to you."

Hereupon the lady, in presence of her husband, laid the child on its little bed and that very instant it opened its eyes, crying, "Papa! Mamma!"

❧

A Baker from Hamme-Zogge Writes:

"In 1902 my son, seven years old, was declared incurable by the physicians. For the last two years he had suffered greatly in his head. The attacks in the morning and evening were particularly severe and lasted several hours. The child lost his reason and it became impossible for him to go to church or to school.

"The good God finally gave us the idea of taking him to the tomb of Father Paul. The third time we were there, we seated ourselves together on the tomb and after some prayers I said to my son, 'Now ask Father Paul in a loud voice if he would please make you well?' He did so, and from that moment he suffered no longer and now enjoys perfect health."

∽

For Several Years Charles Theyns,

an inhabitant of Oostduinkerke, suffered very much from cancer of the stomach. In September 1907 the condition of the patient became so desperate that the curate of the parish administered the last sacraments. In the meantime Madam Crahay of Antwerp, who happened to spend a vacation in Oostduinkerke, came and asked me for a small piece of the habit of Father Paul of Moll in order to place it over the breast of the sufferer. She also advised him and his family to make, with great confidence, novenas in honor of Father Paul, and made him promise that, in case of a cure, he would go to thank Father Paul at his tomb. The patient was unable to take the least food, not even a drop of water, besides he vomited black and bloody matter. The curate coming back to see him, said that he would not live through the day. The physician also said that death was imminent. But during the first days of the novena, to the great astonishment of both the curate and the physician, the condition of the dying man began to improve. The improvement became more apparent from day to day, and in the course of a second novena he was restored to perfect health. Since then he works and travels and says he never felt better in his life.

Here is the statement of his physician:—

"The undersigned, physician of medicine, surgery and obstetrics at Oostduinkerke, certifies that he treated, for some time, one named Charles Theyns of this village for cancer of the stomach, but without any great result, and that actually he is now completely freed from his disease."

DR. FEYS. OOSTDUINKERKE, NOV. 21, 1907.

CRUD

A Gentleman from Thielt

paid a visit to Father Paul at Steenbrugge. In the beginning of their conversation, Father Paul noticed a fly flying through the room and quickly proceeded to catch it, saying, "These flies are the cause of so many diseases."

In Congo, the fly tsé-tsé, whose bite causes the sleeping-malady, is a real plague, and science is still seeking for an effectual remedy. The sleeping-malady is a contagious disease and has been brought into Europe from other countries. Many cases of it have been discovered in Belgium.

In Hamme, a farmer had been afflicted with the sleeping-malady for three months. Two physicians treated him but without success. Finally the farmer placed himself under the protection of Father Paul and made some novenas to him. He was entirely cured. On July 1, 1913, he made a pilgrimage to Father Paul's tomb to thank him.

CRUD

The Burgomaster of Buezet

inquired of me in a letter where he could get a photograph of Father Paul, as he would like to become acquainted with him. He said that his son, twenty-one years of age, had been afflicted with a paralyzed finger.

"The physician wished to amputate the finger," wrote the Burgomaster, "but we prayed to Father Paul, and the finger was restored to life, and is completely cured."

CRUD

A Farmer in Oostcamp

who was an intimate friend of Father Paul, says: "I went to Father Paul's tomb with the great annual pilgrimage of 1913. There I said to our good saint: 'We are anxious to take in our hay. But we are having so much rain, please help us!' Now, on Saturday, July 5th, although the weather was threatening, I made up my mind to take in the hay, quite confident in Father Paul's protection. My sisters tried in vain to dissuade me, saying that the rain would spoil it all. Nevertheless, I gave orders to scatter the heaps of hay once more for a final drying before loading. We had scarcely begun work, when it rained again, but not a drop fell on our hay. At the close of the day, it was taken in perfectly dry and fragrant."

In 1906, the Servant of a Restaurant Keeper

in Termonde had on her neck a terrible cancer which had already been cauterized several times. Two physicians were successively consulted and both advised an operation at the hospital. But her mistress proposed first to make a novena in honor of the late Father Paul. On the last day of the novena the cancer disappeared without leaving a trace.

Sayings of Father Paul

Preliminary Remarks.

A conversation with the Rev. Father was always a real treat to his intimate friends. His advice and counsels were given with surprising precision and appropriateness.

The Rev. Father showed himself well informed on all subjects, and solved the most difficult questions in a few words. He gave his friends instructions on a multitude of subjects, God, the angels, the saints, religion, the future life, human sciences, art, everything in fact, as though he possessed infused knowledge and wisdom.

What pleasant and consoling remembrances! But, also, what a pity that all his precious communications were not at once written down for future reference!

We have recalled to mind, and gathered up some of these sayings and conversations, and the brief specimens which we give will, we hope, induce all the friends of Father Paul to record likewise their own personal recollections concerning this matter.

Father Paul attributed the wonders which he worked to the intervention of his holy Father Benedict.

"As for me," he would say, "I am only the doorkeeper of St. Benedict."

"They say that St. Benedict is minister of heaven. We must often speak to him."

"St. Benedict is our Father, he is *obliged* to take care of us."

"I have no need of any one, the Blessed Virgin and St. Benedict are sufficient for me."

Some one reminded Father Paul that, according to tradition, people obtained all that they demanded from a certain saint on his feast day.

"Every day," he replied, "is the feast of St. Benedict."

A friend from Oostcamp once complained of a pain in his eyes, and said he had consulted a physician.

"All right!" replied Father Paul; "but have you already addressed St. Benedict? He is the best physician."

To show the great power of the medal of St. Benedict, Father Paul maintained that one medal was sufficient to put out a conflagration.

The death of a young lady brought sorrow to a numerous family. They spoke of it to Father Paul who showed himself deeply effected and said,—

"A medal of St. Benedict would have cured her."

"Lightning and the noise of thunder have always been the cause of terror to me. When it thunders I tremble like a leaf," said a man from the country to Father Paul.

"Here is a medal of St. Benedict," he replied; "wear it around your neck, you will not be afraid any more, and will have nothing to fear from lightning."

In the beginning of his residence at Steenbrugge, Father Paul said to his friends, "St. Benedict is not well enough known."

"When I have a visit to make, I do not trust to myself for what I have to say, and I do not get my speeches ready; but I pray to the Holy Spirit to enlighten me, and aid me."

"Parents in heaven intercede unceasingly with God in behalf of their children on earth."

"By their prayers and good works, children augment the accidental glory of their parents who are in heaven."

"The souls in purgatory are aware of the discord of the members of their families on earth, and this knowledge increases their sufferings."

Speaking of the soul of a lady deceased, Father Paul said, "She remained only one hour in purgatory, and she did not stay there any longer because she brought up her children so well." He added that by a special privilege, this lady had undergone the hour of her purgatory on the chair in which she had expired.

A lady having died after a long and painful sickness her daughter went to Steenbrugge and asked Father Paul if he thought that her mother went straight to heaven, after so many sufferings.

"Madam," he replied, "your mother would be already in heaven, if she had not spoiled her children so much. She is still in purgatory pray hard for her."

"A good means of avoiding a long stay in purgatory is *to die entirely resigned to the holy will of God.*"

A lady had met her death in a terrible railway collision near Ghent. Father Paul said that her soul had gone straight to heaven because, at the last moment, the lady cried out, "Lord, may Thy will be done."

A person from the village of Ursel complained to Father Paul that an ecstatic had told her that her father, who had died a short time before, was in purgatory.

"I became angry with this girl," she said, "because my father was an excellent Christian and died completely resigned to the will of God; I cannot believe that his soul is still in purgatory!"

Father Paul sweetly replied, "Why do you refuse to believe what this ecstatic girl asserts? Of course, you are not obliged to do so. Your father was very good, but are you quite certain that he died entirely resigned to the will of God?. . .For the rest, do not be so anxious; it is not sure that your father has to suffer in purgatory. A great many souls endure no other suffering than the delay of their admission to heaven; and to many of them permission is given to hover in the church before the Most Holy Sacrament."

"In order to go straight to heaven, one must make a close acquaintance with the Queen of Heaven."

A young girl from the country asked Father Paul to say a Mass for the success of a certain affair. "Rather have that Mass said for the repose of the soul of your mother who is deep down in purgatory," he replied.

Father Paul used to relate that the soul of a sister appeared to him and said, "Oh, my father! purgatory is more terrible than you have described!"

"The cold which certain souls endure in purgatory is as terrible as fire."

A subscriber to an irreligious journal having died at Saint-Michel, his wife would not give up the paper, although she refrained from reading it.

Father Paul maintained for certain that the widow would have to remain long in purgatory, for having tolerated the introduction of a journal of that kind into her house.

"There are souls condemned to stay in purgatory till the end of the world."

Father Paul often asserted that the souls in purgatory who were delivered by his prayers came to thank him.

Sometimes, at the request of the relatives of those that had died, Father Paul told them how long the souls of these departed ones had to stay in purgatory. But usually he avoided letting them know when they were delivered, because, as a rule, he said, the friends then cease to pray for their souls, and yet the prayers offered up for them increase their accidental happiness in heaven.

He also said that a great number of suffering souls continually came to him to ask his prayers for their deliverance, and that at night, his bed was surrounded by suffering souls.

In the confessional Father Paul said to one of his penitents, "If you were to die now, you would have three days of purgatory, and I could diminish your punishment by only one day."

"None of my near relatives are any longer in purgatory."

Father Paul said to a Carmelite nun, "You can avoid passing through purgatory, if you carefully observe the Rule of your Order."

Father Paul said that he gave himself the discipline every day for the following intentions:—

1. The perseverance of the just.
2. The conversion of sinners.

3. The holy Church.

4. The souls in purgatory.

5. The happiness of his friends and benefactors.

He used to say that a great many suffering souls would then appear to him and cry out, "For me, if you please! For me! For me!"

"On each of her feasts, the Blessed Virgin descends into purgatory, consoles all the suffering souls, and delivers many of them."

A Beguine from Antwerp having died suddenly, her servant was deeply grieved. As Father Paul was visiting a lady acquaintance of his, she spoke to him of the servant's grief.

"Oh!" said the Father, "She ought not to be sad, her old mistress will be in purgatory only for eight days, and she does not suffer there."

A merchant was on the point of having recourse to a banker, but he thought it best to consult Father Paul first.

"For my part," he replied, "I would rather address myself to the souls in purgatory than the banker, for these souls are always grateful when we pray for their release, and they then obtain from God all we ask and even more."

Father Paul was always on the lookout for an opportunity of enrolling members in the Confraternity of the Blue Scapular,* and advised the new members to gain every day, as far as possible, all the plenary indulgences applicable to the suffering souls.

The members of this Confraternity can gain a great number of plenary indulgences for the souls in purgatory, as often as they recite six Our Fathers, Hail Marys and Glory be to the Father, etc., and this without the necessity of approaching the sacraments.

---

* The Blue Scapular is from an apparition of the Virgin Mary to Sr. Ursula Benincasa [1547-1618], founder of the Theatines of the Immaculate Conception of the B.V.M. The Scapular can be blessed by Theatine Fathers, and Marians of the Immaculate Conception, who promote the Confraternity. See Appendix.

At Termonde, in 1894, a man was the victim of a terrible accident which cost his life. Father Paul spoke of this unhappy case as follows: "He had no religion and never went to church, but his soul is not lost because, at the last moment, he offered up his life in expiation of his sins. All the same, he will stay a long time in purgatory."

"A lady from Antwerp writes: "Very often we had the happiness of having the good and saintly Father Paul at our house. During the evenings, in the intimacy of a holy friendship, he would entertain us with pious topics, and when he spoke to us of the love of God, it was with the burning words of a seraph, he would go on repeating:—

" 'O love of God! Love so little known! so little loved! Who can describe the love of God for us? No, the love of all the mothers united to the love of all the angels and saints is only an atom compared to His divine love!'

"When he spoke to us of the passion of our Savior he shed abundant tears, and his face was, as it were, transfigured.

"He told us once that his sermons had been criticized because he never failed to speak of the love that God has for us.

" 'And then,' he said, 'I took some notice of these remarks; but God gave me to understand that I had not done right, and He commanded me to speak, at each sermon or conference, of His great love for man.'

"The souls in purgatory had a great comforter in Father Paul. 'One day,' he told us, 'I was very sick in my cell, and leaning with my elbow on the back of my chair, I heard quite close to me, groans and lamentations. I turned around and beheld a soul enveloped in flames and completely tied up with chains. This soul asked me to remember her in my prayers, and especially in the holy sacrifice of the Mass. I said to her, 'Pray for me; I shall pray for you.' At that very instant the soul disappeared and I found myself cured. Shortly afterwards this soul was released and came to thank me.' "

Father Paul related one of his visions to a person from Knesselaere in the following manner:—

"The Blessed Virgin appeared to me, holding the Divine Infant in her arms; he was crying bitterly and did not cease to complain. I asked Mary what was the cause of the sorrows of the little Jesus, and she replied, 'It is because priests do not remind the faithful sufficiently of the love of God for man, and of the passion of our Savior.'

"Thereupon I promised to treat of these two subjects in my next sermon, and immediately the sadness of the Infant Jesus was changed into great joy. He threw His little arms round the neck of His Mother, and embraced her tenderly."

A lady acquaintance from Knesselaere paid a visit to Father Paul and found him very ill, his head, and left arm and leg were much swollen. Father Paul explained the cause of his condition in these terms: —

"I had great pains in my head and suffered so intensely from them that I complained to Jesus. He replied to me, 'How insignificant your sufferings are, compared with the martyrdom I suffered, when crowned with thorns!'

"Then I asked Him that I might experience the pain of only one of those thorns and, at the same instant, the torture became so great that I fainted."

From a letter to the Mother Superior of a convent: "It is by love that one can overcome the All-powerful God; He is so sensitive to love that He can refuse us nothing."

Extracts from Letters from Father Paul

To a Lady in Knesselaere.

"God is astonishing in His love. The more we love Him, the more He loves us. He pays us back in tenfold love, the love which we have for Him."

"Man will be all the more glorious in heaven, the greater his love for God has been on earth."

"The love of God is as beautiful for men who love Him, as it is terrible to the demons and the damned."

"The more a man loves God, the more beautiful he grows in the eyes of God."

"God being infinite love, we can always love Him more and more."

"O love! O infinite love! O eternal love! O sweet love of God!"

"Man finds his greatest consolation in faithfully keeping the commandments of God and the holy Church, and in having a great devotion to Mary."

Father Paul once said to a person in Antwerp, "I never cease saying, 'O love! O great love! O infinite love of God!' If men knew how pleasing this is to God, they would repeat it without ceasing; several persons have become saints in this way."

Father Paul once said to a lay sister, a penitent of his: "When you enter the church in the morning it will be like a burning furnace; fire everywhere, the fire of the love of God to welcome you. You will not see this fire, but the whole church will be full of it."

"A sigh of love for God is worth more than a whole year of penance" (penance performed habitually or in our own will).

"God will not ask, 'Have you done much?' but, 'Have you worked for the love of God?' Quantity is not sufficient, it is quality that is necessary."

"On rising in the morning, many persons offer to God all the actions of the day saying, 'All for the glory of God!' But they should say, 'All for the love and glory of God!' because love surpasses all."

"Very early one morning, Father Paul seeing a peasant who had come a long distance through a terrific snowstorm, to hear Mass in the church at Steenbrugge, said to him: 'If you could see the immense merits which your courage has procured for you, you would be astonished, and you might yet increase them in a measure incredible, by saying, 'All for the love of Jesus.' "

To a servant girl in Antwerp Father Paul said, "Before eating, sleeping, opening or closing a door, or any other action, always have the intention of doing all for the love of Jesus. In this way you will continually reap a rich harvest for heaven."

"The devil can promise everything, but can give nothing."
"Humility renders men great in the eyes of God."

"When making the Way of the Cross, try to have compassion for the sufferings of Christ; for all those who took part in His sorrows became saints as, for example, Simon of Cyrene, Veronica, the good thief, the holy women and so many others."

"The power of the demons and their allies among men is not very terrible, because their activity is quickly rendered sterile by want of harmony in their camp, where the troops always end by fighting among themselves."

"The devil cannot go any farther than the length of his chain will allow." (In Flemish: De duvel kan toch maer loopen zoo verre alz zijin keten lang is.)

"The devil becomes still more active at the approach of great festivals; and you will observe that then, especially, he stirs up dissensions in families."

"When a demon suggests a bad thought, it is easy to resist the temptation; but if one does not immediately repel it, a second demon comes at once to help the first. Afterwards, in proportion as resistance is delayed, still other demons come and combine their efforts, and when one has to battle against seven devils all at once, it is very difficult not to succumb."

To pregnant women, Father Paul gave the advice to go to the priest and ask him to recite over them the prayers appointed for that purpose in the ritual, so as to guard themselves, as well as the children to be born, against all possible misfortune.

"It is before and at the moment of birth that the Evil One is most intent upon doing mischief to human beings, and consequently there is some risk in not having recourse to the special prayers of the Church."

One day Father Paul was seen with a large wound on his forehead. He explained that it was the effect of a blow which the devil had given him.

Father Paul said that one day, after hearing a man's confession, he was forcibly lifted up by the devil to the ceiling of the confessional; at the same time he heard a voice crying out to him, "I am . . . ." (giving here the full name of a certain person).

Father Paul once said to a friend, "I have just seen our Savior and immediately afterwards there filed past me a large troop of men on horseback, all clad in armour, like cavaliers of the Middle Ages: they were so many demons! When anything good happens, the devil at once interferes."

There was a talk in the presence of Father Paul of sorcerers and sorceresses, of diabolical Sabbath meetings and interferences of evil spirits. Asked to express his opinion, Father Paul said, "In our days the action of the evil spirit is less to be feared than formerly. His power diminishes with the ever increasing number of priests; for the almost continual offering of the holy sacrifice of the Mass victoriously neutralizes the efforts of Satan."*

During a storm that was accompanied by vivid flashes of lightning and the deafening crash of thunder, Father Paul said; "At the last judgment the sentence pronounced against the reprobates will crash like this over their heads, but with a noise a thousand times more terrible."

A young lady writes, "One day at Steenbrugge, Father Paul exhorted me to pray daily in union with the anguish of Jesus crucified and the sorrows of Mary† at the foot of the cross. The Rev. Father said that he did it also, and to these prayers he attributed the great number of sinners who came to confession to him; and for that reason the devil had vowed a special hatred against him.

"One night," he added, "the devil came to my cell and leaped on my neck with an indescribable rage, in order to strangle me."

"But, Father!" I exclaimed, "how did you get rid of him?"

"Oh, well, my child, I invoked Jesus in His love and said, 'O love! O infinite love! O ocean of love! How great was your goodness for men to allow Yourself to be tempted in the desert by Satan!' And immediately the devil fled, grumbling in a horrible manner and filling my cell with a pestilential odor. He often comes to torment me."

Father Paul told a sister in Antwerp that the devil gave him volleys of blows, and in a thousand different ways, often handled him very roughly.

"But one must not complain of it," he added, for if you knew how beautiful heaven is, you would ask to suffer everything in order to get there."

---

* Before 1898, the year of Fr. Paul's demise.
† See Appendix for a rosary of the sorrows of Mary.

He told her also that the Blessed Virgin appeared to him very frequently; and when he spoke of heaven which, he said, he saw in ecstasy, he would never come to an end.

To another person Father Paul said that on a certain Christmas night, he had never seen the heaven of the elect look so beautiful as on that occasion.

"Last night," Father Paul said to a farmer, "the devil lifted me violently from my bed and threw me rudely on the floor." "Although I am not naturally timid," the farmer replied, "I assure you that, in a similar case, I would tremble in all my limbs. And were you not afraid?"

"Not at all," Father Paul answered, "what we ought to fear far more is the world where devils swarm, and where the devil reigns supreme."

"It is useless to seek perfection among men; perfection is found in heaven alone."

In the case of ecstatics, if they give into the slightest thought of pride, the devil at once interferes with their actions."

Someone complained to Father Paul about an ecstatic. "Then do not believe," he said, "that these saintly souls have no faults. No saint in this world is exempt from faults."

"*The devil cannot endure humility;* it is his great enemy; as soon as he perceives its presence anywhere, he becomes helpless and runs away."

"A good way of finding out for sure whether an apparition is diabolical, is to ask the blessing of the being that has appeared; for the devil has no power to impart a blessing."

During a conversation in which Father Paul spoke of the great power of holy water which, through ignorance, is not sufficiently appreciated, some one said to him:—

"Once when I had warts on my hand, a friend assured me that an excellent means of getting rid of them was to plunge these warts into holy water and then make the sign of the cross with that hand. He said I should do this once a day for three days in succession. I followed his advice and the warts disappeared. This remedy received the approval of the Rev. Father.

Father Paul was not pleased to see people enter the church without taking holy water. To a gentleman who did not stop to bless himself he said,

"Take holy water; there at least, the devil is not present."

October 14, 1881, a furious hurricane swept over a building in course of construction, belonging to the Marais Congregation in Bruges. The building was completely overturned so that hardly a stone remained upon a stone. The roof was taken off by one blast, then the solid walls of the grand building were entirely overthrown. This catastrophe astonished even the contractors and builders, and the architect when informed of this misfortune, was so terribly shocked that he died soon after. Father Paul explained the cause of the disaster in these words:—

"This is quickly done. Satan places a demon against each stone and at the first signal, the whole collapses!" The Rev. Father also recommended that one or several medals of St. Benedict be placed within the material of the new building, in order to protect it.

During one winter there was continual bad weather. Now, with the least blast of wind one or more panes of glass were broken in a convent, situated not far from the monastery of Steenbrugge; the glazier alone enjoyed the benefit of these mishaps.

The proper thing to do in this case was to complain to Father Paul; people had to live at a great distance in order not to have recourse to him in every vexatious circumstance. So the sisters went to Father Paul and he said, "I saw a demon in your garden; it is he who makes use of the wind to break your windows. Here is a medal, fasten it to your door on the inside, and fear no more." From that time forward the glazier lost his job of putting in new windows at the convent.

"The Liberals are the devil's sorcerers: they will cut a droll figure once when they arrive in the other world."

"The Nihilists of Russia are a scourge, like the grasshoppers: the more that are imprisoned, the more come."

"Socialism here is but a passing wind."

"People complain of socialism, but it will spread a great deal more, and this, because people do not sufficiently venerate the Most Holy Sacrament."

On the morning after the elections for the legislature, by which the late "liberal" ministry in Belgium was defeated, Father Paul said, "The liberal party has lived. Now there are but two parties, the Catholics and the Socialists."

"The perfections of God are infinite. In heaven the saints will see the divine perfections succeed each other without ceasing: every moment a new perfection will be revealed to them, and so it will be through all eternity."

A country girl having told Father Paul that she had been warned against the book known as "The Prayers of St. Gertrude,"* he replied that it was a great mistake and added, "Of all prayer books, *this is the most beautiful*."

---

* This book may be obtained through Caritas Publishing.

"If it were permitted to one of the elect to live again in this world, he would submit with joy to all the sufferings that men have ever endured here below, in order to add to his merits that which he would acquire by the recital of one *Ave Maria*."

Father Paul related the following vision to a young lady of Knesselaere: —

"I am in the habit of reciting daily the rosary of our Lady of the Seven Dolors;* but one day, when I was on a journey, I unwillingly omitted this pious exercise. The following night the Blessed Virgin appeared to me, her heart pierced with the seven dolors; her eyes were bathed in tears, nor did she utter a word. Having made the sign of the cross, I set out at once to say my rosary, and noticed that the Blessed Virgin joined her hands. Having finished the meditation and prayers of the first group of seven beads, one of the seven dolors of Mary emitted a celestial light. And as I recited the following groups of seven beads, the other six dolors were also illumined with the same splendor.

"Having finally recited three Hail Marys in memory of the tears of the Blessed Virgin, I saw the tears of Mary dissolving into a heavenly smile; the divine Mother greeted me, blessed me and disappeared."

A person living in Thielt reports the following stories as told by Father Paul: —

" 'One evening, in 1895, after our spiritual exercises, I was walking through the cloister in the abbey, reciting, according to my custom, three Hail Marys in honor of our Lady to obtain her maternal blessing, when all at once I saw this good Mother clothed in a robe of dazzling white. She approached and made a little cross with her thumb on my forehead. The emotion which I felt is indescribable, and if the apparition had lasted two minutes longer, Father Paul would be no more of this world; for I would not have been able to support this brilliancy any longer.'

"After Father Paul had told me the above, he fell into an ecstasy which lasted about five minutes."

* See Appendix

Here are two other visions related by Father Paul to the same person: —

" 'One day while I knelt in adoration before the Most Holy Sacrament exposed, I saw Jesus standing before me. He wore a white garment, and was of dazzling beauty.' "

Again: " 'A very pious young girl was saying the rosary in our church, in honor of the nine choirs of angels.* I saw above her head nine silver strings which continually moved up and down. This symbolized the joy felt by the angels of the nine choirs at the homage which was paid to them.'

"Father Paul loved to propagate this devotion to the nine choirs of angels."

From a young lady of Heusden (Ghent) we heard the following story:

"At a visit to Father Paul, in 1895, he said to me, 'If I were to tell you something, would you believe me?'

" 'Yes, Father.'

" 'The Blessed Virgin appeared to me, and before disappearing she placed her hand upon my shoulder.'

"He also said to me, 'There are souls in the fire of purgatory who ask your prayers for their deliverance. You knew these persons well, and now they are forgotten by their children.'

"He also told me that my father is in heaven."

In the confessional, Father Paul said to a friend from Oostcamp:—

"From the time of the Ascension of our Lord, the most Blessed Virgin communicated every day and by a special privilege, the host remained intact within her up to the moment of the next Communion, so that Mary always guarded, in her interior, the humanity and divinity of Jesus Christ; and thus was able to keep up a continual conversation with her Divine Son."

* See Appendix

Father Paul said to a person from Oostcamp, "In an ecstasy, a saint has seen the body of St. Joseph preserved intact in a tomb, the site of which is yet unknown. The more the glorious Spouse of the most Blessed Virgin is honored, the sooner will the finding of his body take place, which will be a day of great joy for the Church."

"At the time when the Church is most persecuted, God raises up in the world the greatest number of saints."

To a Trappist lay brother Father Paul once said, "A single act of humility is worth more than fasting a hundred years on water and bread; for humility always remains a virtue, whilst fasting is often accompanied with pride."

"Never has there been so much faith as at the present day."

Someone remarked to the Rev. Father that our generation was not so good as the preceding one.

"You cannot say that!" he replied.

"When God works miracles in our favor, He is pleased most often to produce them in a manner which seems quite natural."

"Every communication coming from the Father of Lights is made in clear and very concise terms, leaving no place for doubt or double meaning."

Once when Father Paul was sick, he said, "I cannot ask for my recovery, but others can ask it for me. I can ask everything for others."

Speaking of certain persons whose faithful friendship for himself he praised highly, Father Paul gave the assurance that these friends would never suffer any misfortunes.

"During the consecration of the three Masses on Christmas I obtain everything I asked for."

"In order to be heard, it is not always sufficient only to pray oneself, one should also ask the prayers of others."

The Mother Superior of a convent complained to Father Paul that he came so seldom to help the community with his counsels.

"I am so often in the midst of you without your seeing me," the Rev. Father replied.

The following extract we copied from the letter of Father Paul, addressed from Termonde, Aug. 30, 1894, to a person in Ghent whom he had visited that day:—

"I arrived home safe, without seeing or hearing anything on the way. While you were still looking at me, I was already at home."

Are not these lines calculated to suggest the idea of bilocation?

"It is better to make novenas in the morning than in the evening."

Father Paul advised a countryman to make a novena to St. Benedict.

"I shall have to wait a few days," he replied, "for I have commenced a novena to St. Joseph."

"Nothing prevents you from making the two novenas at the same time, in heaven, there is no jealousy among the saints."

Father Paul blamed those very much, who habitually spent part of the night in work or in pleasure. He said: "The night belongs to God."

Father Paul sometimes made use of pleasantries in order to make people remember his advice. He asked a farmer who went to him to confession, "Until what hour do you stay out in the evening?"

"That depends; when I amuse myself, I do not come home till eleven or midnight."

"How many commandments of God are there?"

"Ten."

"There you see! If it were good not to come home till eleven, there would be eleven commandments . . . Believe me, go to bed at ten, and you will feel much better for it."

In the presence of Father Paul, some one made fun of an absent person who was very scrupulous.

"Scrupulosity," he said, "is one of the saddest maladies. Be very careful not to make fun of scrupulous persons, for you may one day become scrupulous yourself."

A very scrupulous person asked for a way out of her scruples. Father Paul laughingly replied, "Well, then, don't be scrupulous any longer!"

"The good God is not pleased with scrupulous people."

"It is the saints who have to endure the greatest temptations in this world."

The good and saintly Father Paul loved cheerful dispositions. "You will see," he said to some religious, "That in convents and everywhere the persons who are sad are always the least to be recommended.

They keep their eyes cast down and give themselves the air of a "Saint-don't-touch-me;" being full of restlessness, nothing gives them pleasure. Always the last where duty calls, they go there without fervor, but with their false air of habitual compunction.

"Whilst with persons who are always gay and full of joy, work becomes easy and brings forth good and salutary results."

Father Paul opposed making vows. "This often causes trouble later on," he said, "it is preferable to say, 'I resolve to do this or that.' "

A friend asked for prayers to obtain a certain favor. Father Paul replied, "I shall ask for what you demand when Our Lord comes."

Regarding these divine visits Father Paul once said to another friend, in a most suggestive tone of voice, "Have you read how familiarly St. Mechtild conversed with our Lord?"

"The remedy for cancer exists, but is not yet known."

"The physicians know the streets, the places and the houses of the human body quite well, but they do not know their inhabitants."

"When I have to take medicine, I never fail first to dip a medal of St. Benedict into it."

One day in summer, when the Rev. Father was in the garden with his friends, some one cut off a few small branches of a fruit tree and said jokingly, "The tree won't complain of it, it does not feel these cuts."

"You know nothing about it," replied Father Paul in a very suggestive tone.

"Must then everything that has life on earth be subject to the law of suffering?"

"Very often those who retain the goods of others die without making restitution."

"If a sinner were, for a single moment, to see the state of his soul, he would at once die of fright."

To a lady whom he had cured, Father Paul said, "Will you be kind enough to induce all your friends and acquaintances who are sick to come to see me? I shall cure them all!"

"I can obtain nothing for those who have the habit of blaspheming."

Father Paul said that he gave his blessing to his friends three times every day.

"All those who shall have suffered on my account will be associated with me in my glory."*

"People will publish the good which I have done, but will be silent as to what I have suffered. . ."

* Expressions of this sort have appeared strange to some readers of the First Edition, and appear to be little in accord with the humility of a saint. But history furnishes many examples of similar expressions from the lips of canonized saints. To cite but one example, the numerous authors who during many centuries have written the life of St. Godelieve of Ghistelles unanimously mention this prediction of the illustrious martyr: "The day will come when I shall he raised above all the women of Flanders." How often have not the saintly souls of this world been, as it were, the mouth-pieces of God? And have not the prophets of the Old Testament been the inspired and docile instruments of which the Almighty made use in order to announce and foretell to the nations His immutable and eternal decrees?

"Only at the last judgment will it be known how much I have suffered," Father Paul said to a friend.

"The simplicity of the just is turned into ridicule," says St. Gregory, and so it was with the good and saintly Father Paul. He was conscious of the raillery, at times very bitter, of which certain people made him the object, and most probably he also foresaw the injuries which would be heaped on his memory by some of his implacable enemies. Be that as it may, his friends love to recall a very suggestive remark of his,—

"My friends will be the last to laugh, and nothing will prevent them from laughing forever."

The good and saintly Father Paul was often calumniated and persecuted. He remarked one day to a friend, —

"Those who dig a pit for me, will themselves fall into a deeper one."

About the year 1888, Father Paul said to a person at Watervliet, that God had decided to punish the whole world with terrible chastisements; but that finally He had spared mankind, in answer to the prayers and penances of one single religious.

Father Paul did not tell the name of this religious.

In the confessional, an ecstatic said to Father Paul that in a dream she had seen the Rev. Father's soul carried to heaven by angels and there placed near the choir of angels. He replied simply, "Yes indeed, my place is there." Then he asked, "Do you know your place in heaven?"

"No."

"Well, I know it."

We may here remark that other ecstatics of our country likewise say that the Rev. Father Paul has a high place in heaven, and that he is a very powerful protector. But the Church alone has the authority to confirm these assertions.

To a friend Father Paul said, "Oh! we all know our places in heaven!"

"It is wrong to imagine heaven as a place whose inhabitants enjoy the same happiness. Heaven is a dwelling place where every work of charity, "werk van liefde," enjoys an eternal recompense."

In the confessional, Father Paul said to a servant girl from Thielt at the very beginning, "I know everything that you are going to confess, but, nevertheless, you have to tell it yourself."

As an ecstatic was making her confession to Father Paul, he interrupted her, saying, "Do you not see our Lord?"
"No."
"But I see Him, He is at your side."
To an ecstatic Father Paul said, "You will not work any miracles during your life-time, but you will after your death."

A short time before his departure from Steenbrugge, on a Sunday at Mass, Father Paul addressed the congregation from the pulpit as follows: —
"I shall not stay here much longer. Let all those who are suffering, or whose hearts are suffering, come to see me; I shall help them all!"

To one of his penitents Father Paul said, "Always obey me blindly, I shall be your guide during my life and after my death."
One day this same person said to the Rev. Father that, if he died, she would deserve to be pitied very much.

"On the contrary," he replied, "it will be so much better for you, when I am in heaven; for then you may ask me continually and my power will be still greater."

To a poor working girl of Thielt Father Paul said, "I will protect you all my life, and much more so after my death."

To another poor woman he said, "I will give you a loaf of bread which will never get mouldy, and a cup which will never be drained."

As Father Paul was visiting the wife of a blacksmith in Steenbrugge whose child was about to be buried, he said to her, —

"If I had been allowed to come, your child would not have died."

After a day of consultation, Father Paul was on the point of leaving Antwerp when some one spoke to him of a mother whose child was sick. He replied, "It is a great pity that this child was not brought to me, for all the sick children that came today have been cured."

Surprise was once expressed in the presence of Father Paul at the great number of children he cured.

"It is not surprising at all," he said, "these children have not yet done evil."

Married couples who were desolate because they had no children, also applied for help. But in order to have their wishes granted, the Rev. Father insisted that these couples should come to him in person and ask his prayers.

A friend of Father Paul failed to obtain a good photograph of an artistic object. Having lost patience, he wrote to the Rev. Father and received the following reply: —

"If you think that the devil is interfering in this matter, put a medal on the object that is to be photographed, and all will go well."

"Do not forget to attach a medal to your easel," said Father Paul to an artist painter.

While Father Paul was visiting a chateau in the neighborhood of Bruges, he was informed that a friend had met with a railway accident. Father Paul remarked,

"This gentleman had a medal of St. Benedict in his pocket-book: if he had worn it about his neck, he would not have had this accident."

A friend having demanded the prayers of Father Paul for a relative living in Paris, the Father gave him a medal to be sent and earnestly advised him to tell the patient not to put the medal in his pocket-book, but wear it around his neck, as also his scapular, as that was the only proper way of doing to experience the effect of blessed objects.

The friend found out later that the patient in Paris carried his scapular in his pocket-book.

Father Paul strongly disapproved of the manner in which blessed objects, such as scapulars and medals, are sometimes worn around the neck in a covering completely closed. He said that the covering should be open at the lower end; and when he was asked, why this should be so, he simply replied, "That is a mystery. "

When Father Paul visited some farmers in Oostcamp, a young lady who was sick asked him to cure her.

"Make use of your medal of St. Benedict and you will get well."

"I don't know where it is . . . "

"What? don't you wear the medal? And I, a religious, would not dare to be without the cross and the medal about my neck; and you, a simple lay person, do not wear it!"

"When we arrive up there, St. Peter will ask, 'Have you suffered much on earth? If you have, enter; if not, there is no room for you here.'"

A young girl from Scheepsdaele complained to Father Paul that she had very little time for her devotions, and even the few prayers she did say were said with many distractions.

"Oh! in that case," Father Paul replied, "you can remedy the matter by saying, in the evening, 'May all my imperfections of this day be changed into perfections!'"

A good country woman from Lichtervelde went to Steenbrugge to see Father Paul. He said to her, "You find it very difficult to pray, don't you?"

"Yes, Father!"

"Well, then, look here: when you wish to pray, place your hand on your heart and say, 'Good Jesus, You know very well what that means!' That is enough, for it says everything."

"When you say the *Our Father*, say it with the intention of obtaining the highest place in heaven."

A servant girl said to Father Paul, "I am sometimes afraid of going mad."

"No, no!" the Rev. Father replied, "you will never go mad: you are not proud enough."

Father Paul did not read any newspapers. "What's the use," he said. "What they print today is denied tomorrow." And showing his crucifix, he said, "This is my newspaper."

"Without the murderous attack of which he was the victim, the President of the French Republic, Carnot, would never have been converted."

A young girl inquired if the misfortunes that befell her family were divine punishments.

"No," replied Father Paul, "they are trials which the good God sends you in order to make you a little more like Him." Thereupon the girl asked what would become of her.

"An angel in heaven," he said.

To a friend from Oostcamp he once said, "Ik weet alles regtstreeks van onzen Lieven Heer." "I get all my information directly from our dear Lord. "

Conversing with some friends, Father Paul asked them what they would do to protect themselves against a mad dog. After every one had declared his plan, Father Paul, in his turn said, "As for me, I would take a medal of St. Benedict* in my hand, and would pass on quietly, without troubling myself: the mad dog would not come near."

A young man having told Father Paul that he had been sent in ridicule a sarcastic caricature, because, when invited to a feast on a fast day, he had abstained from forbidden meats, the Rev. Father replied that this derision would merit for him and his family great honor in the other world.

Entering a convent, Father Paul asked the Mother Superior, "Have you already thanked the good God for all the pains which He has sent you? . . . No? Well, then, I shall do so for you."

* We may remark here that at the celebrated basilica of St. Hubert, in Luxemburg, which is frequented by people bitten by mad beasts, medals of St. Benedict are distributed.

Apropos of the great St. Hubert is it not strange to see of late so many people of Belgium and the north of France, when bitten by dogs, have recourse to the Pasteur treatment which does not guarantee a cure? Numerous cases prove that. Whereas the experience of twelve centuries conclusively shows that the cure ("la taille") at St. Hubert works infallibly!

A young man wrote to Termonde, asking that his mother be cured. Father Paul replied: "In answer to the prayer which I have offered, your mother ought to be completely restored by this time."

Here is another proof of the goodness and patience of Father Paul. Speaking of a family in Antwerp, he confided to a friend that these good people consulted him in all their affairs, and added, "They would not change a nail in their house without asking me if I approved of the change."

When Father Paul refused to be interested in an affair, it was a bad sign. Whilst the Count of Chambord was still living, a visitor spoke to him of that pretender to the throne of France, hoping to receive some light as to his chances of success. Father Paul coldly remarked, "I do not occupy myself with this matter."

The New Year's letters which Father Paul sent to his friends always contained, under the guise of good wishes, real seasonable gifts; for all the good things he wished were realized. To give but one example. Writing to business people in Contich, Father Paul said, "I wish you the payment of all bills outstanding." These people had, in fact, debtors of long standing, but had given up all hope of ever receiving payment. However, soon after receiving the good wishes of Father Paul, the old debts were unexpectedly paid.

A religious was preaching a retreat at Thielt, and a servant girl had been present at the opening sermon in which the preacher said that the souls going to heaven were as few in number as the leaves that remain on the trees in winter. This remark caused so great a displeasure to the woman that she stayed away from the rest of the sermons. When she mentioned this occurrence later on to Father Paul, he said,

"You did right, for in making such a statement the preacher outraged the infinite goodness of God."

Father Paul was an excellent patron of the post office. The number of letters which he answered is incredible. There are many friends of the Rev. Father who have saved three, four or five hundred of his letters. Generally, a letter of the Rev. Father contained from twenty to thirty small lines written in a style as concise as it was familiar. He made use of odds and ends of all kind of paper, seldom using an entire letter sheet, and wrote standing; or, as he himself once told the sisters in a convent, he would kneel on the floor on one knee and write upon the other. . .

A friend seeing him overwhelmed with business, offered to act as his secretary.

"Impossible!" Father Paul replied, "it is a question here of heavenly affairs."

A young man who wished to marry a Parisian, asked Father Paul if he considered her a suitable choice from a religious and moral point of view. The Father replied, "T' is eerste klasse voor Parijs." "It is first class for Paris."

A young man besought Father Paul to tell him who the person was that he ought to marry. "The good God never tells that beforehand," he replied.

A rich young lady was praised very much for her great devotion to good works. Father Paul simply remarked, "Zy moet wel!" "It is her duty!"

It was one of the dearest wishes of the good and saintly Father Paul to crown the series of his works by the foundation of a beautiful Abbey at Antwerp. All the necessary means had been abundantly provided, and his numerous friends of that wealthy commercial metropolis hoped to see him soon establish his residence in their midst; they already calculated the immense good which the presence of the celebrated Benedictine would procure for their city. But a determined opposition on the part of the secular clergy caused the failure of that beautiful project. Father Paul resigned himself with humility, although, as he himself said, he could have overthrown all opposition by one word.

As a matter of fact, speaking of this project to his friends from Antwerp, the Rev. Father told them that all he needed to do, was to apply directly to the Pope, Leo XIII. He added:—

"I know His Holiness, and he knows me. . . . The Pope is a saint."

Speaking once, in detail, of facts referring to the first centuries of the Christian era, and wishing to impress upon his hearers how he came to know these facts, Father Paul said, "This is not difficult; for God, there is neither past or future, everything is present to Him."

Father Paul generally declined to answer useless requests or those that were too worldly. He related one day that he received a letter from America with a request for prayers that the writer might win a big prize in a lottery. The letter remained unanswered.

Father Paul said to a friend from Oostcamp, "It has never happened to me that I prayed for a recruit who recommended himself to me, without having obtained for him freedom from military service."

A friend wrote to the Rev. Father asking him to obtain a good number for a recruit. Father Paul replied that the person must himself ask him for it.

But sometimes a request made through a third party was favorably received.

Speaking of France, Father Paul said that this country was going to be purified by great chastisements.

In Flemish, "Dat nest moet gezuiverd worden."

Speaking of the end of the world, Father Paul said, "I think that our Lord came to redeem mankind in the middle of time."

If this opinion is prophetic, the world would yet exist for about two thousand years.

In his prophecies which have already been fulfilled, Father Paul most frequently employed this expression "I think that . . . ."

"The Bible," Father Paul said, "contains no error, but. . .men know nothing."

To preachers he said, "It is necessary to return to the simplicity of the Gospel."

"There are no two angels alike in heaven. How great then must the power of God be to have been able to create, *in a single instant*, these innumerable legions of heavenly spirits!"

In Antwerp, Father Paul said of a young girl who was recommended to him in her sickness, "I can do nothing for her because she consults a fortune-teller."

As Father Paul was once quizzed about the lamentable state of his old hat, he remarked with a smile, "I put up with this one, in order to have a fine one in the other world."

During a visit paid by Father Paul to some good friends of his, a young man inadvertently overturned a beautiful porcelain vase which broke into a hundred pieces. At the very moment Father Paul said to the young man in a low voice, "Ask now that the vase be restored to its former state."

But as the attention of the young man was turned elsewhere he neglected the Father's obliging invitation. Later on, when they recalled the words of the good religious, they regretted very much not to have seized the occasion of seeing the performance of a miracle.

A young lady visiting Father Paul was invited by him to go to the church, saying that she would see our Lord in person in the sacred host which was exposed. But as she did not take his suggestion seriously, she replied that she had no need of seeing such a wonder, in order to believe in the Real Presence.

"Very well," Father Paul said, "Your faith causes me great joy."

After the death of the Rev. Father, this young lady, hearing of the great number of persons who had received a like invitation from Father Paul and had actually seen our Lord in the Blessed Sacrament, cried out with most keen regret, "Oh! if I had only known!"

"When I distribute Holy Communion," Father Paul said to a friend from Oostcamp, "it is the Infant Jesus in person, that I see in the host."

On the day of his death, Father Paul, literally exhausted, was hardly able to reply by a feeble sign to the questions that were put to him.

A lay-brother said to him, "When you are in heaven, ask that I may join you soon. "Making a supreme effort, the good Father found strength enough to reply slowly, "You cannot demand such a thing."

But at least," the lay-brother said, "Will you demand that I may be near you in heaven?"

"Yes."

Father Paul once said, "I have been persecuted during my life. . . and I will still be persecuted after my death!"

"We must not want to penetrate the mysteries of religion, because that awakens pride. The bad angels did so, and they ended by saying: "We shall be like unto the Most High!"

Affectionate Salutations

Wherewith the Servant of God, Father
Paul of Moll, Addressed Mary.

I greet thee, Mary, Daughter of God the Father.

I greet thee, Mary, Mother of the Son of God.

I greet thee, Mary, Spouse of the Holy Spirit.

I greet thee, Mary, Temple of the Blessed Trinity.

I greet thee, Mary, white Lily of the resplendent Trinity.

I greet thee, Mary, fragrant Rose of the heavenly court.

I greet thee, Mary, Virgin full of meekness and humility, of whom the King of heaven willed to be born and nourished by thy milk.

I greet thee, Mary, Virgin of virgins.

I greet thee, Mary, Queen of martyrs, whose soul was pierced by the sword of sorrows.

I greet thee, Mary, Lady and Mistress, to whom all power has been given in heaven and on earth.

I greet thee, Mary, Queen of my heart, my sweetness, my life and all my hope.

I greet thee, Mary, Mother most amiable.

I greet thee, Mary, Mother most admirable.

I greet thee, Mary, Mother of beautiful love.

I greet thee, Mary, conceived without sin.

I greet thee, Mary, full of grace, the Lord is with thee, blessed art thou among women, and blessed be the fruit of thy womb.

Blessed be thy spouse Saint Joseph.

Blessed be thy father Saint Joachim.

Blessed be thy mother Saint Ann.

Blessed be thy angel Saint Gabriel.

Blessed be the Eternal Father who hath chosen thee.

Blessed be thy Son who hath loved thee.

Blessed be the Holy Ghost who hath espoused thee.

May all those who love thee bless thee.

O Blessed Virgin, bless us all in the name of thy dear Son. Amen.

The venerable Father Paul assured one of his friends, that those who devoutly venerate Mary with these affectionate salutations may rely on her powerful protection and blessing.

Once, whilst giving a copy of these Salutations to a girl from Eecloo, Father Paul said to her, "These Salutations are so beautiful! Say them every morning. From on high, in heaven, the Blessed Virgin will then give you her blessing.

"Yes, yes, would to God that you could see her! The Blessed Virgin blesses you then; I know it quite well."

He said further that it is impossible not to be heard favorably when we recite these Salutations to Mary for the conversion of sinners.

LETTERS OF FATHER PAUL

∽

PRELIMINARY REMARKS BY THE AUTHOR.

We have shown how very busy the Rev. Father Paul was. From morning till night he received a crowd of visitors, or went to visit those who called for his assistance. He heard confessions sometimes until eleven o'clock at night, and as he could not neglect the divine office, nor the many prayers which he had promised to his wards, one asked where he found time for his voluminous correspondence: every day he answered about thirty letters! Did he sacrifice his night's rest for that purpose? It is probable.

There is likewise a very great number of souvenirs or pious pictures, on the back of which he had written in Flemish charming verses, nearly all treating of the love of God. Father Paul, a born poet, wrote verses with the most astonishing facility. There exist a few pious treatises which he had printed, also some manuscripts treating of the love of God, which he perhaps intended to publish.

Father Paul has truly been called the *singer of divine love*. In his conversations, his letters, his sermons, everywhere he drew attention to the love of God. This divine love with which his heart was inflamed seems to have dictated the following letters, addressed to one of his penitents, an ecstatic.

Translator's Note. Most of Father Paul's letters are headed and closed by a pious expression of love for Jesus. In the original Flemish we find these words at the head of the letters: "Uyt liefde *tot* Jesus," the French equivalent of which is "Par amour *pour* Jesus," in English literally "*With love for Jesus.*" At the end of these letters he writes in Flemish, "Uyt liefde *van* Jesus," French, "Par amour *de* Jesus," which in literal English means, "*With love from Jesus.*" In the English pamphlet this distinction has been overlooked; we prefer the literal translation.

～

With Love for Jesus!

Dearest Sister in Jesus Christ,

I have not been able to reply sooner to your New Year's greetings. I also wish you a happy and salutary New Year, a year of love, a heart of love; let all your actions be love; all your words, love; all your thoughts, love; all your sensations, love; all that you see, love; all that you hear, love; all that you desire, love of God.

O love! O infinite love! Yes, I may well say so, for the love of God is a boundless ocean of love, one drop of which is sufficient to set man's heart on fire with love.

May I not then say, O love! O infinite love? The love of God for man is so great that God forgets, so to say, His infinite justice, in order to be able to show His infinite love.

May I not then say, O love! O infinite love? A mother knows how dearly she loves her children, but what is the love of a mother in comparison with the love of God for us? Less than nothing.

May I not then say, O love! O infinite love? Before man was created, God already loved him with so tender a love that he said, I will give him My flesh, My blood, My divinity; I shall dwell in Him with all My perfections, for love of him.

May I not say then, O love! O infinite love? O my God! O God of infinite love, I thank Thee and I ask of Thee that I may be able to love Thee ever more and more; that I may be able to love Thee with a burning love!

I have not been able to reply sooner: so many letters are waiting for an answer. Do everything for the love of God; say, "Everything that I shall do this year, O my God, I shall do for love of Thee!"

In your sufferings, no matter how great they may be, do not complain so long as you are able to love.

O God of infinite love! give me a heart of love! I shall ask it for you.

I pray much for you that you may become more and more inflamed with the love of God.

Here is my name: Praised be Jesus Christ!

With love for Thee, Jesus.

Dearest Sister in Jesus Christ,

O God, behold my heart in desolation,
Bereft of love, it is in bitterness;
My heart so steeped in sadness and dejection,
Fulfil its longing by the gift of love divine.

One sigh of love is of more value than the whole world, so that for one sigh of the love of God you may renounce the friendship, the honor, the glory and the riches of the world. Therefore, never be sad if I do not write to you or speak to you of love; give one sigh of love for God, and think that you then possess more than all the world can give you. If you suffer, think that God, who is infinite love, wills it, and say, O love! O infinite love!

Live alone with God, that is to say, live apart from the world, but near to God; reveal to no person the intimate sentiments of your heart, only to God alone, and show Him how your heart sighs for His love. Be hidden to men, after the example of the saints. I shall ask for you much love. Always recall to yourself the presence of God, burning with a love greater than the ocean; be convinced that he desires ceaselessly to communicate to you His love, His burning love, in order that you, also, inflamed with love, be transformed into His love. Desire as much as possible to love God more and more. God imparts His love sometimes in peace, and sometimes also in misfortunes or in sufferings; we must praise and thank God for all He does, whether it be pleasing to us or not.

Thank God that He has made known to you His love, yes, that you are able to possess that love, that you are a child of the love of God.

Be so good as to ask love for me, I shall also demand the love of God for you.

With love for Jesus, I am. . .

O love! O infinite love of God!

You may write to me always, I shall reply to you by a short or a long letter, according as it may be possible for me.

(We have rarely seen Father Paul's letters dated.)

With Love for Jesus!

Sister in Jesus Christ,

How astonishing is God in His infinite love! We ought to cry out ceaselessly with the greatest enthusiasm, with all our force, with our whole soul, O love! O infinite love! O astonishing love of God!

When the most beautiful angels contemplate the sanctity of God, they sing with one voice and with the greatest astonishment, Holy! Holy! Holy! is the God of all eternity! And, at sight of that astonishing love, they cry out in the same manner three times, O infinite and eternal love of God!

A great number of the children of love, see Jesus in the Holy Sacrament. They have seen Him first in Antwerp. They see our Lord in the great host exposed at the benediction, and they see Him differently at the same time; as a shepherd carrying a lamb on His shoulders or in His arms; in His passion, bleeding; or in the form of a white dove.

As for myself I have seen Him, Oh! I do not know how. M. J. has seen Him often already, under different forms, and she is in ecstasy over it.

They see Jesus distinctly in such a manner that there can be no doubt.

M. J. and two other young ladies have seen the same prodigy in Eecloo.

Several persons from Watervliet went to Eecloo last week, but have seen nothing.

With love from Jesus!

∾

With Love for Jesus!

Sister in Jesus Christ,

I prostrate before the infinite love of Jesus, imploring an ocean of love for God. I am sad, God alone with His love can console me.

The fear of not going to heaven, you must consider as a suggestion of the devil. You complain that no one speaks to you of the love of

God and you even dare almost to complain that I do not write to you of the love of Jesus.

Few persons have had the great happiness that you have had in being instructed in the love of Jesus. You are like those who have made their studies to become a priest, lawyer, or doctor, they know enough in order to follow their profession. Thus I have taught you of the love of God all that is necessary, in order to advance unceasingly in love.

The devil will do all in his power in order to turn you aside from the love of Jesus. Mary, the Mother of beautiful love, will defend you, all the saints will help you, and I shall pray for you in order that you may always remain a child of love, and make great progress in the love of Jesus.

With love from Jesus,

Your humble servant, D. P.

∽

With Love for Jesus!

Dearest Penitent,

O love! O infinite love of Jesus! O excess of love! When shall I be able to love Thee enough, when shall my will be inflamed with love for Thee, O boundless ocean of love? When shall all my desires be desires of love, so that I may be able to love Thee and to love nothing else but Thee and Thee alone, O my God, O infinite love? I shall seek until I shall find Thee, I shall knock until Thou shalt open for me, I shall pray until Thou shalt give me an ardent love and shalt suppress in me all other sentiments.

Love surpasses incomparably, both in value and in beauty, all satisfaction. God, by His nature, is infinite love, and it is with this infinite love that He loves man so much.

To understand, or, at least, to get an idea of His infinite love, think of His infinite perfections. If you wish to have an idea of the love with which He loves man, see with what love God loves Mary.

He has given so much to Mary that she is called the Mother of beautiful love. This great love was granted to her as Mother of God. Mary being truly our Mother, how could God love our Mother so much without loving her children? If God reserved that ardent and great love for Mary, our Mother, this love would not be fully agreeable to her because Mary, as Mother, would not be happy to see that her children did not share that true happiness. What does a mother desire, if not to see her children share her happiness? God Himself, the infinite Love, has not thought differently, for see what an incomprehensible love He has for the children of Mary!

Is it not for the children of Mary that Jesus suffered so much? It was in order to prove His love for the children of Mary. Jesus did not suffer for Mary, for she never was guilty in the eyes of God, she never had to render an account; but, through sin, her children have made themselves culpable before God, and it was in order to satisfy for sin that Jesus came. But Jesus has done much more than was necessary: all that He suffered more, He endured for the love of man in order to prove to him His love.

Every time you see a crucifix you may say, O excess of love! Every time Jesus scourged comes into your mind you may say, O love! O infinite love! When you see Jesus carrying the cross you may say, O excess of the infinite love of Jesus! God has given so much love to Mary that she is called with reason the Mother of beautiful love, and all the children of Mary are equally children of beautiful love, and those who are not, have rejected that right through sin. That right lost can be restored through the infinite merits of Jesus, merits which He has acquired for us in His love for us.

When then you see Jesus in His passion, you see Him at the same time in His excess of love. Often contemplate Jesus enduring outrages, humiliations, mockeries, derision, and say, O love! O infinite love of Jesus! When you think of the Most Holy Sacrament, when you receive Jesus or when you make spiritual communions, or when you adore Jesus, you may say, O infinite love of Jesus!

Have an ardent desire to be a child of the love of Jesus. The love of Jesus is a great treasure beyond comparison.

I wish you a good and happy year, a year of love, so that you, also, may be a child of beautiful love as your Mother Mary is the Mother of beautiful love.

With love from Jesus.

⌒⌒

With Love for Thee, Jesus!

Dearest Sister in Jesus Christ,

I should wish to write you a long letter, but I have no time; I must preach the Lenten sermons, preach at the Masses and teach catechism to the children.

O love! O infinite love of Jesus! I give Thee my heart, to Thee alone, not once, but throughout eternity.

On the days when you have but little or no love, do not murmur against Jesus, do not speak to anybody of it; you can tell it to me. In heaven you will be able to live without being separated from the love of Jesus, but not so on earth. Only say, O Jesus of infinite love! I feel, or, I have no love, but be it according to Your desire, I accept it for love of You and in the hope that You will grant me more. See, however, I experience the hunger and thirst for Your love, I long for You as the fish longs for the water out of which it has been taken; You cannot nor would You abandon me, You only wish to try me; You act very well, but do not make me languish without Your love; I make the resolution never to love anything but You.

I ought to tell you yet much on the subject of poor sinners, who do not know God or who do not love Him; I must yet very much exhort you to praise and thank God, but I have no time.

During the time of Lent often take into your hand the chalice of bitterness. O love! O infinite love, would that you could set on fire all hearts!

⌒⌒

With Love for the Sacred Heart of Jesus!

Dearest Penitent,

O love! O excess of the love of Jesus! I give Thee my heart, to Thee alone, not once, but always, unto eternity, and with so great a love as no person ever has done. The excess of the love of God is not contained within the infinite perfections of God, but that love is found wherever it is possible. It is found in the souls in purgatory, it is found upon earth. I cannot say that upon earth, it is less brilliant than in purgatory, for can we see that love more clearly than in the Holy Sacrament of infinite love, and in the passion of Jesus?

Jesus allowed Himself to be so horribly scourged as thereby to become unrecognizable. Jesus, so beautiful, behold how disfigured He with blood and wounds is now, so that one cannot recognize Him except by His love: to those who did not know His love He became completely unrecognizable.

In purgatory, His infinite love is known, although the souls are not as yet fully satiated with it; but in heaven, they will be eternally filled with it; love will satiate them in a manner incomprehensible. There the souls see the infinite grandeur of God; unceasingly they see and receive continual effusions of love, resembling the torrents of a boundless ocean of love.

The grandeur of God is incomprehensible, and it is as if He were great and powerful only to show His love, to bestow love and to receive the love of man in order to unite Himself always with man through love.

What is the Holy Sacrament of love if not a union of the love of God with man? Therefore it is that I encourage all children of love to the constant practice of spiritual communion and sighs of love. They unite us equally to God through love, much less, it is true, than real Communion, but yet they help to receive Jesus with so much greater love in Holy Communion.

I desire most ardently that this love may be known by the hearts of all men that they may be inflamed with love for God. The incomprehensible and burning love of God continually fills man, that God may reign in his heart; but mortal sins constantly push back that love. God Himself says, "I do not want the death of sinners, but I want them to live that I may love them, and be united with them through love."

Those who are in the state of grace, but do not know His love, God loves with an incomprehensible love because God loves everything that is good; but we shall never understand the love that God bears towards His children of love, and how much He desires to unite Himself with them by love.

It is on account of this love for man that Jesus had the will to suffer, with great patience, all outrages, contempt, and pain. With what satisfaction can we not suffer, and desire to suffer to show our love for Jesus!

If it is given you to take part in the love of Jesus, then take part, also, in His dolorous passion. If Jesus often comes to console you with His sweet love, take likewise and joyfully your part of pity for Jesus in His excess of suffering, as was done by the sorrowing women.

How can one contemplate Jesus in the excess of His suffering, for the love of man, without being touched and saying, "I want to give my love to Jesus!"

I recommend to you again the devotion to the Sacred Heart of Jesus. O Sacred Heart of Jesus! O Sacred Heart of Jesus! O ocean of love!

I do not know as yet if the love for Jesus will make me depart from here.* I shall demand for you love for Jesus.

With love from the Sacred Heart of Jesus, I am your humble servant in Jesus,

D. P. relig.

∾

With Love for Jesus!

Dearest Sister,

O love! O infinite love of God for man! How astonishing God is in the love with which He loves man! For all that you see He has made in His infinite love. Look at the Sacred Heart of Jesus, and you will hear Jesus tell you, "Behold the heart that has loved men so much." Look at the Most Holy Sacrament. What is the Most Holy Sacrament? It is an excess of love. Look at the holy Face, that holy Face says to you, "O love! O infinite love of Jesus!" Look at Jesus crucified, and must you not cry out, "O love! O infinite love of Jesus! Is it possible, that love can go so far?"

Was His love held up by the cross? Ah, no, this Jesus with His Sacred Heart, and in the Most Holy Sacrament and crucified, went

---

* This letter was written by the Rev. Father near the end of his stay at Steenbrugge.

to heaven. There He is seated upon a throne of infinite glory; from there, He pours forth His infinite love into all the hearts open to His love. Every sigh of love, every desire of love is a new opening of your heart, allowing the love of God to penetrate.

Unite yourself to God through love, and rejoice in such great happiness; thank God for this great benefit, and be so much the more ardent in the love of God.

I am overburdened with work, it happens sometimes that I am unable to write more, do not expect it of me.

With love from Jesus, I am . . . . . .

⌒↩⌒

With Love for Jesus!

Sister in Jesus Christ,

O love! O infinite love of God for man! One word escapes from my lips and plunges me into the greatest astonishment, O love! O. . .

It is not given to any man to tell what the infinite love of God is, not even to make any comparison of it. All that can be said about it is still nothing.

Imagine all the love of one hundred thousand mothers for their children. It is nothing in comparison with the infinite love of God. One may say that a drop of water is a portion of the ocean; but all the love we can imagine cannot give us an idea of the least part of the love of God for man.

I wish you would allow me never to say more than, O love! O infinite love of God! I can hardly say anything more or anything better, for these words contain all that is necessary to induce us never to do anything except for the love of God; they are sufficient to satiate us with the love of God, and make us desire Him more and more.

When meditation becomes impossible for you, think of the love of God.

God, the saints and the souls in purgatory are my sole occupation. Pray for me and the souls in purgatory, I will pray for you.

With love from Jesus,
D. Paul, relig.

188

꧁

With Love for Jesus!

Sister in Jesus Christ,

With the grace of God, I must tell you that nothing occupies my heart more than the love of God. I wish to love the God of most tender and amiable love, and I cannot desire or wish anything better to others, yes, to all persons of the world.

For this reason the devil persecutes me much and, as happens very often in a similar case, the instruments of which he makes use are the very ones who owe me the greatest gratitude, thus rendering the humiliation still more painful.

I thank you for your good wishes. I wish you likewise a beautiful and happy year, a year of love; for that end I recommend to you three inexhaustible sources of love: —

1. The Most Holy Sacrament.
2. The sorrowful passion of Jesus Christ.
3. The Sacred Heart of Jesus, there to establish your dwelling and nourish yourself with the infinite love of God.

Your humble servant,
O love! O infinite love of God!

꧁

With Love for Jesus!

Sister in Jesus Christ,

Cry out and repeat a thousand times, O love! O infinite love of God for man! For God is infinite love, and to man alone He has given a heart of love in order to love God and be loved of Him. For this reason we ought to have a high regard for all men; if they are not already children of love, they may become so.

This obliges me to give an impressive notice to all the children of love; be prudent, for not every one is as yet a child of love, nor does every one understand what it is to be a child of love.

For this reason the impossible will be attempted to hinder the children of love from going where they can nourish themselves with love. Alas! if one knew the love of God, one would not act contrary to it. It is my duty to cry out: Do not go to such and such a place, for love is in danger there. Help me to nourish the children of love; if they say or do anything against you, pass on and say, What does it matter? It is a child of love.

With love from Jesus, I am,

D. Paul, relig.

ᕙᕗ

With Love for Jesus!

Dearest Sister in Jesus Christ,

For the love of Thee, Jesus, I demand of Thee, I pray Thee, I beseech Thee to inspire me in this writing; give me to know Thy holy will. O love! O infinite love! I give Thee my heart, to Thee alone, not once, but continually and for eternity. We shall never be able to proclaim nor admire worthily the infinite goodness of God. God is infinitely great and has an incomprehensible love for miserable man, so inclined to evil and so indifferent towards God. When a man, the greatest enemy of God, truly contrite, asks pardon of God by going to confession, the love of God is so great that He gives Himself at once, soul, body, and divinity, and wants to love that man, love him always more and more. No matter how miserable he may be, provided he is no longer in the state of mortal sin, God loves him with an incomprehensible love.

How can one despise or not love one whom God loves so tenderly, so paternally? What a great crime to do evil to one whom God loves so much?

Why is there more joy in heaven over one sinner who does penance than over ninety-nine just? Because in heaven they see the joy which the fact of being able to love that man once more, procures for the heart of the infinite love of God.

The heavenly spirits are absorbed in the abyss of the infinite love of God, and they see much better than we are able to understand, what an inexpressible joy it is for the infinite love of God to be able to love again a man who, by mortal sin had rejected the love of God.

What can there be more agreeable to the heart of the infinite love of God than to pray for the conversion of those who are in the state of mortal sin? To be a child of love, is to sacrifice oneself to the love of God for the conversion of sinners.

I rejoice at the one word, the conversion of sinners! If we had to pray hundreds of years in order to have a man brought back to the love of God, we would have reason enough to rejoice on account of it.

God demands now that you be and remain a true child of love, and that your love grow greater unceasingly. Ask God that all your actions, from the beginning of your existence, be actions of love for God, performed in union with the sorrowful passion of Jesus.

O Jesus! my Well-beloved, do You permit Yourself to be ill-treated so frightfully? Is it to give proofs of Your love? O Jesus! You have already given sufficient proofs; no person can ever say that You have not given enough pledges of Your love. O Jesus! grant me the joy of being able to prevent You being ill-treated so much.

O holy blood! O blood of love! would that I could imitate Thee!

I had no time to answer you sooner.

With love from Jesus, I am. . .
Praised be Jesus Christ!

ⵥⵥ

With Love for Jesus!

Dearest Sister in Jesus Christ,

O love! O infinite love of my God! O love without beginning and without end, how great you are, how sweet, how agreeable!

O love of my God! You are great, because you are infinite; you are sweet, because whoever has tasted you is famished with love. The more one has of it, the more one desires; always more and more inflamed with love; never satiated with love; for the more one tastes of it, the sweeter it is, the more intense is the desire for love, the ardent love for God.

Love is agreeable, for from the moment one knows it, one can scarcely love anything else but the love of God. Therefore, St. Augustine has said, "Lord God, if I had known Thee sooner, I would have loved Thee sooner." Love is so agreeable that whoever knows the love of God, scarcely loves anything but that agreeable love. Why should it not be agreeable to the heart of man, since God Himself has said, *I shall be all things to you*, that is to say, all the good we can imagine to ourselves, such as all sweetness, all harmony.

Does not a son enjoy the riches of a good father? How agreeable it is for a child to enjoy with his father his great riches! Which are the riches of God? They are His infinite perfections, and the ability to be loved by an infinite love, and to be able to love.

So then, when you have some love for God, you may esteem yourself happy on account of it, according to the degree of your love for God, and in that case, you may consider all other things as nothing, such as riches and pleasures, persecution and sufferings, outrages and contempt; and suffer all, because then you have a chance to prove your love for Jesus.

It is easy to show one's love for Jesus in prosperity and good fortune; but to show a beautiful love in bitterness. . . With you it is not as with many others who seem to have much love as long as everything turns out according to their wishes, but whose love is all eclipsed in the time of adversity.

From the moment a man knows God, his first action is to love Him, to give Him his love, and that need of loving is so much the greater the better he knows his God.

Never shall one know God well, so long as one is attached to men and the world: we must not attach ourselves to them except in so far as they lead us to the knowledge and love of God.

If Adam had not sinned, love would be the sole desire of man; but sins have diminished and obscured in man his desire for the love of God. We may revive that desire by prayer, by ardent and earnest prayer, by detachment, by a perfect life, and thus arrive at ardent love for God.

Hence, never become discouraged if it costs you much to have a little of the love of God; for one sigh of love is of more value than all that the world can procure.

With love from Jesus.

Extracts from Letters.

Addressed by the Rev. Father Paul to a lady of Audenarde.

God is impenetrable, His wisdom is infinite. Jesus has shown His love for us by incomparable sufferings. It is the divine will that we show our love for God throughout everything and in everything, but especially in our sufferings.

In suffering one recognizes true love. One suffers, but it is for the love of Jesus.

An act of love for God in suffering causes the astonishment of the angels; an act of love for God in suffering is formidable to the demon; an act of love for God in suffering will shine in heaven for all eternity.

If one could understand the value of an act of love for God in suffering, one would experience the greatest grief at being obliged to pass a single moment without being able to make this meritorious act. Happy is he who, in suffering, makes acts of love!

Madam, I recommend you to the Sacred Heart of Jesus, you and your whole family. Often say with devotion: O Sacred Heart of Jesus of infinite love and mercy without end, give me a heart of love, and give Thy grace to poor sinners, that they may be enabled to know Thee and love Thee.

I shall commence a novena for you on Wednesday, and from now on, I shall give you my blessing twice a day, at half past five in the morning and towards eight in the evening. You may always write to me, without fear of troubling me.

❧

God is infinitely good and wise. He shows His goodness towards you by sending you crosses. The more bitter your pains, the more meritorious they are.

Every cross is a blessing from heaven, a blessing which surpasses all the happiness of the world. If one were able to understand the full value of crosses, it would be a terrible torment to be deprived of them.

I shall pray that God may make you know the value of crosses, so that you may appreciate them all the more, and I shall demand for you great patience. Suffer everything, henceforth, in thanksgiving for this special grace. In heaven you will see how true is all that I tell you.

cv

Extracts from Letters of the Rev. Father Paul.

To a member of his family.

I wish you particularly the grace to see what God is in His infinitive love, in order to love Him with your whole heart, during your whole life, and to be hereafter united with Him for all eternity. We cannot comprehend how much God loves us, and all that He does to show His great love to men: but we comprehend still less what He will do in heaven for His children of love.

If it were given you to see one little ray of His great love, you would never be able to say anything else but, "O love! O infinite, O beautiful love of God!"

God does not demand of you, in order to be a child of love, that you should do more than you are able to do, but all He says to you is, "My child give me your heart!" And I add thereto, Do everything for love of Jesus.

Often say, before all your work, "For love of Thee, Jesus." Often think of the love of God, and principally of three things wherein He has shown His great love, in the Most Holy Sacrament, in His sorrowful passion, and in His Sacred Heart.

When you communicate, recall His great love, then unite yourself with God through love, give your heart to God, demand a heart that will love Him always more and more; above all think of the sorrowful passion of Jesus, principally on Friday; and when you have to suffer anything, consider with what love He has suffered, that you also may suffer everything for the love of Jesus in His Sacred Heart, the source of infinite love.

At my next visit we shall again talk of the infinite love of God. Love to go to Holy Communion and often make spiritual communions. Never attach yourself to the world, but flee from it. . .

cv

The love which God devotes to man, and that with which he is loved ought to be considered the greatest treasure He can give us. In order to understand this, it would be necessary for us to be able to know God, a thing impossible, because God is infinitely perfect. It is the same with regard to His love, the more you were to consider the love of God, the more you would have to say, "O love! O infinite love of God!"

Unite yourself often with God through love, at your morning and evening prayer, and say, I shall do everything for the love of God that all my actions may be acts of love. Ask for that love through the intercession of Mary. Suffer and endure everything for the love of Jesus, as Jesus has suffered everything for love of us.

I wish you an ardent love for God, it is the richest and most beautiful treasure you can wish or desire. All other treasures will disappear like smoke; but the treasure of love shall remain forever in heaven.

Ask God for this beautiful treasure, for it must come from Him; men cannot procure it for you. For this reason often ask God for a heart of love that you may love Him ever more and more, and like a child of love. Add to your morning and evening prayers, "All that I shall do today, or tonight, I shall do for the love of God, so that all my actions may be actions of love. I unite myself today, or tonight, with all the acts of love made to God, both in heaven and on earth." Say quite often during the day, when you commence to do something, were it only moving a chair, opening or shutting a door, or any other action, "For love of Thee, Jesus."

When you have to suffer anything say, "I want to suffer it for the love of Jesus, just as Jesus has suffered all for love of me."

Have a great devotion to the Most Holy Sacrament of love. Communicate as often as you can, and never say, "I am not worthy to do so!" Nobody is sufficiently worthy of it, but the great love of God calls you. Often have a desire of receiving Jesus.

Devotion to the sorrowful passion of Jesus.

Devotion to the Sacred Heart of Jesus.

Everywhere we can find the great love of God, at home, in the fields, in the street, in the convents, in good health, in sickness, in adversity, in poverty, everywhere except in the riches, the honor, the glory and the pleasures of the world.

I shall ask for you also a share of the love of God.

Pray much for the souls in purgatory.

∾

Other Extracts from Letters of the Rev. Father Paul.

The love of God is my desire, my riches, my joy, and my best food, yes, all!

O God of infinite love! Give me two wings to fly towards Thee, that I may rest in Thee and be satiated with Thy beautiful love; a wing of love, to draw me without ceasing toward Thy beautiful love, and a wing of confidence in order to help me to perform all my actions, all my steps, all my prayers for the love of God.

Who shall ever be able to understand the love, infinitely great, wherewith Thou, O God, lovest man! We should wish to express, to describe that love; one word only escapes our powerless lips: O love! O infinite love of God! O sweet love, sweeter than honey! O ocean of love! inflame my heart with the sacred fire of Thy holy love!

My name is

Love.

∾

O love! O infinite love of Jesus! O Jesus give me a mouth of love so as to entertain all men with Thy infinite love! Give me a heart of love so that nothing else may come forth from it but for Thy beautiful love. Give me eyes of love that I may see nothing else but Thy love in all things, even in my sufferings and in everything that goes against me. Give me a taste of love, that I may taste Thy love in everything I eat and drink. Give me hands of love that I may write of Thy beautiful love to all the children of love. Give me feet of love that I may go and entertain those who suffer, with Thy beautiful love and Thy ignominious and painful death, so that they may not complain any longer of their crosses.

O love! O infinite love of God! Thy love, O my God, is my nourishment, my treasure, my consolation, my life! I do not need any one but those who speak to me of Thy beautiful love. O love of

Jesus! Thou art my consolation, my all. Nothing against Thee, everything for Thee!

O love! O infinite love of Jesus!

Thus my name is written.

∽

I offer up this day (or this night) for the greater glory of God. Everything that I shall do today (or tonight) I shall do for the love of God, that all my actions may be acts of love.

I unite myself today (or tonight) with all the acts of praise and thanksgiving that are elicited in heaven and on earth.

I unite myself with all the acts of love that are made by the Sacred Heart of Jesus.

I unite myself with all the sentiments of pity that ever have been felt and ever will be felt for Jesus in His pains. I make the intention of saying each time when God or His holy name is blasphemed: "My God, be Thou praised and blessed forever and ever! Thy holy name be praised and blessed forever and ever!"

I consign myself today (or tonight), body and soul, into Thy hands.

I unite myself with all the acts of adoration and love that are made in the Most Holy Sacrament of infinite love.

During the day make frequent spiritual communions, when entering or leaving the church, when retiring and in other circumstances.

Unite yourself often with God by ejaculatory prayers, and elevate your heart to God. Think often of the passion of Jesus, and suffer everything for the love of Jesus, the same as Jesus suffered everything through love for you.

As often as I shall recite seven Our Fathers and seven Hail Marys, I resolve to say, "In honor of the drops of blood shed for us by Jesus! and to obtain the graces which Jesus has attached thereto, and to complete the number thereof."

When going out I say at the door, "Through love for Thee, Jesus!" And when I am alone I recite five Our Fathers and five Hail Marys for the conversion of sinners, and the six Our Fathers, six Hail Marys and six Glory be to the Father etc., connected with the blue scapular, and I consign the indulgences into the hands of Mary.

Letter of Rev. Father Paul to a working woman of Thielt.

O love! O infinite love of God! How astonishing, beautiful and amiable is God in His love! O God of infinite love! I ask Thee for the grace to be able to write to Mathilde of Thy love.

Exclaim then anew with myself and with all the children of love, and also with Sister Luitgarde, "O love! O infinite love of God! Give me a heart to love Thee, O my God! and to love Thee with an immense love."

A sigh of love for God, brought forth with devotion, is of more value than the whole world; the world will perish completely, but the sigh of love for God is for eternity. If it were given you to heave, with devotion, but *one* sigh of love for God in your whole life, you would still be obliged to say, "An eternity even were too short to thank God for it sufficiently."

Offer your sufferings to God for the love of Jesus, as Jesus has suffered all for the love of us.

I hope you will not die yet; but if God wills it, die with love for Jesus, the same as Jesus has died with love for us: be then without fear.

You are still able to say, "I want to suffer everything for the love of Jesus, as Jesus has suffered everything for love of us, in order to obtain the pardon and expiation of my sins, and to be able, at once after my death, to unite myself with Jesus through love and for all eternity."

Sister Luitgarde may read this letter and I will have her admitted among the children of the beautiful love of Jesus.

With love from Jesus,
D. Paul relig.

A Few Recent* Favors Obtained through
the Intercession of Father Paul.

❧

SAN ANTONIO, TEX. The St. Benedict's Medal that had touched Father Paul's relic and which you sent to the sick lady, has done wonderful work here; but the good lady had to part with it, to save the life of a dying man, who had not approached the sacraments since he made his first Holy Communion. After it was placed on his neck and dipped into water for him to bathe in, he immediately became better. There was a lady here who had not been to confession or Mass for twenty years. Some one gave her a St. Benedict's Medal to put on last Tuesday and on Saturday she went to confession.

OHIO. A priest writes: Father Paul's life is one of the most interesting lives I ever read. Through his intercession I have received some marked favors recently. The devotion to St. Benedict and Father Paul is rapidly increasing in this parish. Spiritual and temporal favors have been granted through their intercession. A wonderful, religious spirit is manifesting itself all about the parish. I have received great blessings through the intercession of Father Paul during the past year and I wish to show my gratitude by distributing a few copies of his life.

MT. VERNON, OHIO. A Protestant lady came to me two weeks ago. She had a large, angry looking lump on the upper eyelid. I told her to go to the doctor at once; but she did not like the idea. So I said: I will give you a Medal of St. Benedict, to use on your eye and to wear on your neck. Last Thursday she sent me word that the evening before, as she was sitting before the grate-fire the lump fell off in her lap. She was so thankful and intends to wear the Medal all her life. I feel sure of her conversion. As she wanted to read something about the Saint that cured her, I gave her the life of Father Paul to read.

* As of 1914.

DETROIT, MICH. I asked the intercession of Father Paul of Moll in a very serious matter and I promised to have a holy Mass said in his honor for the repose of the poor souls, if my request were granted. I am more than grateful to say that my prayer was indeed heard in a very extraordinary manner. It goes to show, how great is the power of the saintly monk.

SAN FRANCISCO. Father Paul of Moll has been a good Father to me in the past year, he has obtained for me a number of favors, one special great one, the cure in a serious illness.

SACRED HEART CONVENT, N. DAK. I will mention to Father Paul's honor what he did for us. Last November I fell and broke my shoulder in three places; the physicians said I could never use that arm again; I made two novenas to St. Benedict and Father Paul. Now I have the use of this same arm (right one) as I had before the accident.

IOWA. Another priest from Iowa writes:—

Father Paul has been a striking revelation to me. I have read the wonderful book twice and am treasuring up the heavenly light that shines in it and the divine wisdom of his sayings. When the world at large will know completely of Father Paul, he will become a new St. Anthony of Padua and countless blessings he will obtain for those who call upon him in their distress.

MISSOURI. A Redemptorist Father writes: —

Our aged Father . . . . has great confidence in the intercession of Father Paul of Moll. Whenever he suffered from a pain in his head, he invoked Father Paul and was at once relieved. Later on he invoked him, when suffering from a long-standing, intermittent pain in the left side. He was suddenly cured after invoking him and the pain has not returned since.

NEWPORT, KY. Our one year old baby took very sick with bronchitis, then pneumonia, then inward convulsions. His heart got very bad. His temperature at times would be over 103. He took vomiting and diarrhea. He was indeed a very sick baby. Besides our doctor we had a specialist. We prayed to the Sacred Heart, to the

Blessed Virgin and to St. Anthony. The nurse was a Protestant. At night she would read the book of Father Paul of Moll for pastime. One evening the nurse said, "Why don't you make a novena?" I said, "My goodness, Ida, I have prayed so much, let God's will be done!" However, she insisted on starting a novena that night; she would help us pray. A queer remark for a Protestant. We started a novena that night to Father Paul of Moll and on the tenth day the baby was pronounced out of danger.

A Short Sketch
of the
Life of Father Paul of Moll

"Transitt benefaciendo."
"He went about doing good."

February 29, 1896, an Antwerp newspaper published the following:—

"Last Monday, February 24, 1896, there died peacefully in the Lord, in the Abbey of Termonde, after a long, serious illness, the sympathetic and celebrated Father Paul. Dom Paul (in the world Francis Luyckx), a Benedictine monk, had a profound knowledge of the human heart, which he carefully concealed beneath an exterior of the greatest simplicity.

"Animated by an unbounded love for the people, he was the refuge of the poor, and especially of the afflicted. Although the lowly and humble were particularly dear to him, he was also the counselor and the confidant of persons of rank and high station in our own country, as well as in England, France, Austria, and Italy. All who came in contact with Father Paul were captivated by his mysterious influence upon them, the effects of which never left them.

"At Brussels, Bruges, Antwerp, and in the Campine, he wonderfully but unpretentiously spread the devotion to his holy Father St. Benedict. In all those places he was an honored guest, and regarded as an angel of peace and consolation.

"The services which Father Paul rendered suffering humanity are incalculable; yet many did not obtain publicity. Although his biography would supply enough material for an extensive and excellent work, it may be briefly summed up in these two words of the Gospel: '*Transiit benefaciendo.*'—'He went about doing good.'

"May he receive from the Almighty, as the reward of his labors, the eternal companionship of his blessed Father St. Benedict, whose great power of intercession he labored so energetically to make known. May his soul rest in peace."

The Long-looked-for Biography.

The many friends and admires of the Rev. Father Paul have repeatedly expressed the desire to see this long-looked-for biography published. Many of them, anxious to possess a memorial of this good religious, insisted that we publish a few modest pages, recording certain facts, mostly unknown but none the less remarkable, which adorned the saintly career of Father Paul.

"I would like, before dying," remarked an aged father of a family, "that the blessed memory of our great friend and benefactor be religiously transmitted to all my posterity. For I am convinced that Father Paul is no less a powerful intercessor in heaven, than he was a benefactor on earth."

As we were honored by the esteemed friendship of the Rev. Father for many years, we gladly comply with their desire, and embrace this as a most favorable opportunity of offering our tribute of reverence and gratitude to his cherished memory.

It is not a biography of Father Paul that we publish, but rather a collection of certain incidents in his life that came to our knowledge. We follow, strictly speaking no specified order in the following work: but simply relate facts with a scrupulous regard to their authenticity. We present them in unadorned simplicity and truthfulness, and in that order which is best calculated to attract the reader's attention. Added thereto are some of the Rev. Father's letters, and a number of his familiar sayings.

In conformity with the decrees of Pope Urban VIII, dated 1634 and 1641, we attach no value to the facts herein related other than that which is purely human, and we humbly submit them to the judgment of holy Mother Church.

It suffices to have been a witness of the profound veneration in which Father Paul was held, to form an idea of the eagerness with which anything referring to his life, will be received by those who were wont to call him, "the holy monk and the great wonderworker."

Now especially is it providential, that God deigns, through the instrumentality of the humble, to work strange but consoling wonders thereby to confound the Voltairians and other skeptics of our day. Before presenting our readers with marvelous examples of the wonders Father Paul wrought we shall call attention to the various periods of his religious life, and the missions entrusted to him, and endeavor to sketch the characteristic traits of this celebrated Benedictine.

Father Paul was born at Moll, a village in the province of Antwerp, January 15, 1824, and in baptism received the name Francis. He was the son of Vincent Luyckx and Ann Catherine van Balen. Francis made his primary studies at the village school of Milleghem, Moll, and completed his course at the college of Gheel.

From early childhood Francis realized that he was called to the religious life, and great was his joy, on June 25, 1846, when he obtained admission into the Benedictine monastery of Termonde. The following August he was invested with the holy habit of St. Benedict.

Then began his preparation for the great day, when he would forever renounce the fleeting, foolish hopes of the world, and be definitely numbered as a member of the great family of the Patriarch of the monks of the West. After a year of probation, he was admitted (Sept. 30, 1849) to profession, and united himself irrevocably to his Savior by pronouncing the vows of poverty, chastity, and obedience.

In 1856, he went to Italy to continue his theological studies in the celebrated college of the Benedictines at Parma, and it was in that city that he for the first time ascended the steps of the altar to offer the holy sacrifice for the living and the dead. He returned to his own country in the year 1859, and remained at Termonde until 1869, in which he was intrusted with the task of reestablishing the abbey of Afflighem. In 1879, he founded the monastery of Steenbrugge, about a mile and a half from Bruges, of which he was prior until 1886, and which he left in 1887, to return to Termonde.

A Friend of the Poor.

Remembering his former life at Termonde, the good Flemish people realized that Providence had restored to the monastery a man of extraordinary virtue, and the renown of Father Paul spread rapidly. It is estimated that a million persons had recourse to him; and being of an amiable and kindly disposition, he received all with open arms. He was above all the protector and friend of the poor, as the following incident testifies. A lady in the neighborhood of the monastery was dangerously ill, and being asked if he had visited her,

Father Paul replied, "I never visit the rich unless sent for, but with the poor it is different."

It seemed to be an innate desire of his charitable nature to afford assistance to his neighbor. Often when taking leave of his visitors he would inquire, with touching insistence, if they had no further request to make. On receiving a letter from a learned acquaintance, he pushed it aside with a gesture of disappointment saying, "He does not ask for anything." To a friend in Oostcamp he said, "*Ask of me whatever you desire, and it will be procured for you. And continue to ask, for when I am in heaven, my power will be greater.*"

So little repose did Father Paul enjoy, that he was ever ready to render a service. A monk of the abbey of Termonde remarked, "Whenever we came to the chapel for the midnight Office, Father Paul was always the first absorbed in prayer, although the younger fathers quickened their pace to reach the chapel before him. He was seldom seen without his rosary in his hand." Another Benedictine father observed in regard to Father Paul, "Never was there a monk in our Order more devoted to penance and prayer."

Profound Humility.

Although Father Paul commanded the elements, healed the sick, read the secrets of the human heart, and foretold future events, he nevertheless shunned all praise, and delighted in saying, "I am nothing, and I know absolutely nothing."

In conversation with his brothers in religion he rarely referred to the wonders he wrought in favor of those who had recourse to him. The day after the good Father's death, there was general astonishment depicted on the countenances of the Benedictines, at the reports from every quarter of the innumerable and wonderful cures he had effected.

The monks were doubtless aware of Father Paul's popularity, judging from the fact that the majority of the many visitors called for him; but they never suspected that their humble confrére possessed such great power, although his fame was almost universal. Many were the visitors and the letters that he received from France, England, Germany, Holland, Italy and America, where Father Paul had a host of most illustrious personages as clients.

And not least among the prodigies accredited to him was the graceful tact with which he concealed his good works from the plaudits of men. Some other instances of his profound humility are recorded, which are worthy of our attention.

A Silent Jubilee.

Father Paul was ordained priest in Pavia, Italy, Sunday, Nov. 21, 1858. Twenty-five years later he observed the silver jubilee of his priesthood, and celebrated his holy Mass with more than usual fervor increased by the sentiments of joy and gratitude, which on that memorable day filled his happy heart. A friend who met him remarked, "The feast of the Presentation of our Blessed Lady has ushered in a charming, spring-like day, on the eve perhaps of a long, dreary winter."

Father Paul replied, "Especially joyous is this day to me, for it introduces the twenty-fifth anniversary of my priestly ordination."

"I congratulate you. I presume you celebrated your silver jubilee with your religious brethren."

"Oh, no, but two knew of it, my guardian angel and myself."

What the Bishop Thinks.

Father Paul related to one of his acquaintances the circumstances of his last visit to Monsignor Faict, bishop of Bruges.—"Before leaving Steenbrugge I called on the bishop, and kneeling, said to him, 'My Lord, I come to ask pardon for all the evil I may have done during my stay in your diocese.' 'Rise, I am not worthy that you kneel before me: you have done nothing but good, and you may return to my diocese whenever you wish.' "

A curate once asked the same bishop what he thought of Father Paul: and his Lordship answered, "Father Paul is a saint."

The interests of the Belgian Benedictines certainly could not have been entrusted to one better qualified than Father Paul. He founded the abbey of Steenbrugge: and reestablished the ancient and renowned monastery of Afflighem. And in the accomplishment of this extraordinary task, Father Paul received no material aid save that which Divine Providence furnished—asked for nothing, while he profusely distributed favors which gold could not purchase; and the gratitude of the recipients provided all that was needed for the completion of his work.

Daily Besieged by a Large Crowd.

The monastery of Termonde was daily besieged by a large crowd, as early as five o'clock in the morning, and in turn every one was received by Father Paul. The sick, the blind, and the paralytic, were either instantly cured, or requested to recite a prayer, or make a novena in honor of St. Benedict; and their prayers always brought forth good results.

Father Paul performed wonders indeed wherever he went, and he profusely exerted the supernatural power given to him. It sufficed for the afflicted and miserable to come in contact with him, in order to experience that all their sorrow and suffering had vanished, and to feel peace and joy pervading their happy hearts.

His memory is fondly cherished and affectionately enshrined in the hearts of the people of Antwerp where he visited frequently; and where the clients, who anxiously awaited his coming, might be numbered by hundreds.

Father Paul's misson was not only the healing of corporal and spiritual maladies. By his prayers and counsel, those involved in business difficulties, were benefited and helped out of embarrassment. Malicious persons often came to ridicule Father Paul, but at the sound of his voice, or a glance of his eye, they abandoned their design, and followed him to the confessional, where he revealed to them the most secret deeds of their life. The discouraged and despondent he uplifted by the promise of a happier and brighter future.

He Visited Bruges, Ghent, Antwerp, and Brussels.

Nor were Father Paul's labors confined to the neighborhood of the monastery, his ardor and zeal extended their limits. He visited

Bruges, Ghent, Antwerp, Brussels, and Malines; and all are indebted to him for many favors.

There were but few convents in the villages and towns through which he passed which Father Paul did not visit. The praise bestowed by the religious brothers and sisters may convey some idea of the joy they experienced while entertaining him. The Rev. Mother of one convent thus expressed herself: "If the blessing of a priest be profitable, what may we not expect from the blessing of so great a saint as Father Paul."

Neither charitable institutions, nor hospitals, nor even prisons were forgotten. Father Paul always found the sick to be cured, the unhappy to be cheered, and aching hearts to be consoled.

His words were ever charming in their simplicity. "You are ill. I shall pray, and tomorrow it will pass." Or again, "Be at ease, do not worry—all will go well; you will be astonished at all the happiness in store for you." There is no misery to which human nature is heir, that did not find relief through the mediation of Father Paul. We have abundant evidence to show that, even after death, his protection still continued, as will be seen in the following pages.

His Death.

Our dearly beloved and deeply lamented Father Paul died at the abbey of Termonde, Feb. 24, 1896, and his funeral took place the Thursday following. As the papers were not notified of his demise they contained no obituary, yet an immense throng of people attended the funeral solemnities, and accompanied the remains to the cemetery, thus showing their veneration—which was the crowning glory of Father Paul's obsequies.

Father Paul accounted for the extraordinary mission which he had received from heaven in the following manner: —

"In the beginning of my religious life, I was so ill, that my life was despaired of. (Father Paul was dying of consumption.) I have been cured miraculously, and I have but one lung. Our Savior appeared to me, accompanied by the Blessed Virgin, Saint Joseph, and Saint Benedict. Our Lady held my hand, while our Savior placed his right hand on my head, and said:

"Be cured; henceforth you will live for the consolation of a great number of persons. I grant you everything that you shall ask of Me for others."

We leave it to the reader to judge whether the divine promise has been fulfilled—and the life of Father Paul may be appropriately summed up in the motto of this book:

"Transiit benefaciendo."

"He went about doing good."

BOOK TWO

The Medal of

Saint Benedict

THE MEDAL OF SAINT BENEDICT

ITS ORIGIN, MEANING, AND PRIVELAGES*

INTRODUCTION.

THE original of this translation was written by the venerable restorer of the Benedictines in France, to propagate a devotion which had already become very popular in Italy and Germany. It is now brought out in an English form, in the hope that it may be the means of making the name of St. Benedict better known, and of spreading devotion to him in this age, which seems specially to need his spirit.

The following account of St. Benedict's mission and life is extracted from Abbot Guéranger's " Liturgical Year."†

With what profound veneration ought we not to celebrate the name of this wonderful Saint, who as St. Gregory says, " was filled with the spirit of all the just! " If we consider his virtues, we find nothing superior in the annals of perfection presented to our admiration by the Church. Love of God and man, humility, the gift of prayer, dominion over the passions, form him into a masterpiece of the grace of the Holy Ghost. Miracles seem to constitute his life; he cures the sick, commands the elements, casts out devils, and raises the dead to life. The spirit of prophecy unfolds futurity to him; and the most intimate thoughts of men are not too distant for the eye of his mind to scan. These superhuman qualifications are heightened by a sweet majesty, a serene gravity, and a tender charity, which shine in every page of his wonderful life; it is one of his holiest children who wrote it—St. Gregory the Great. It is this holy Pope and doctor who had the honour of telling posterity all the wonders which God vouchsafed to work in His servant Benedict.

---

* This second book is a compilation of texts from the 1914 edition of *The Very Rev. Father Paul of Moll* , and material from Dom Prosper Guéranger's *Liturgical Year.*
† See English Translation. Lent, March 21st

Yes, posterity had a right to know the life and virtues of a man whose salutary influence upon the Church and society has been so observable during the ages of the Christian era. To describe the influence exercised by the spirit of St. Benedict, we should have to transcribe the annals of all the nations of the Western Church, from the seventh century down to our own times. Benedict is the Father of Europe. By his Benedictines, numerous as the stars of heaven, and as the sands of the sea-shore, he rescued the last remnants of Roman vigour from the total annihilation threatened by the invasion of barbarians; he presided over the establishment of the public and private laws of those nations which grew out of the ruins of the Roman Empire; he carried the Gospel and civilization into England, Germany, and the northern countries, including Sclavonia; and to conclude, he saved the precious deposit of the arts and sciences from the tempest which would have swept them from the world, and would have left mankind a prey to a gloomy and fatal ignorance.

And Benedict did all this by that little book which we call his " Rule." This admirable code of Christian perfection and prudence disciplined the countless legions of religious by whom the holy Patriarch achieved all these prodigies. During the ages which preceded the promulgation of this " Rule "—so wonderful in its simple eloquence—the monastic life in the Western Church had produced some few saintly men, but there was nothing to justify the hope that this kind of life would become, even more than it had been in the East, the principal means of the Christian regeneration and civilization of so many nations. But before this " Rule " all other rules, one by one, disappeared as the stars fade away when the sun rises. The West was peopled with monasteries, and from these monasteries flowed upon Europe all those blessings which have made it the privileged quarter of the globe.

An incredible number of saints, both men and women, who look up to Benedict as their Father, purify and sanctify the world, which had not yet emerged from the state of semi-barbarism. A long series of Popes, who had once been novices in the Benedictine cloister, preside over the destinies of this new world, and form for it a new legislation, which, being based exclusively on the moral law, is to avert the threatening prevalence of brutal despotism. Bishops innumerable, trained in the same school of Benedict, consolidate this moral legislation in the provinces and cities over which they are appointed. The Apostles of twenty barbarous nations confront their fierce and savage tribes, and, with the Gospel in one hand, and the " Rule " of their Holy Father in the other, lead them into the fold of Christ. For many centuries the learned men, the doctors of the Church, and the instructors of youth, belong, almost exclusively, to the Order of the Great Patriarch, who, by the labours of his children, pours forth on the people the purest beauty of light and truth. This choir of heroes in every virtue, of popes, of bishops, of apostles, of holy doctors, proclaiming themselves his disciples, and joining with the universal Church in glorifying that God whose holiness and power shine forth so brightly in the life and actions of Benedict—what a corona, what an aureola of glory for one saint to have!

St. Benedict was born* of a noble family at Nursia.† He was sent to Rome that he might receive a liberal education; but not long after he withdrew to a place called Subiaco, and there hid himself in a very deep cave, that he might give himself entirely to Jesus Christ. He passed three years in that retirement, unknown to all save to a monk, by name Romanus, who supplied him with the necessaries of life. The devil having one day excited him to a violent temptation of impurity, he rolled himself amidst prickly brambles and extinguished within himself the desire of carnal pleasure by the pain he thus endured. The fame of his sanctity, however, became known beyond the limits of his hiding-place, and certain monks put themselves under his guidance. He sharply rebuked them for their wicked lives: which rebuke so irritated them that they resolved to put poison in his drink. Having made the sign of the cross over the cup as they proffered it to him, it broke, and, leaving that monastery, he returned to his solitude.

---

* A.D. 480.
† About fifty miles east of Rome, in the province of Umbria.

But whereas many daily came to him, beseeching him to take them as his disciples, he built twelve monasteries, and drew up the most admirable rules for their government. He afterwards went to Monte Cassino,* where he destroyed an image of Apollo, which was still adored in those parts; and having pulled down the altar and burned the groves, he built a chapel in that same place, in honour of St. Martin, and another in honour of St. John.† He instructed the inhabitants in the Christian religion. Day by day did Benedict advance in the grace of God, so that he even foretold, in a spirit of prophecy, what was to take place. Totila, the King of the Goths, having heard of this, and being anxious to know if it were the truth, went to visit him; but first he sent his sword-bearer, who was to pretend that he was the king, and who, for this end, was dressed in royal robes and accompanied by a royal retinue. As soon as Benedict saw him, he said, " Put off, my son, put off this dress, for it is not thine." But he foretold to Totila that he would reach Rome, cross the sea, and die at the end of nine years.

Several months before he departed from this life, he foretold to his disciples the day on which he should die. Six days previous to his death he ordered them to open the sepulchre wherein he wished to be buried. On the sixth day he desired to be carried to the church; and there, having received the Eucharist, with his eyes raised in prayer towards heaven, and supported in the arms of his disciples, he breathed forth his soul.‡ Two monks saw it ascending to heaven, adorned with a most precious robe, and surrounded by shining lights. They also saw a most beautiful and venerable man, who stood above the saint's head, and they heard him speak thus: " This is the way whereby Benedict, the beloved of the Lord, ascended to heaven."

There is an ancient tradition, which says that God revealed to St. Benedict that his Order should not disappear from the world's stage until the Last Day; and that, in the fierce times preceding the Judgment, it should prove a support to the Church and strengthen

---

* Seventy miles south-west of Rome.
† St. John the Baptist.
‡ A.D. 543.

many in the faith. Some think we have entered upon the last days. Certain it is that the sons of the holy patriarch are increasing in number and influence. Perhaps the reason is, that the evils of an age resembling in many points those times for which St. Benedict laboured and prayed, call once more for the spirit and example of the great Patriarch.

There is no way more common of making known a saint, of inspiring the faithful with his spirit, and of drawing down his protection, than by Medals bearing his effigy and struck in his honour. This method of preaching devotion to St. Benedict has been peculiarly successful in the Church for some centuries. God has blessed it by singular favours granted in the most varied circumstances of life, and in the most distant countries. Moved by these tokens of Divine favour, the Church has approved of the Medal of St. Benedict, and in the form of blessing prays God, by the intercession of St. Benedict, to give those who wear it health of body and mind, to protect them from the frauds and snares of the demons, to grant them His grace and indulgence, to preserve them, amid the dangers of the times, stainless and pure in His sight, and through the sufferings of Jesus Christ to bring them safely to the heavenly country.

J. B. M.

St. Edmund's, Douai,
Lent 1880

When using the Medal for any pious purpose, the following prayer may be said:—
May the intercession of the Blessed Patriarch and Abbot Benedict render Thee, O Lord, merciful unto us; that what our own unworthiness cannot obtain we may receive through his powerful patronage: Through Christ our Lord.

Author's Preface

Man has no right to pass judgment on the effects which God deigns to produce by his power and goodness. In order to assist us in our necessities, God, in his wisdom and providence, sometimes makes use of extremely simple means, thus to keep us in humility and filial confidence. A Christian whose faith is but weak is surprised at this, and even tempted to be scandalized, inasmuch as it seems to him that the means by which God works are not in keeping with his greatness. Such a thought as this is nothing less than pride or ignorance, for whenever God puts himself within our reach, he must needs stoop down to our lowliness.

And yet, does he not show his greatness when he selects simple material objects as the medium of communication between himself and us, as in the case of the Holy Sacraments? Does he not thereby show us how he is the absolute Master of all, even so far as this —that he can embody his grace in such lowly and apparently commonplace forms as these ? The Church, which is guided by his Spirit, delights in imitating this his mode of acting, at least in some slight way, and hence she communicates the divine virtue which she possesses to those objects which she sanctifies as helps and consolations for her children.

This little work treats of one of these sacred objects; one which is honoured with the approbation and blessing of the Church, and which unites in itself the triumphant power of the holy cross which redeemed us, with the memory of one of God's most illustrious servants. Every Christian that loves and adores Christ who redeemed us, or who believes in the intercession of the Saints who are now reigning in heaven with Him, will look on the Medal of St. Benedict with respect; and when he hears of any of those heavenly favours of which it has been the instrument, he will give thanks to God, who authorizes us to make use of his Son's cross as a shield of protection, and to rely with confidence on the assistance of the Saints in heaven.

We have collected together in these pages a certain number of facts which prove that God deigns to protect, in a special manner those who put their confidence in the sacred signs marked on the Medal. These facts, to which we in no manner wish to attribute the name of miracles properly so called, have been told us by persons in whom we have the fullest confidence. The reader is at liberty to form his own judgment upon them, and believe them or not, as he pleases. Numerous as they are, we could easily have given very many more, of all of which we have received the particulars; but we thought it advisable to limit ourselves to those we have related, and to aim rather at variety than number.

In publishing this work upon a subject which to many may seem ill fitted for an age like this, when Rationalism is so rife, our only object is to render a service to our brethren in the faith. During life they will be placed in circumstances when they will feel that they need a special help from Heaven. Let them, at these times, have recourse to the Medal of St Benedict, as so many Christians are in the habit of doing ; and if their faith be strong and simple, they may depend on the promise of our Lord—such faith shall not go unrewarded.

CHAPTER I.

On The Figure Of The Cross Represented On The Medal.

THERE is a great wish on the part of many Catholics to have clear ideas regarding the celebrated Medal which goes under the name of the great Patriarch of the Western Monks. It is true that several notices have been already published, some more, some less correct, have been already published ; but not one of them—so it seems to us—having fully satisfied the wishes of the faithful, we thought it would be well to offer to their devotion a more complete explanation of an object, which has become so dear to them. That there may be order in what we are going to say about it, we will begin with the description of the Medal.

A Christian needs but reflect for a moment on the sovereign virtue of the cross of Jesus Christ in order to understand how worthy of respect a Medal is on which it is represented. The cross was the instrument of the world's redemption; it is the saving tree whereon was expiated the sin committed by man when he ate the fruit of the forbidden tree. St. Paul tells us that the sentence of our condemnation was fastened to the cross, and blotted out by the blood of our Redeemer.* In a word, the cross, which the Church salutes as *our*

---

* I Col. ii. 14.

219

only hope, "Spes Unica," is to appear at the last day in the clouds of heaven, as the trophy of the victory of the Man-God.

The image of the cross excites in our minds the liveliest sentiments of gratitude towards God for the benefit of our salvation. After the Blessed Sacrament, there is nothing on earth so deserving our respect as the cross; and it is for this reason that we pay it a worship of adoration, which is referred to God, whose precious blood was spilt upon it.

Animated by sentiments of the purest religion, the primitive Christians had, from the very beginning of the Church, the profoundest veneration for the image of the cross, and the Fathers seem never to tire in the praises they give to this august sign. When, after three hundred years of persecution, God had decreed to give peace to His Church, there appeared in the heavens a cross, on which were these words, " In this sign shalt thou conquer; " and the Emperor Constantine, to whom was granted this vision, promising him victory over his enemies, would henceforth have his army go to battle under a standard bearing the image of the cross with the monogram of the word " Christ." This standard was called the *Labarum.*

The cross is an object of terror to the evil spirits; they ever crouch in terror before it; they no sooner see it than they let go their prey and take to flight. In a word, of such importance to Christians is the cross and the blessing it brings along with it, that from the times of the Apostles, down to our own age, the faithful have ever been accustomed frequently to make the sign of the cross upon themselves, and the priests of the Church have constantly used it over all the objects which', in virtue of their sacerdotal character, they have the power to bless and sanctify.

Our Medal, therefore, which firstly offers to us the figure of the cross, is in strict accordance with Christian piety, and worthy, even were there no other motive than this, of all possible veneration.

CHAPTER II.

Of The Effigy Of St. Benedict Represented On The Medal.

THE honour of appearing on the same medal with the figure of the holy cross has been given to St. Benedict, with the intention of expressing the efficacy which this holy sign had, when made by his venerable hand. St. Gregory the Great, who has written the Life of the holy Patriarch, tells us how, by the sign of the cross, he overcame his temptations, and by the same sign broke the cup of poisoned drink which was proffered to him, thus unmasking the wicked designs of those who had plotted to take away his life. When the evil spirit, in order to terrify his Religious, made the monastery of Monte Cassino appear to be on fire, St. Benedict immediately dispels the artifice by making over the fiery phantom this same sign of our Redeemer's Passion.* When his Religious are troubled interiorly with the suggestions of the tempter, the holy Father bids them take the remedy, and it is to make on their breasts the sign of the cross.†

In his Rule, he prescribes that the brother, who has been reading the solemn engagement of his profession at the foot of the altar, should immediately affix to it the sign of the cross, as an irrevocable seal of the deed on which his vows are written.

The disciples of St. Benedict have had a like confidence in this sacred sign, and have worked innumerable miracles by it. Let it here suffice to mention St. Maurus giving sight to a blind man; St. Placid curing many who were sick; St. Richmir liberating captives, St. Wulstan preserving a workman in the very act of falling from the top of the church-tower; St. Odilo drawing out from a man's eye a splinter of wood which had run through it; St. Anselm of Canterbury driving away from an old man the horrid spectres which were tormenting him in his dying moments; St. Hugh of Cluny quelling a storm; St. Gregory the Seventh arresting the conflagration at Rome, &c. : these, and a thousand other such miracles, which are related in

---

* See his Life, chap. x.
† Ibid., chap. xx.

the "Acts of the Saints of the Order of St. Benedict," were all worked by the sign of the cross.

The glory and efficacy of the august instrument of our salvation have been celebrated with enthusiasm by the children of the great Patriarch; they loved to extol it, for their hearts were full of gratitude towards it. Not to speak of the little Office of the Holy Cross which St. Udalric, Bishop of Augsburg, used to recite, and which was also said in choir in the abbeys of St. Gall, of Reichenau, of Bursfeld, &c.; the blessed Rhabanus Maurus and St. Peter Damian consecrated their talent for poetry in singing the praises of the holy cross; St. Anselm of Canterbury has written its praises in the form of most exquisite prayers; Venerable Bede, St. Odilo of Cluny, Rupert of Deutz, Ecbert of Schonaugen, and a long list of others of the Order, have left us sermons on the holy cross; Eginhard wrote a book in defence of the worship paid to it against the Iconoclasts, and Peter the Venerable defended, in a set treatise, the use of the sign of the cross, which had been attacked by the Petrobrusians. A great number of the most famous monasteries of the Order of St. Benedict were founded under the title of " Holy Cross." Of these, let it suffice to mention the celebrated monastery built at Paris by the Bishop, St. Germanus; the monastery built by St. Faron in the diocese of Meaux; the abbey of " Holy Cross " founded at Poitiers by St. Radegonde; the monastery of " Holy Cross " at Bordeaux built by Clovis the Second; those of Metten in Bavaria, Reichenau in Switzerland, Quimperld in Brittany, and the five famous monasteries in the Vosgian country which were founded by St. Hydulph, and which he so situated that they formed a cross.

The Saviour of the world seems to have entrusted, by a special favour, to the children of St. Benedict a large portion of the cross on which He died for the redemption of man. Large fragments of this sacred wood have been confided to their keeping, and a Christian might almost glory in having seen the instrument of his salvation, were all the pieces to be put before him, which have been possessed by different monasteries of this Order. We may mention the following amongst the houses thus privileged:—In France, St. Germain-des-Prés, in Paris, St. Denis'; Holy Cross at Poitiers; Connery, in Touraine, Gellone, &c.; St. Michael's de Murano, in Venice; Sahagun, in Spain; Reichenau, in Switzerland; St. Ulric's and St. Afra's at Augsburg, in Germany; St. Michael's, at Hildesheim; St. Trutpert's, in the Black Forest; Mœlk, in Austria; the celebrated monastery of Gandersheim, &c.

But the most glorious mission given to the Benedictines in what relates to the glory of the holy cross is that of having carried this instrument of salvation into so many countries by preaching the gospel to their pagan inhabitants. The greater part of the West was converted by their zeal from the darkness of infidelity; and the reader need scarce be told that England was converted by St. Augustine of Canterbury; Germany by St. Boniface; Belgium by St. Amandus; Holland and Zealand by St. Willibrord; Westphalia by St. Swithbert; Sweden and Denmark by St. Anscharius; Austria by St. Wolfgang; Saxony by St. Ludgerius; Bavaria by St. Corbinian; Poland and Bohemia by St. Adalbert of Prague; Prussia by St. Otho of Bamberg; Russia by St. Boniface the Second.

Such are, in brief, the facts which give to the person and name of St. Benedict a special connection with the holy cross; it is, therefore, with a most evident appropriateness that the effigy of this holy Patriarch has been put on the same medal with the figure of the cross of our Lord Jesus Christ.

We see still more clearly why this should have been done when we refer to what is related in the Acts of the two great disciples of this servant of God, St. Placid and St. Maurus. Both of them, when working the miracles, which we meet with in almost every page of their lives, were wont to join together with the invocation of the holy cross the name of their holy Father, Benedict, thus establishing, at the very beginning of the Order, the pious practice, of which the Medal was to be, in after times, the symbol and the expression.

St. Placid had scarcely bidden farewell to the holy Patriarch on leaving Monte Cassino to repair to Sicily, when arriving at Capua he was besought to heal the dean of the church of that town. His humility made him for a long time resist such a demand; at length he consents, and placing his hand upon the head of the priest, who was sick of a mortal disease, he immediately cures him, whilst pronouncing these words: " In the name of our Lord Jesus Christ, who, by the prayers and virtue of Benedict our Master, drew me safe and sound from the midst of the water, may God reward thy faith, and restore thee to thy former health."

Immediately there comes a blind man, begging in his turn to be cured. Placid makes the sign of the cross upon his eyes, at the same time adding this prayer: " Lord Jesus Christ, Mediator of God and men, who didst come down from heaven to earth that thou mightest enlighten those who were sitting in the darkness and shades of death; thou who hast given to our blessed Master Benedict the gift of healing all maladies and all wounds, deign, by his merits, to give sight to this blind man, to the end that, seeing the magnificence of thy works, he may fear and adore thee as the Sovereign Lord." Then addressing himself to the blind man, Placid thus continued: " By the merits of our most holy Father Benedict, I command thee, in the name of him who created the sun and moon to be the ornament of the heavens, and gave to him who was born blind the eyes which nature had denied him, arise, and be thou healed! go now and tell all men the wonderful works of our God." The blind man immediately recovered his sight. We might quote several other miracles from the life of St. Placid, such as healing the sick or driving out devils from those possessed, in which the invocation or the mention of St. Benedict, still living, was united with the making of the sign of the cross. In some of these miracles, we find the sick themselves acknowledging and proclaiming this mysterious connection.

St. Maurus, having been sent by the great Patriarch into Gaul, there to establish his Rule, soon began to work numerous miracles. As we noticed before, these miracles were wrought by means of the holy cross, but the saintly abbot was also accustomed to join to the divine virtue of the instrument of our redemption, a prayer invoking the intervention of St. Benedict. He bore testimony to this himself when, on occasion of his having saved one of his fellow-travellers from death, he made this declaration: " If," said the saint to those who had witnessed the miracle, " the Divine Majesty hath deigned to work this miracle by the wood which redeemed us, it is plainly not to man, but to the Redeemer himself that we must give the glory of it, although none of you can doubt, but that *the merits of our most holy Father Benedict* have obtained this grace of him for us."

From these facts it is evident that, even from the very commencement of the Benedictine Order, this method of having recourse to the divine goodness was practised with wonderful success. St. Benedict was still on earth, and his disciples invoked his name when they were asking favours of Heaven; if such confidence in his merits was, even then, thus blessed by God, how great must the power of his intercession be now that he has been raised to his throne of glory in heaven!

Chapter III.

Origin of the Medal.

The origin of the Medal probably dates back to the time of St. Benedict himself, of whom we know that in his frequent combats with the evil spirit, he generally made use of the sign of the cross, and wrought many miracles thereby. He also taught his disciples to use the sign of our redemption against the assaults of Satan and in other dangers. St. Maurus and St. Placid, his first and most renowned disciples, wrought their numerous miracles through the power of the holy Cross and in the name and by the merits of their holy Founder.

The Medal of St. Benedict became more widely known through the following wonderful occurrence. Bruno, afterwards Pope Leo IX., had in his youth been bitten by a venomous reptile, in consequence of which he was seriously ill for two months. He had lost the use of speech and was in a short time reduced to a skeleton. All hopes of his recovery had been abandoned, when suddenly he beheld a luminous ladder that reached to heaven, from which descended a venerable old man wearing the habit of a monk. It was St. Benedict, bearing in his hand a radiant cross, with which he touched the swollen face of Bruno, and instantly cured him. Then the apparition disappeared.

Bruno, who had been healed in such a miraculous manner, later on entered the Order of St. Benedict. He ascended the papal throne in the year 1048, under the name of Leo IX. and was renowned in the Church for his sanctity, his devotion to the holy Cross, and to St. Benedict. Through this Pope the Medal of St. Benedict was enriched with special blessings, and its veneration spread everywhere. The use of the Medal was solemnly approved and recommended to the faithful by Pope Benedict XIV. in 1742.

CHAPTER IV.

Description of the Medal.*

ON one side the Medal has a cross, the sign of our redemption, the protecting shield given us by God, to ward off the fiery arrows of the evil spirit.

In the angles of the cross are found these four letters: **C. S. P. B.** They stand for the words: **C**rux **S**ancti **P**atris **B**enedicti. "The Cross of the Holy Father Benedict."

On the perpendicular bar of the cross itself are found the letters: **C. S. S. M. L**. And on the horizontal bar of the cross: **N. D. S. M. D**. They signify:

---

* We distinguish two types of the Medal of St. Benedict. The ordinary Medal and that of Monte Cassino, which is known as the Jubilee Medal. The latter has been enriched with a great number of indulgences, especially with the famous *Toties Quoties* plenary indulgence, on All Souls' Day. .

In the year 1880, the Venerable Benedictine Order celebrated the 1400th anniversary of the birth of its glorious Founder. The beautiful Jubilee Medal was struck on this occasion and since that time the Monastery of Monte Cassino has the sole privilege of striking this Medal. Hence all Jubilee Medals must be procured from the Monastery of Monte Cassino.

Crux Sacra Sit Mihi Lux,
Non Draco Sit Mihi Dux.
May the holy Cross be my light,
Let not the dragon be my guide.

Round the margin of the Medal, beginning at the right hand on top, we have the following letters: **V. R. S. N. S. M. V.; S. M. Q. L. I. V. B.** They stand for the verses:

Vade Retro, Satana;
Nunquam Suade Mihi Vana.
Sunt Mala Quæ Libas;
Ipse Venena Bibas.

The English words are: "Begone Satan! Suggest not to me thy vain things. The cup thou profferest me is evil; drink thou thy poison."

The reverse of the Medal bears the image of St. Benedict, holding in his right hand the cross, in the power of which he wrought so many miracles, and in his left hand bearing the holy rule, which leads all its followers by the way of the cross to eternal light.

Round the margin is the inscription: "Ejus in obitu nostro praesentia muniamur."—May his presence protect us in the hour of our death.

CHAPTER V.

The Blessing of the Medal of St. Benedict.*

THE Medal of St. Benedict must be blessed by a Benedictine Father† or by a priest especially authorized. There are three solemn prayers of the church for the blessing of the Medal.

The first prayer is an exorcism of the wicked spirit, to make void his evil influence, with the earnest petition that the Medal be for the welfare of body and soul of the wearer.

The second prayer is a fervent petition and reads as follows: —

---

* See Appendix for the full Blessing.

† In 1968 the Sacred Congregation of Rites issued the instruction that this formerly reserved Blessing may now be given by any priest. (Instr., 26 Sept. 1964; Can. 1168)

O Almighty God, the Giver of all good gifts, we humbly beseech Thee, that Thou wouldst bestow through the intercession of the holy Father St. Benedict, Thy blessing upon these Medals, their letters and characters designed by Thee, that all who wear them and strive to perform good works may obtain health of body and soul, the grace of salvation, the indulgences conceded to us, and by the assistance of Thy mercy escape the snares and deceptions of the devil and appear holy and stainless in Thy sight.

The third prayer is very impressive in virtue of the detailed and solemn commemoration of the agony, sufferings and death of our Lord.

After the blessing, the Medals cannot be sold, nor after use, can they be given away, lent or exchanged; otherwise the blessing is lost. Medals must, therefore, be bought before they are blessed; those which are found must be blessed again.

Chapter VI.

Of The Use To Be Made Of The Medal Of St. Benedict.

After having described the Medal of St. Benedict, and given its origin, we will now explain the use which is to be made of it and the advantages to be derived from it. We are aware that in this age of ours, when the devil is thought by many to be an imaginary rather than a real being, it will seem to be strange that a medal should be made and blessed, and used as a preservative against the power of the wicked spirit. And yet the Holy Scriptures give us abundant instructions upon the ever-busy power of the devils, as also upon the dangers to which we are exposed, both in soul and body, by the snares they set for us. The not believing in the existence of devils, or the ridiculing of the accounts which are told of their operations, is not enough to destroy their power, and, in spite of this incredulity, the air is filled with legions of these spirits of wickedness, as St. Paul teaches us.*

* Eph. ii. 2, vi. 12.

Were it not that God protected us by the ministry of the holy angels, and this generally without our being aware of it, it would be impossible for us to escape the countless snares of these enemies of all God's creatures. But if there ever was a time when it would seem to be superfluous to prove this existence of wicked spirits, it is now, when we find reappearing amongst us those dangerous and sinful practices, which were used by the pagans of old, and now again by Christians, for the purpose of eliciting an answer from spirits, though these can be no other than evil and lying ones. Surely our age is credulous enough in the existence of devils, when we find it so fashionable to be using again all those consultings of the dead, and oracles, and superstitions, which Satan employed for keeping men under his power during so many hundred years.

Now such is the power of the holy cross against Satan and his legions, that we may look upon it as the invincible shield which makes us invulnerable against all their darts. The brazen serpent raised up in the desert by Moses, in order to cure those who were stung by the fiery serpents, is given to us by our Saviour himself as a figure of his cross.* The mark made on the house-doors with the blood of the Paschal Lamb by the Israelites preserved them from the terrible visit of the destroying Angel.† The prophet Ezechiel tells us that they were God's elect, who had Thau on their foreheads; and it is this same mark which St. John, in his Apocalypse, calls the sign of the Lamb.‡ It would even seem that the pagans had some idea of the power which this sacred sign was to exercise, at some future period, against the devils; for on occasion of the destruction of the temple of Serapis at Alexandria, under the Emperor Theodosius, there was found engraven upon its foundations the letters *Thau*, which is the figure of the cross, and the symbol which was venerated by the pagans as expressive of the future life. The very adorers of Serapis used to say, agreeably to a tradition which they had, that when this symbol should be made known to the world, idolatry would cease.

---

* St. John iii. 14.
† Exod. xii. 23.
‡ Apoc. xiv. I.

History informs us that the pagan mysteries were sometimes rendered powerless on account of there being in the crowd, a Christian who made the sign of the cross. Tertullian tells us in his " Apology," that even pagans, who had witnessed what wonders the Christians wrought by the cross, would themselves successfully employ this mysterious sign against the artifices and attacks of the wicked spirits. St. Augustine assures us that the same was done in his time: " Nor ought we," says he, " to be astonished at this; these men are, it is true, strangers who have not joined our ranks; but it is the power of our great King, which makes itself felt on these occasions."*

After the triumph of the Church, the great doctor, St. Athanasius, thus expressed his own convictions and confidence in reference to this important subject: "The sign of the cross," he says, " has the power of dispelling all the secret charms of magic, and of rendering harmless all the deadly draughts it employs. Let any one but try what I say; let him make the sign of the cross in the midst of the demons, and of pretended oracles, and magical spells; let him invoke the name of Christ, and he will see for himself how the devils fly from this sign and this name, how the oracles are struck dumb, and how magic and its philters lose their power! "†

So that this power of the cross is, at the same time, an historical truth, and a dogma of our faith; and it is only because our faith is weak, that we so seldom have recourse to it, and so seldom experience help from it. The snares of Satan are laid for us on every side; we are surrounded by dangers both of soul and body: let us imitate the early Christians and defend ourselves by making a more frequent use of the sign of the cross. Will the happy time ever come again for our country when we shall be allowed to have the crucifix as our protection in our towns and highways and fields, and be permitted to reverence it in our public squares as well as in our own houses, and not be insulted for wearing it openly on our breast besides loving it secretly in our heart ?

And now, applying these considerations to the medal which is the subject of these pages, we come to this conclusion, that it must

* De Diversis Quaestionibus, Quaest. lxxxix.
† De Incarnatione Verbi, cap. xlviii.

be profitable to us to use with faith the Medal of St. Benedict on occasions when we have reason to fear the snares of the enemy. Its protection will infallibly prove efficacious in every kind of temptation. Numerous and undeniable facts attest its powerful efficacy on a thousand different occasions, in which the faithful had reason to apprehend a danger, either from the direct agency of Satan, or from the effects of certain evil practices. We may also employ it in favour of others as a means of preserving or delivering them from dangers, which we foresee are threatening them. Unforeseen accidents may happen to us on land or on sea; let us carry about us this holy Medal with faith and we shall be protected. Even in the most trivial circumstances, and in those interests which regard solely man's temporal well-being, the efficacy of the holy cross and the power of St. Benedict have been felt. For example, the wicked spirits, in their hatred of man, sometimes molest the animals which God has created for our service, or infest the various articles of nourishment which the same Providence has given to us. Or again, it is not unfrequently the case that our bodily sufferings are caused or protracted by the influence of these our cruel enemies. Experience has proved that the Medal of St. Benedict, made use of with a proper intention and with prayer, has frequently broken the snares of the devil, procured a visible improvement in cases of sickness, and sometimes even effected a complete cure.

Let us state here that we do not ascribe any unknown or hidden power to the Medal; a power, which the superstitious ascribe to their charms. We know wherein its power lies and we protest that the graces and favors are due, not to the gold or the silver, the brass or aluminum of the Medal, but to our faith in the merits of Christ crucified, to the efficacious prayers of the holy Father St. Benedict and to the blessings which the holy Church bestows upon the Medal and upon those who wear it. This Medal excludes every power or influence which is not from above.

Through the pious use of the Medal of St. Benedict thousands of miracles and wonderful cures have been obtained. We would here mention that in the last few years we have received a number of letters relating most remarkable cures and extraordinary favors obtained by the devout use of the said Medal. It is, indeed, edifying to see how the faithful love and venerate this highly blessed Medal and how anxious they are to obtain this holy article which has proved to be a remedy for almost every evil.

The Medal of St. Benedict is powerful *to ward off all dangers of body and soul coming from the evil spirit.* We are exposed to the wicked assaults of the devil day and night. St. Peter says, "Your adversary, the devil, as a roaring lion goeth about seeking whom he may devour" (1. Peter 5, 8). In the life of St. Benedict we see how the devil tried to do harm to his soul and body and also to his spiritual children. Father Paul of Moll frustrated the evil doings of the spirit of darkness chiefly through the use of the Medal of St. Benedict, which has proved a most powerful protection against the snares and delusions of the old enemy. Missionaries in pagan lands use this Medal with so great effect, that it has been given the remarkable name, "The devil-chasing Medal."

The Medal is, therefore, a powerful means:

- To destroy witchcraft and all other diabolical influences.
- To keep away the spells of magicians, of wicked and evil-minded persons.
- To impart protection to persons tempted, deluded or tormented by evil spirits.
- To obtain the conversion of sinners, especially when they are **in** danger of death.
- To serve as an armour in temptations against holy purity.
- To destroy the effects of poison.
- To secure timely and healthy birth for children.
- To afford protection against storms and lightning.

Finally, the Medal has often been used with admirable effect, even for animals infected with plague or other maladies; and for fields when invaded by harmful insects.

The Medal may be worn about the neck, attached to the scapular or the rosary, or otherwise carried devoutly about one's person. For the sick it can be placed on wounds, dipped in medicine or in water which is given to them to drink.

The Medal is frequently put into the foundation of houses, or in walls, hung over doors, or fastened on stables and barns to call down God's protection and blessing. It is also buried in fields as the saintly Father Paul of Moll advised his friends to do. He reminded them, however, not to use the same Medal for their own person and for the cattle or the field, but to have for these different purposes special Medals.

No particular prayers are prescribed, for the very wearing and use of the Medal is considered a silent prayer to God to grant us, through the merits of St. Benedict, the favors we request. However, for obtaining extraordinary favors it is highly recommended to perform special devotions in honor of the holy Father St. Benedict, for instance on Tuesday, on which day the Church commemorates the death of the holy Patriarch. The Way of the Cross is also highly recommended or a novena to St. Benedict. His feast is celebrated March 21st, two days after the feast of St. Joseph.

CHAPTER VII.

The Miraculous Effects Of The Medal Of St. Benedict In The Seventeenth Century.

THOUGH the Medal of St. Benedict has been given to the faithful as a protection in the various necessities in which they may be at any time placed, yet as its use is only private, and almost always secret, we cannot be surprised that there has never been published an official account of the salutary effects it has produced. We are going, however, to mention some few facts which attested its powerful efficacy during the seventeenth century, the period of its first introduction into France. We take them from the pious and learned Bucelin, in his " Benedictus Redivivus " (Veldkirk, 1679, pp. 267-269).

The Medal, which had become well known throughout Germany after the event at Nattremberg, passed into France through the province of Franche-Comté.

In 1665, at Luxeuil in France, a young man possessed by the wicked spirit was most cruelly tormented. His parents had employed every means to free him from this state, but all had failed. In this extremity it came into their minds to have recourse to the Medal of St. Benedict. They made their son drink some water into which they had dipped the Medal. Scarcely had the boy raised the cup to his lips, than the devil began to torment his victim with such unusual violence, that the bystanders were struck with terror. The parents, however, were consoled by hearing the devil declare, by the mouth of their son, that he felt himself controlled by a superior power, and that he would go out of the boy at the third hour of the night. So in effect it happened: the infernal spirit went out at the time mentioned, and the boy was restored to peace of mind and health of body.

The following fact took place at Luxeuil about the same time. A young girl was irresistibly compelled by the wicked spirit to utter, at every turn, the most obscene words. One would have thought that the devil had taken up his abode on the lips of his victim. In order to free her from this violence of the enemy of every virtue, her friends gave her also, some water to drink which had been sanctified by contact with the Medal of St. Benedict. Immediately she felt herself freed from this wretched compulsion, nor did she ever after transgress in her words the rules of Christian modesty.

The same year, 1665, there was a man who had a sore on his arm, but so large and so inflamed, that no remedy seemed to have any effect on it. It was suggested that the next time the sore was dressed, there should be also tied on his arm a Medal of St. Benedict. This was done, and the next day, on taking off the bandages, the sore was found to be in a healthy state, and after a few days was perfectly healed.

About the same time, another sick man was reduced to such a state that nothing seemed to give him relief, and he was despaired of. In this sad condition, he asked to be given to drink some water in which the Medal of St. Benedict had been dipped, and very soon afterwards he was restored to perfect health.

In the year 1666, the castle of Maillot, not many miles from Besançon, was infested by devils. Its inmates were being continually alarmed by hearing strange noises, and numbers of their cattle were dying from unknown distempers. At length, such was the terror, that the building was abandoned. Some pious persons recommended the Medal of St. Benedict being hung up here and there on the walls of the castle, and the event justified their confidence. Instantly all cause of fear disappeared, the house was perfectly quiet, and the inmates lived in it henceforth without being molested.

In 1665, a village of Lorraine was being laid waste by frequent fires. Every day some house was burnt down, and no one could discover any cause for these destructive fires. After twelve houses had been thus destroyed, the inhabitants went in despair to a neighbouring monastery, and asked what they had better do under this calamity. The monks gave them several Medals of St. Benedict, advising them to hang them on the walls of the houses which were still spared. The villagers followed this advice, and from that time they had no more cause to fear further ravages from fire.

In a certain part of Burgundy a distemper broke out amongst the cattle, and so virulent was it, that the cows gave blood instead of milk. They were perfectly cured on being made to drink water into which the Medal of St. Benedict had been put. This fact happened in the same year, 1665.

The owner of a brick-kiln complained of not being able to bake the clay, no matter how intensely the kiln was heated. A Medal of St. Benedict was fastened to the wall; the fire immediately regained its power, nor did the unnatural phenomenon again appear. This event happened about the same year as the last.

CHAPTER VIII.

The Effects Of The Medal Of St. Benedict In The Nineteenth Century—Cures Obtained By It.

DURING the last few years the grace of God has produced a change in the minds of the faithful of these Northern countries, by reanimating many of them with a respect for what is supernatural. This also in its turn revived confidence in the holy practices from which our ancestors received so many blessings. The Medal of St. Benedict, which was on the point of becoming a secret, known only by a few pious souls, has now been brought so much into notice that thousands have recourse to it in their necessities, and their confidence has been rewarded.*

We proceed to give several instances of the protection granted to those who have used this holy Medal, and we begin by those which relate to the cure of bodily ailments.

In the early part of July, in the year 1843, a lady, who was taking the waters at Néris (France), was suddenly seized with a violent bleeding at the nose. The doctor is called in; he perceives the danger, but the remedies he prescribes for stopping the bleeding only seem to increase it. Things continue in this state till the evening of the third day, when, at nine o'clock, the danger visibly increases, and the doctor can no longer conceal his fears. The landlady of the hotel goes out of the room in a state of great excitement, and, as if by inspiration, she asks if any one in the house has a Medal of St. Benedict. Fortunately one is found; the sick person, who was a woman of strong faith, accepts the Medal, and immediately the bleeding stops. She washes her hands and face, and goes to lie down, which she had not been able to do for three days and two nights. The person who had lent the Medal found, on returning home, a letter dated Rome, July 8, 1843, in which was written: " I have not yet been able to meet with the book of the ' Benedictine of Prague.'† However, I send you a little book on the same subject, given me by our Benedictines of Rome." Now, in the list given in this little book of the miraculous effects of the Medal of St. Benedict we

* See "Vie de M. Dupont, mort à Tours en odeur de sainteté le 18 Mars 1876. Par Abbé Janvier." This work was reviewed in the "Tablet" of February 7, 1880. The subject of the memoir is said to have made great use of the Medal of St. Benedict as a means of defeating the malice of Satan, and his Life is full of most interesting examples of wonderful graces obtained through its use.—Ed.

† The book here alluded to is that of Benno Löbl, Abbot of St. Margaret's of Prague, entitled, " Disquisitio sacra numismatica, de origine, quidditate, virtute, pioque usu Numismatum seu Crucularum S. Benedicti, Abbatis, Vienna, Austria, apud Leopoldum Kaliwoda, 1743." We have this work, and have consulted it in drawing up this notice.

read this amongst this rest: " It is a most efficacious remedy against haemorrhage,"*

About the same time, a young person, who was laid up with the typhus fever, had been obliged to sit for ten days in an arm-chair, as the reclining position of lying in bed had become unsufferable. At nine in the evening, a friend of the family, who had come to see her, spoke to her of St. Benedict's Medals, and slipped one into her handkerchief. Scarce five minutes had elapsed, when the sick person got into bed, and on the morrow, after sleeping soundly during the whole night, found herself perfectly recovered from the terrible fever, which up to that time had baffled all the skill of the doctors.

In January of 1849, at T——, the Reverend Father P——, a Jesuit, called at the house of an intimate friend who lived close by, and asked him if he could recommend some cure for a toothache, which was almost driving him wild. The friend began to tell him about St. Benedict's Medal. After a short explanation of it, the good Father accepts of one. The very moment it touches his hand he utters a cry, like that which dentists so often hear from their patients, and then says, " My tooth is broken." He puts his finger on the place, and is surprised to find the tooth all right and the aching quite gone.

In 1858, a Benedictine of St. Paul's in Rome, having heard that a child, to which he had stood godfather, was taken dangerously ill at Juliers, in Rhenish Prussia, sent to the mother a Medal of St. Benedict. Inflammation of the lungs, accompanied by spasms in the stomach, had gradually reduced the child to the last extremity. One night, the mother, seeing the child almost at the point of death, was suddenly minded to make use of the Medal which she had received a few days before. Distracted with grief and trembling with anxiety, she lays the Medal on her child's breast, and then throws herself on her knees at the foot of the bed in fervent prayer. That very moment the poor little sufferer quietly fell asleep, and after some hours of the most tranquil slumber, got up full of life and free from the disease, which up to that time had seemed incurable.

In the summer of the same year, 1858, the cholera was raging at Tivoli, in Italy, and a man, who lived not far from Subiaco, was

* " E'rimedio efficacissimo pel jetto di sangue."

237

seized with the most excruciating pains. In a few hours this terrible malady had made such progress, that his friends ran in great haste to bring the priest, that he might administer the last sacraments. In the meantime the danger became so great that the sick man thought himself at the point of death, and swooned away from the violence of the pain. A few moments after he returned to himself, and felt that his sufferings were still increasing. The cramps in his stomach were more violent than ever, and in endeavouring to allay them by the pressure of his hands, he touched the Medal of St. Benedict, which he always wore. This reminded him to have recourse to the holy Patriarch, for whom he entertained the most lively devotion. His pains immediately disappeared; he gets up, leaves his bed, and seeing the priest, who, out of breath, with the perspiration running down his face, had just come into the house, "Father," he exclaimed, "I am cured;" and showing him the Medal, he added, "See what has saved me." The good man paid a visit not long after to the Benedictine abbey of St. Paul at Rome, taking with him the certificates of both the priest and doctor, which bore testimony to the truth of this extraordinary cure.

In February 1861, a colony of Benedictines from the same abbey of St. Paul at Rome, established itself near the town of Cleves, in Rhenish Prussia. They began in March to build an enclosure round the little garden of the new monastery. The man who acted as superintendent of repairs of the parish church, which was served by the Benedictine Fathers, offered to go and purchase for them the wood they required for the building of the enclosure. Accordingly, he repaired to the place where they were felling trees in the Government forests. This man had had given to him the Medal of St. Benedict, and he carried it on his person with great devotion. After having loaded his cart with several large trunks of oak, he started back for the monastery; but just as the cart began to move, one of the trees, which had not been properly fastened, came rolling down. The good man was at the back of the cart, and not being able to get out of the way in time, was knocked down and his right leg almost crushed to pieces.

He was carried home. The Prior of the monastery, on hearing of this frightful accident, said to the bystanders, " It was in the service of St. Benedict that he got wounded, and St. Benedict will cure him."

One of the religious mentioned this to the poor sufferer, who had already been thinking of having recourse to his Medal, which he never ceased to wear. Placing it then on his leg, which was so fearfully crushed, he fastens it there with a bandage. In a very short time he falls fast asleep, and continued so till late the following morning, when he awakes, gets up without the slightest difficulty, and finds the wounds as perfectly healed, as though there had been no accident at all.

In 1861, at Chambéry, in the convent called " St. Benedict's," one of the sisters had been suffering for three months most acute pains in her legs, brought on by her having been exposed to draughts and unusually heavy work. She could not make up her mind to tell her sufferings to any one, nor had she employed any remedy. At last she resolved on making a novena in honour of St. Benedict, and during it to make use of the Medal in order to obtain the protection of the holy Patriarch. During the nine days, she used often to press the Medal strongly upon her legs, first on one, and then on the other, at the same time invoking the aid of St. Benedict, and each time the pains were relieved. She went on, however, with the heavy work which her duties in the house required of her. The first novena not having produced any other effect than mere momentary relief, she decided on a second. This was blessed with perfect success, and entirely removed the pain. The same sister, being afterwards afflicted with sore eyes, had recourse to the same remedy, and having bathed her eyes with water into which she had dipped the Medal, her sight was immediatcly strengthened, and in a few days became as good as ever it had been.

About the same time there lived in Savoy a little girl six years old, who had been, for several weeks, suffering the most excruciating pains. The child's nerves had become contracted, and to touch her, even with the tip of the finger, caused her to feel agonies of torture. In such a state as this, she could neither eat nor drink. Her parents had employed all the remedies which medical skill could suggest without success. The case was evidently an incurable one. Two sisters of the convent of St. Benedict, which we have just mentioned, went to visit the little girl (for she belonged to the school which they managed), and to offer some consolation to the mother. On reaching home they bethought themselves of the Medal of St. Benedict. They immediately sent one, with word that it should be put round the child's neck, and that she should be persuaded to swallow something into which the Medal should have been previously dipped. The mother of the little sufferer faithfully complied with the pious prescription. An immediate change was visible, and after a few days the child got up perfectly cured.

In the same country, but in the preceding year, two women were cured—one of the miliary fever after confinement, and the other of a dangerous attack of dropsy on the chest—and both of them by drinking something into which the Medal of St. Benedict had been put.

In the district of Westmoreland, Pennsylvania, during the month of August 1861, Mrs. X., a Catholic, perceived that one of her daughters was taken with a violent attack of diphtheria. It began about evening, and kept getting worse every hour. It was the more distressing owing to the difficulty of finding a doctor in that part of the country. The nearest was almost twelve miles off. The mother had great faith in the protection of St. Benedict, and had one of his Medals in her possession. She resolved on putting this Medal into a tumbler of water, and making her child drink it. She did so. The child drank the water thus sanctified by the contact of the Medal, and next morning was out of all danger.

In the early part of the year 1863, at Montigny-le-Roy, there was a woman who had been suffering for a long time the most severe attacks of earache. Clots of blood and bad matter would occasionally come forth from the ear, showing the diseased state of the organ. At length deafness came on, and the poor woman was unfit for any work. Having had a Medal of St. Benedict given to her, she put it to her ear, and said a Pater and Ave in honour of the holy Patriarch.

The moment after, she was completely cured, and could hear as well as ever she had done in her life.

The same year, at Andabres (Dep. de Hérault), Miss R. G—— was for two years threatened with a cancer on the forehead. A painful gland had formed on it, and had resisted all the remedies which medical men had employed to cure it. One evening, before retiring to rest, this young lady thought of placing on her forehead, during the night, a Medal of St. Benedict, at the same time earnestly recommending herself to the holy Patriarch's protection. She slept most soundly that night, and next morning, after taking off the Medal, found to her surprise, that the gland had entirely disappeared.

At Limoges, in the year 1864, in the house of the Sisters of St. Joseph, a postulant came to show one of her superiors her arm, in which some foreign body had entered. She was suffering most acute pains, and this led to the conjecture, that a needle had entered the flesh; and on feeling the arm it seemed evident, that certainly something of that nature must have entered. A surgeon was sent for, in the hope that by lancing the arm the poor creature might be somewhat relieved. All at once, before the doctor arrived even, the idea struck the assistant sister of having recourse to the Medal of St. Benedict. She placed it straightway on the wounded arm. After having recited together five *Our Fathers* and five *Hail Marys*, with the invocation to St. Benedict, the postulant said, " Suppose I try to draw out the needle?" "Try," answered the assistant sister. Their efforts were not of the slightest avail, and tended only to increase the pain. The assistant then said to the sister, " Press with the Medal on one side." The sister obeyed. Scarcely had she pressed it upon one side of the arm, than the needle appeared on the other, and they were able to draw it out easily, and that without causing pain. When the surgeon arrived, his services were not required.

At Montauban, in the year 1865, an invalid lady, unable to move, was confined to her bed for two years and a half, and everything seemed to forbode that she would remain thus helpless the rest of her life. One day after the priest had brought her Holy Communion, a Sister of Charity, who had just come on her accustomed visit, with some difficulty managed to place the Medal of St. Benedict between her fingers, and succeeded with great exertion in bringing the hand of the sick lady to rest upon her breast, hoping the touch of this sacred object would produce some good result. Immediately the invalid felt a thrill throughout her whole being, a copious perspiration broke out, and these words escaped her lips, " I am cured! " At once life returned to her limbs; she attempted to rise, and ridding herself of the flannels in which she had been swathed for so long a time, put on once more the clothes which she had been in the habit of wearing before her sickness. As early as the following day, she betook herself to the church to give thanks to God for her sudden cure.

Madame A. S., a lady of the diocese of Le Mans, in the year 1868, suffered intense pains in the head from neuralgia, which was caused by a decayed tooth. All ordinary remedies had been tried, and none had had any effect. The patient had recourse to the Medal of St. Benedict, and pressing it close to her cheek, held it there; but it gave her no relief. After the lapse of about half an hour, all the time holding the Medal to her cheek, she received a visit from a neighbouring friend, who had just been acquainted with the news of her illness, and the sick woman gave him an account, in a disconnected manner, of the violence of her sufferings. Her visitor, seized with compassion, suggested that perhaps a little brandy kept in her mouth for a short time, would at least deaden the pain a little. As there was no brandy in the house, he sent to his own home a person who was present, to get some, charging him to return with it quickly.

Scarcely had the messenger closed the door behind him, than the pain stopped suddenly, never more to return. St. Benedict, whose Medal had been used, only after medical aid had proved useless, would not allow material means to succeed, after use had been made of the glorious emblem of his power, and the cure of the poor sufferer was instantaneous.

CHAPTER IX.

On The Spiritual Favours Obtained By The Use Of The Medal.

THE greater number of favours obtained during our own times, by means of St. Benedict's Medal, have reference to the instantaneous conversion of sinners, who had been callous to all that had previously been tried, in order to bring them to God. We will mention a few of these instances.

In a provincial town of France, there was living a gentleman in very comfortable circumstances, who had I once held a Government appointment. His sister, an I exceedingly pious widowed lady, nursed him with the most affectionate care during his frequent attacks of illness, but was, above all, most anxious to induce her dear brother to think upon doing something for his salvation. Hitherto, all her efforts had been fruitless. No matter how gentle or indirect her attempts, they were all met with this cold answer, " Do not talk to me about seeing a priest: I cannot bear to hear the subject mentioned." The sister went, at last, to a friend, and told him in confidence of her trouble, and he said to her, "Pay no attention to your brother's answer; persevere in your entreaties. If by your silence you suffer him to fall into hell, he would surely not excuse you/' In this way several years elapsed.

In the December of 1846, after a short illness, there were evidences of gangrene; the doctors not only pronounced such to be the case, but moreover, that an operation would be useless, and finally, that the sick man could not live two days longer. The friend who had advised the sister not to be deterred by the words of her brother, one day came to see her. She was overwhelmed with grief, but declared, that not even now, had she the courage to put the question to him. "Well, then," says the friend, "take these two Medals of St. Benedict: keep one for yourself that the devil may not hinder you from doing your duty, and put the other under your brother's pillow." She took his advice, and five minutes had scarcely passed, when the following conversation took place between the brother and sister:—" Dear sister! " said the sick man. " Well, brother, what is it?" "My dear sister, do you not think it would be right to send for the priest ? "

The priest was accordingly sent for, and soon arrived: the sick man received him with joy, and all the rites of the Church were administered. Two days after he died in the most edifying dispositions.

In 1854, in an hospital of incurables, there was a woman advanced in years, who was almost entirely paralysed, and quite bedridden. With no more religion about her than that of an impious lunatic, she would utter at times such disgusting language and such horrid blasphemies, that many persons looked upon her as one possessed by the devil. There were reasons for suspecting that she kept near her certain articles, which prompted her to all this wickedness. It happened that on a day, when the ward had to undergo a thorough cleaning, she was obliged to be taken from her bed, and put for the time in a room near at hand. She screamed, or rather howled, with rage, but she was obliged to yield. The nuns of the hospital found under the mattress a bag filled with objects of a most suspicious character. They took it away, and put in its place a Medal of St. Benedict. In an hour or so the poor woman was carried back to her bed, without of course being told of what had been done. Scarcely, however, did she come near the bed than she began to abuse the sisters for having taken away her treasure, of which no doubt the devil took care to tell her. In spite of all this, she was laid on the bed, when suddenly her screaming ceased, and she became as quiet as a lamb. The hideous look she ordinarily put on was changed into one of joy. The poor creature then asked for a priest. A few days after the infirmary was arranged as a chapel, prettily lit up, and flowers placed here and there, to receive our Lord, who was coming to, comfort and cure this soul, now set free, like a captive bird, from the snares of hell.

In 1859, a poor woman was telling her troubles to a person, who knew something of the efficacy, with which our Lord has enriched the Medal of St. Benedict. Her husband, though a clever workman, was a great drunkard. All they earned was regularly spent at the end of the week, and, of course, there was nothing in the house but wretchedness. The person to whom she spoke gave her one of the Medals, advising her to touch with it the bottle of wine, which she put before her husband at meals, though she herself was obliged to be satisfied with water. When he had tasted the wine, he exclaimed, "What wretched stuff! give me some water, for it is better than such wine as this. I will make up for it after." When he had finished his dinner, he made his wife give him some money, and went to his old place, the neighbouring public-house, from which he was always accustomed to come back home, late at night, intoxicated. In about a quarter of an hour he came home, telling his wife that he was sure this was a plot against him, for the wine at the tavern was worse than their own. It was a happy night for both. Next day, and the next few days, water was the only beverage the poor man could bear to touch. When this much was gained, his wife, who was an excellent Christian, had not much difficulty in persuading him to fulfil henceforward his religious duties.

In the same year, 1859, at T——, there was a woman, eighty years old, who had declared that she was determined to die without going to confession; it was upwards of sixty years since she had been to the Sacraments. The priest, who was asked by a friend to visit her, was prepared for a refusal. A Medal was put into the priest's hand, and the person who gave it to him said, " Go, and fear not." On his entering her room, the old lady turned her face towards the wall, saying aloud that she intended going to sleep. " Do so," replied the priest, " but take this Medal, I beg of you, and meanwhile I will say a little prayer." He knelt down by the bedside, and before he had time to finish the Memorare, the old lady turned towards him, told her relatives to leave the room, and began her confession.

On the 14th of March, 1859, a pious layman happened to meet in the street a priest, who was much distressed about a young man of seventeen who had come home from Paris so ill, that the doctor was of opinion that he could not live many days. The priest had been three times to the house, but the family would not receive him. The layman on hearing this, spoke to him about the wonderful efficacy of St. Benedict's Medal, gave him one, and encouraged him to make another trial. The priest went, and at first met with the same reception. He then brought forth the Medal, which he said he wished to give to the young man. " Oh, if that is all," said the person, who was speaking to him, " you may come in." Finally, he got into the room of the young man, who no sooner saw him than he hid his face in the bedclothes. " My dear friend," said the priest, " accept this little present from me." Immediately he uncovered his face, and began his confession with the most admirable sentiments of contrition.

In 1860, an old man was received into one of the Paris hospitals, and falling seriously ill there, it was evident that he had but a very short time to live. He was a Protestant. The sisters, who had the care of the hospital, seeing that there was no chance of his recovery, lost no time in making every possible effort to secure to him the life of his soul. For this end they had made novena after novena; private and general communions had been offered up, and they had got a great many Masses said. It seemed, however, to be all of no avail. It happened one Sunday, that a friend having come to the hospital to visit the sick, and being informed of the poor Protestant who was so near death, advised them to give the sick man a Medal of St. Benedict, and in case he should refuse it, to put it under his pillow. The advice was instantly followed, and the Medal was put round the neck of the dying man. The next time the same person came to the hospital, he had the consolation of hearing, that the very Sunday he advised them to use the Medal, the Protestant had asked at twelve o'clock at night to be received into the Church. They offered to send for either of the two nearest parish priests, but he refused, saying that he would prefer the chaplain of the house, whom he happened to know. This latter, not having the faculties necessary for receiving the sick man's abjuration or for absolving him from heresy, leave was obliged to be sent for to the Archbishop, so that in spite of all the diligence that was used, it was not possible to administer the Sacraments to the sick man before nine o'clock the next morning. The old man received all the rites of the Church with great devotion, and died tranquilly in the evening of the same day.

An English Puseyite minister, a young man full of information, happened to be at T—— in 1861. He was fond of controversy, and had therefore sought an introduction to three parsons who had become zealous converts, and lived out in the country not far from the town. For nine days had the amicable discussion been going on with no result. The tenth day, May 14th, was fixed by Divine Providence for the close of these disputes, which were destined to prepare the way for an extraordinary conversion. The Puseyite minister was going back to the town, and one of his three friends being obliged to take a party of children to see the circus, which was at that time being exhibited in a field adjoining the market-place, invited him to go there with them. He did so. They reached the circus and took their tickets. Whilst the children were enjoying the amusements, our two controversialists resumed their discussion, and as their neighbours could not understand them, they were under no restraints. The entertainment was about half over, when the Puseyite interrupted the dispute, saying, " I have had quite enough; let us have no more: you can never convince me." Thus abruptly silenced, his Catholic friend was going to give all up, when he suddenly bethought himself of the wonderful things he had heard regarding the Medal of St. Benedict, and taking off the one he wore, he begged his friend to accept it. The Puseyite holds out his hand and takes the Medal. For several minutes there was silence on both sides. Meanwhile the Catholic was praying. Suddenly the Puseyite broke the silence with these words: " My dear friend, I have done wrong by holding all these long disputes. The light now beams upon me, and I wish without delay to be received into the Church." Accordingly, he made his profession of faith five days after, and the Church numbered one more in the fold of Christ.

In the town of Noyon, in France, there was a pious workwoman, who was in great trouble on account of her mother being out of her mind, and having fits from time to time, during which she was perfectly furious. People who brought work to the daughter were afraid of the poor mad mother, who would sometimes seize anything she could get hold of in the room, and throw it out of the window. There was every reason for fearing that some day or other she would destroy herself. This state of things went on for several years. But there was nothing which so afflicted the daughter as the impossibility of her mother ever getting to confession, which was the more distressing as this state of madness had seized the poor creature so suddenly, that she had not had the opportunity of settling the affairs of her conscience. In the year 1861, a pious Christian happened to give her a Medal of St. Benedict, which she contrived to put round her mother's neck. The same instant all her madness ceased—she took the Medal and kissed it unceasingly. Soon after, she made her confession in the most edifying manner. Since then, she has continued to be as gentle and quiet as a lamb, and though the infirmities of old age now oblige her to keep her bed, she never gives way to anything like impatience, and there seems to be every likelihood of her dying a happy death.*

Chapter X.

Protection Against The Snares Of The Devil.†

There is one special influence which the Medal of the holy Patriarch St. Benedict possesses, and which may be called the principal object for which God has given this gift to the faithful—the power it possesses to frustrate the devil's stratagems. We here mention a few facts which will do more than merely interest our readers; they will suggest to them what they themselves may do, should they ever find themselves in circumstances which now-a-days are anything but impossible.

In 1839, a celebrated magnetizer, who had performed several wonderful things in different towns in France, stopped at T——, where he advertised that he was going to give public performances. He took about with him to all these different places a young girl on whom he exercised his mesmerism, and he drew crowded audiences by the extraordinary effects he produced on this poor victim. In the town of which we are now speaking, he attracted an immense crowd by his advertisement. The lecture was to be given in a very large room, which anciently had been a church, but had been turned to profane uses long before this. The hour came; but nothing that the magnetizer did, had the slightest effect, and the girl remained unmoved by all his passes. The audience was dismissed,

---

* See Life of St. Benedict, chap, xxxviii.

† See Life of St. Benedict., chaps, xvi., xxx.

and the money returned to those who grumbled at being disappointed. A few hours after, placards were plastered up all over the town, announcing a second meeting, at such an hour, in the Town Hall. But this time also, the lecturer could do nothing, and after all his trouble and expense, he stole away from the town. Next day came the papers with their scientific explanations of the failure. One would have it that the room had been too hot, another that the gas was too much turned on, and the rest. Of course, none of them assigned the true cause. A nun who had happened to hear of the proposed lecture, and knowing that the Church is opposed to the practice of mesmerism, resolved on thwarting the operations of the lecturer, so far as they had any connection with the devil. All she did was to hang out of her cell window a Medal of St. Benedict, and beg the intervention of the holy Patriarch. The result was what we have related, and the prince of the power of this air,* as the Apostle calls Satan, was vanquished.

In the year 1840, the town council of S—— proposed to widen one of the streets, though it was already quite wide enough for the traffic. The measure was carried, and it was resolved that they should pull down a large portion of a church dedicated to our Blessed Lady, and much frequented by pilgrims. In order to carry out this plan, they began to build a partition wall the whole length of the church. Our Lady's altar was within the part to be taken down, and therefore was to be destroyed by this whim of the street commissioners. The wall had risen twenty feet, and one may imagine the mess and confusion in the church caused by the masons. A gentleman who was passing through the town, was grieved to see such a sad profanation, and going up to the statue of our Lady, which had been brought from its own place into the portion of the church which was to be spared, he put a Medal of St. Benedict on the pedestal. A few days after, the town surveyor, who had been mainly instrumental in this measure, died suddenly. His successor, when coming to inspect the works, soon perceived how totally unnecessary such a change was, even were it not a desecration, and stopped the works. The next day, he went before the town council and submitted to its

* Eph, ii. 2.

249

consideration so satisfactory a report upon the matter, that the first decision was revoked. The wall, which had almost reached as high as the ceiling, was taken down, and the people saw their dear old church given back to them.

In one of our French towns, a certain gentleman of high position, placed over some most important works, had in his employ a man whom the enemy of all good made use of as a tool, to lessen the influence of his master. All hopes of his amendment had been abandoned, and the evil increased day by day, when some one in the establishment put a Medal of St. Benedict over the framework of the room-door of this man who had proved so mischievous in his position of trust. From that time forward to remain in the room became next to impossible for him. On the 20th of March 18—, at twelve o'clock, the hour at which the first vespers of St. Benedict were ending, on account of its being Lent,* he threw up his employment, and on the following day, which was the feast of St. Benedict, he quitted the establishment.

Not far from the city of Rennes, there was a café and billiard-room kept by a good Catholic family. For some years they had noticed strange symptoms of the place being infested with demons. When there was no one at the billiard-table, noises and voices were sometimes heard as though there were a large party playing; pieces of furniture were changed from place to place in the house without any one of the family touching them; doors opened and shut apparently of themselves, and a strange noise was heard in the bedrooms. One Christmas night, the servant had gone up to the attic to get herself ready for midnight Mass, when she found all that part of the house filled with a thick smoke, in the midst of which there was a something, which she could not lay hold of, moving to and fro. She screamed, hurried out of the place, and fainted. But these strange appearances were frequently happening, and of course kept the inmates of the house in a state of continual alarm. They had got

---

* The ancient discipline of the Church was not to break the fast before Vespers (sunset). Therefore in Lent, from the first Sunday, to observe this very ancient tradition, Vespers are anticipated and recited before the time when the principal meal is allowed to be taken.—Ed

many Masses said for the dead, and had had the house blessed with the formula prescribed by the Church for these occasions, but up to that time all had proved ineffectual. Nothing, therefore, remained for the inmates of the house but to abandon it, though it was quite new, and they had hoped to find it a convenient and comfortable home. A pious woman spoke to them about St. Benedict's Medal, and persuaded them to make use of it. They began by putting it over every door in the house, and immediately all was quiet. But they had not thought of placing the sign of salvation in the doorway leading to the cellar, and all the fury of the evil spirits seemed to concentrate there, so great was the noise and disorder which began to be heard from that quarter. The Medal was put there also, and the influence of Satan seemed at last to have entirely quitted the house; not, however, without seeking his revenge by there and then taking possession of the person who related all this to the writer. Cruel indeed were the sufferings which the devil caused his victim to endure both in body and soul. This person, however, obtained, after some time, deliverance from this terrible trial by following the counsels of an enlightened director, who recommended the poor sufferer not to be afraid of the devil, and to pronounce frequently the holy names of Jesus, Mary, and Joseph.

In the year 1863, a community of nuns, who kept a boarding-school at A——, noticed that first the glass-lamps in the study place, and then those in the refectory of the boarding-school, were by turns broken. The drinking glasses of the lay-sisters, in like manner, were found broken in the refectory drawers. No system of supervision was able to bring to light the cause of the mischief, which was of daily occurrence. This state of affairs lasted for several weeks, when the idea came to the mind of one of the sisters of having recourse to the Medal of St. Benedict. The nuns put this Medal in the lamps and in the drawers, and forthwith the accidents ceased. But what was more astonishing still, was, that the lamps which lighted the galleries and the other rooms of the house were now attacked in their turn, and the breakages began again worse than ever. They only ceased, after the sisters had taken the resolution of employing the same means, which had been so successful in the study room and refectory of the establishment. Then at last were they freed from all further annoyances.

Chapter XI.

The Medal A Preservation In Danger.

AMONGST the effects of St. Benedict's Medal, when it is employed with a lively and simple faith, has always been ranked that of protecting us in danger. We here offer to the reader a few recent facts, which will show that the power granted to this Medal by Almighty God is far from being exhausted.

In June 1847, four Christian brothers and two other travellers were going by coach from Orleans to Lyons. They were inside passengers, and one of the gentlemen began to speak to the rest about St. Benedict's Medal, and gave one to each of the party. He was busy explaining to them the meaning of the letters, when on a sudden the horses took fright at something, set off at full gallop, and the driver soon lost all command over them. The road was being mended, and one half of the pavement had been taken up. The stones with which the road was going to be repaved had been piled up in such a manner as to serve as a barrier to keep conveyances from going on the part which was unpaved. The horses dashed across this heap of stones, dragging the coach after them. Though one side was fearfully higher than the other, it was not upset. For two or three minutes it ploughed through the soft ground on the other side of the road, then in the twinkling of an eye was dragged back again, all safe on to the good part ; and as the traces were broken by the violence of the shock, it immediately stopped, much to the relief of the passengers. This happened near a village called Chateau-Neuf (Loiret), which is about six miles from the town of Saint-Benoît-sur-Loire. The people of the village who had witnessed the narrow escape of the conveyance, cried out, " It is a miracle ! What else could have saved it ? "

A few years before this, in June 1843, a diligence was going up the very steep hill near Ecommoy, a village on the highroad between Le Mans and Tours. The horses were not able to proceed, and, suddenly stopping, were dragged back down the hill at a fearful speed. There were three passengers in the front compartment of the diligence. Opening the door, two of them jumped out on the road, but the third kept his seat, and took into his hands his Medal of St. Benedict. That very instant the diligence stopped, and the horses, which had been dragged sideways, quietly returned to the middle of the road.

It was a summer's day in the year 1858, about five o'clock in the afternoon, when a waggon heavily laden with goods was passing along the street called Rue Royale, Saint Honoré, in Paris. It had got opposite No. 4 or 6, when it stopped. It was in the middle of the street, the horses became restive, and a crowd soon collected. One of the traces broke and the front horse turned completely round. He seemed wild with fright. He raised himself upon his hind legs, and throwing up his other two as high as he could, came down with his whole weight upon another of the horses, which he began biting most savagely, and this done, he recommenced his prancing and kicking. The waggoner was most vigorous in his attempts to subdue the poor animal, pulling the reins and dealing the hardest blows he could, on the horse's head with the butt-end of the whip; but all this seemed only to irritate him the more and make things worse. The policeman who was on the spot assisted the driver in his attempts, and the spectators were busy, as usual on such occasions, vociferating their advice, and yet all to no effect. In the crowd there was a good Christian who had learned by experience how powerful is the intercession of St. Benedict. Seeing the danger, he took the Medal in his hand, at the same time addressing a short ejaculation to the holy Patriarch. Scarcely had his lips pronounced the prayer, when the horse, which was still wild with rage, became suddenly quiet, allowing himself to be patted and then led to his place.

One beautiful morning of the same summer, and in the same city, two soldiers in half-uniform had been giving some exercise to the horses of which they had the management. They were returning to barracks and had got opposite the mayor's courthouse of district No. 1, when the following scene took place, and attracted the attention of the idle and curious who were passing along the street called

Rue Anjou, Saint Honoré. One of the horses suddenly stopped, and turning sideways, nothing that his rider did could induce the animal to move.* In front of the courthouse was an open space. It was facing this that the horse stood just as though he were riveted to the earth. Every now and then he shook his whole body. One of the passers-by was a person who had great faith in the Medal of St. Benedict : he had not quite come up to the spot, but as well as he could judge at the distance, he could not help thinking that the enemy of mankind might very possibly have something to do with all this. Afraid of an accident happening, he recited to himself the words of which the initials are engraven on the Medal : *Vade retro, Satana, &c.* No sooner had he finished the formula, than the horse began to prance and rear, and then became immovable as before.

The individual of whom we just spoke, and who was now very near to the courthouse, perceiving that, the rider was still in the same difficulty, took his Medal into his hand, and said this little prayer : " Glorious St. Benedict, beseech our Lord that he, by thy intercession, may make these horses docile to the command of their riders, and deliver them from danger." The stubborn animal at once proceeded quietly onwards, and cantered up to the other, which had been waiting. The unknown liberator asked a woman who was standing on the pavement at the corner of the street Suresnes, if the horses had been standing there a long time. She told him they had been there for a quarter of an hour.

During the winter of 1858-59, the same person was in Paris, and was just turning into the street Miromesnil. His attention was attracted by seeing a crowd standing on the footpath opposite this street; and the stoppage, he found, was caused by a horse which would not stir one inch farther, in spite of all the beating and spurring of the groom who was riding him. Anxious to see what was the matter, he stopped, and saw that the animal obstinately refused to proceed. The groom at length was obliged to rest, and called for a glass of something to drink to revive his courage and strength. Thinking that Satan might have something to do with such strange perversity, the person we allude to, resolved on having recourse to

* See Life of St. Benedict, chap. ix.

his Medal of St. Benedict. Scarcely had he finished the words which are marked on the Medal, than the horse set off at a gallop along the Avenue Marigny. In spite of this, he still feared the snares of the invisible enemy, so whilst proceeding on his way he kept his eyes on the horse and rider. His fears were soon realised, for the horse had not gone half-way up the avenue, when he suddenly stopped again and turned round as before. The good man then took his Medal into his hand, and said this short prayer: " O glorious St. Benedict, ask of our Lord that he may, by thy intercession, render this his creature obedient to man and harmless." The horse instantly became tractable, and the groom turning him to the right into the Champs Elysées, they soon were out of sight.

On Sunday, the 28th of November 1858, Henry S——, a boy of fourteen, who was apprenticed to M. P——, a jeweller in Paris, happened to meet in the street a person whom he knew to be a friend who took an interest in his family. After a cordial greeting and a few words of conversation, the young man received from the friend a Medal of St. Benedict, as a protection against the dangers to which we are all so much exposed. On the following Thursday, which was the 2d of December, our young apprentice was sliding down the banisters of the staircase, when, seeing that some one was coming up, and afraid of coming against him, he leaned forward, lost his balance, and fell down nearly two stories. In his fall, he came with his side against the banister of the lower story, and the violence of the shock sent him back on to the last step of the landing, where he found himself sitting, with no other injury than being stunned by the fall. He immediately returned to the workshop and resumed his employment. His master, however, fearing that such an accident might produce some fatal result, in spite of there being nothing just then which could give the slightest ground of alarm, sent him home for a few days' perfect rest. Nothing, however, like an indisposition came on, and the young man could not help attributing his extraordinary escape to the power of St. Benedict's Medal, which had so very opportunely been given him to wear.

At Tours, in 1859, a young gentleman was taking a lesson of exercises at a public gymnasium of the town. He was going through one of the feats, which consisted in pulling himself up to a horizontal beam, on which he was then to hang, holding on by his hands and feet. He had scarcely accomplished this than the beam gave way, and he fell fifteen feet flat upon his back on the ground with the beam upon him. The master of the gymnasium, who was present, uttered a cry of alarm; but the young man jumped up, and taking his Medal of St. Benedict showed it to him, saying, " I am all right! I assure you I am not hurt! See what has saved me."

In the February of 1859, a nurse happened to be walking with a little child in the gardens of the Tuileries. It was about three o'clock in the afternoon, and the Emperor was passing. The nurse could not resist her curiosity, so she set off running by the side of the Emperor's carriage, was soon lost in the thick of the crowd, and forgot all about her little charge whom she left behind. The little fellow, seeing himself thus left alone, began to make his way home, which was in the street called Rue Saint Florentin, No. 4. There was a perfect stream of carriages passing just at this exciting moment along the Rue de Rivoli, but the brave little fellow was not afraid. He boldly crossed the street and reached home. His parents were alarmed at seeing him come home by himself; they asked him how he had lost his nurse, and when his sister, who was a year or so older than himself, was exclaiming and asking how in the world he had got home without being run over, " I had round my neck the Medal of St. Benedict," said the child very coolly; " and just as I was going to cross the street, the carriages made such a noise! but they let me run across."

In 1859, a community of nuns, whose special object was the education of young ladies, had just finished building a large dormitory for their boarders. It was now ready for use, and both parents and children were delighted with the excellent accommodation which the new building afforded, for besides the dormitory, there were also several parlours on the ground-floor. But not many weeks elapsed, before much alarm was caused by crackings being heard all over the building. At first they were thought to be the creaking which is sometimes heard in rooms newly boarded; but they became so loud and threatening, that the parents began to talk of taking their children from the school. In vain did the architect assure them that the building was perfectly safe; the nuns were obliged to pacify them by removing all the children from the new dormitory, and promising every possible precaution against accident. They would have begun at once to build another dormitory, but they had spent all their available funds over the one which now proved such a disappointment. A friend of the convent, to whom two of the nuns happened to mention their trouble, advised their having recourse to St. Benedict. He recommended them to put a Medal of the holy Patriarch on each story of the new building, and four down into the foundations, one on each side, reciting meanwhile five times Gloria Patri in honour of the Passion, three times Ave Maria in honour of our Lady, and lastly, three times Gloria Patri in honour of St. Benedict. His advice was followed ; nothing more was heard of the noises which had caused so much alarm, and the community returned fervent thanks to God, to our Lady, and to St. Benedict, for the protection thus visibly granted to them.

In July 1859, at Paris a gentleman was passing on horseback up the Avenue Gabrielle. He happened to come up to that part of the Avenue which is at the back of the Elysée Garden, just as one of the gardeners was watering the beds with one of the large tubes. A cart loaded with wood had been stopped in this very place, in consequence of an accident which had happened to a carriage. The gush of the watering machine frightened the gentleman's horse, which suddenly turning round, galloped back some distance. The rider encouraged the animal to return, and shouted out to the gardener to stop watering for a moment whilst he passed. No attention was paid to this request, and the horse again shied, and again galloped back. Once more the rider urged him by spur and whip to the dreaded spot, and at a furious speed he at last passed it, but in doing so, came with such a shock against the wheel of the cart, that the girth of the saddle was torn and the stirrups got twisted. The gentleman had foreseen the danger, and had pulled his foot out of the stirrup, but in doing so he threw himself so much on the other side as completely to lose his balance, and was thrown over the head of his horse, which passed over him without trampling on him. The poor animal had taken fright at the shower of water which came spurting out in every direction, and though the rider had done his best to pull him clear from the cart, which stood, as we have said, upon the road, yet he dashed against it with all his weight. The gentleman had on his person the Medal of St. Benedict, and felt nothing whatever from the fall but a little stiffness in his limbs. The horse was badly cut by the cart-wheel on his side and hind leg, and for twelve days was unfit for use. The saddle was taken to a saddler in the street Suresnes, and several persons who had witnessed the accident expressed to the rider their surprise at his having escaped without a single scar.

A Medal of St. Benedict had been given to a poor woman who had just lost her husband, and was living by herself in a lonely cottage some distance from Rennes (in France). She was extremely nervous at having to live thus alone, and as a protection against danger she accepted the Medal from a good Christian who lived in the town. In the year 1862, an unhappy wretch, who had just come out of prison, was prowling all about the neighbourhood. He at last hit on a plan for getting into some of the houses round about: he would set the widow's cottage on fire—the people of the neighbourhood would leave their houses and run to the spot, and whilst they were out, he might go in and do his work. An opportunity soon presented itself. The poor widow was spending an hour or two with a neighbour. Suddenly she felt unusually anxious, and declared that she must go home. She is no sooner there than she sees a cloud of smoke coming from the little stable adjoining her cottage, and a man running across the field as though he were trying to make his escape. Without giving herself time for reflection, she set off running after the man, and was not long in discovering him to be the very individual who, not long before, had come to her door begging for something to drink. Whilst pursuing him she screamed for help, and a farmer hearing her, rushed out of his house with his servants, and recognised in the fugitive the man who had attacked him only a few nights before. They were not long before they caught him. He was handed over to the police, and finally sentenced to fourteen years' penal servitude. When in court, he confessed publicly that he had done his utmost to set fire to the widow's cottage, but not being able to succeed, he threw a lighted faggot into the stable, and then went his way. His attempt to burn down the house did not do the slightest injury either to the stable or to the house.

During the month of April 1864, M. D——, of the city of Tours, narrated to us the following incident: He was a visitor at the watering-place of Bourbon-Sancy, during the summer months of one of the preceding years, when a thunderbolt happened to strike one of the houses there and reduced it to ashes. One room only, occupied by two poor girls, escaped destruction. No one could explain so unaccountable an escape, so that all the town flocked to gaze at this marvel. M. D—— also betook himself to the spot in company with some of the bathers. After having closely examined the arrangement of the various portions of the building, and listened to the story of the inhabitants, he had no hesitation in believing that there had taken place some supernatural intervention. He even felt within himself that St. Benedict had not been a stranger to the event, and taking from his pocket a Medal of the holy Patriarch, he offered it to these good young girls. But hardly had they caught sight of the little present he was offering them, when they exclaimed, " But we already have that Medal. Yesterday our brother, having been to water some horses, met a person who had some of those Medals, and knowing that it would give us great pleasure, he asked for one, which he brought home to us *some minutes before the storm.* "

CHAPTER XII.

On Devotion To St. Benedict.

GOD has vouchsafed to make choice of his servant Benedict, and to associate the merits of this holy Patriarch with the divine virtue of the sacred cross engraved on the Medal which we have described in these pages. This fact seems to require that we should add, in conclusion, a few words, in order to recommend to the faithful a devotion towards so powerful a protector.

The motive for our having a special devotion to any particular saint, is generally based on the merits of that saint, merits which give more than ordinary power to his intercession with God for us. Now, if we consider all that grace has worked in St. Benedict, and all that St. Benedict has done, by himself and by his children, for the honour of God, the salvation of souls, and the service of the Church, we are led to think that amongst the friends of God, and amongst those whom he has mercifully glorified, there are few whose intercession can be more powerful.

That Rule, so holy and so full of wisdom, which for more than five centuries was the only one in all the monasteries of the West!—may we not justly consider it as dictated by the Holy Ghost, to the man who was chosen to write it, and to give it his own name? Those thousands of saints which it has produced, and who gloried in being children of St. Benedict, are they not so many stars which shine in heaven round this bright sun ? Whole nations converted from paganism to the Christian faith by his disciples, do they not proclaim him to be their father ? The numerous bands of martyrs who honour Benedict with the title of their leader, do they not give him the right to claim a share in the merits of their combats ? That almost countless multitude of sainted bishops who have governed so many churches, and that constellation of holy doctors who have taught the sacred sciences and fought against the heresies of their time, do they not also render homage to him whom they all honoured here on earth as their master ? The thirty Sovereign Pontiffs whom the Benedictine Rule has given to the Church, and of whom so many were engaged in carrying out measures of the highest importance to the defence and well-being of Christendom, do they not also bear testimony to the deep wisdom of the inspired legislator, under whose guidance they passed so many years in the cloister ? In a word, so many millions of souls who have; during the last thirteen hundred years, consecrated themselves to God under the holy and immortal Rule of St. Benedict, do they not form round his venerable head an everlasting crown, which is the admiration of the elect ?

All these motives justify every effort which we can make, to persuade Christians, who love to honour those who have been heroes of sanctity, to cultivate a devotion towards the great Patriarch, in whom God seems to have united everything that can give us an idea of the immense glory wherewith he has crowned him in heaven. Let us therefore have recourse to St. Benedict in our necessities; he has power to grant all we ask him; and that wonderfully paternal lovingness which formed quite a leading characteristic of his soul, whilst he was here on earth, (as we learn from the account of his admirable life given us by St Gregory the Great), that same paternal sweetness is still, now that he is enjoying the happiness of heaven, the peculiarity of his intercession for his clients on earth.*

He appeared one day to St. Gertrude, his illustrious daughter. The holy virgin, overwhelmed with admiration at the contemplation of his merits, reminded him of his glorious death, when in the church of Monte Cassino, on the 21st of March 543, after having received the Body and Blood of Our Lord, supported in the arms of his disciples, and standing, as it were, in the attitude of a valiant combatant, he breathed forth his soul to his God whilst uttering his last prayer. She then ventured to ask him, in the name of this his so precious a death, that he would vouchsafe to assist by his presence, at their last moments, each of her Religious who were then living in the convent of which she was abbess. Relying upon the credit which he possessed with the Sovereign Lord of all things, the holy Patriarch thus answered her, with that sweet authority which accompanied his words even whilst he was here on earth: "Every one who shall honour me for the privilege wherewith my Divine Master so graciously enriched my death, I promise to be present at his death and assist him. I will be to him as a protection against all those snares which the devils will cruelly lay for him; and comforted by my presence, he shall escape them all, and obtain the bliss of heaven, and there be for ever happy."† So consoling a promise made by such a servant of God, and authenticated by such a noble

---

* " Give us great hearts, dear Father!—hearts as wide
　　As thine, that was wider than the world;—
　　Hearts by incessant labour sanctified,
　　Yet with the peace of prayer within them furled."—Faber.

† St. Gertrudis, Insinuationes Divinae Pietatis, lib. iv. cap. II.

spouse of the Saviour of the world, has inspired the children of St. Benedict with the pious thought of composing a special prayer, in accordance with the intention specified by their Patriarch, in order thus to ensure, to those who recite it, the blessing which he has deigned to promise them. We here give this prayer, with the desire that it may become known and used by the faithful, and secure to them a happy death.

Antiphon.

Benedict, the beloved of our Lord, whilst standing in the church, having been fortified with the Body and Blood of the Lord, supporting his failing limbs on the arms of his disciples, with his hands upraised to heaven, breathed forth his soul amidst words of prayer, and was seen ascending into heaven by a path most richly hung with tapestry, and lit up with countless lamps.

V. Thou didst appear glorious in the sight of the Lord.

R. Therefore did he clothe thee with beauty.

PRAYER.

O God! who didst adorn the precious death of most holy Father Benedict, with so many and so great privileges; grant, we beseech thee, that at our death we may be defended from the snares of our enemies, by the blessed presence of him whose memory we celebrate. Through Christ our Lord. Amen.

Another Prayer in Honor of St. Benedict for a Happy Hour of Death.

O holy Father, blessed by God both in grace and in name, who, whilst standing in prayer with thy hands raised to heaven, didst most happily yield thy angelic spirit into the hands of thy Creator; and hast promised zealously to defend against all the snares of the enemy, in the last struggle of death, those who should daily remind thee of thy glorious departure and thy heavenly joys; protect me, I beseech thee, O glorious Father, this day and every day, by thy holy blessing; that I may never be separated from our blessed Lord, from the society of thyself, and of all the blessed. Through the same Christ our Lord. Amen.*

A Prayer of St. Gertrude in Honor of St. Benedict.

I salute thee, through the Heart of Jesus, O great St. Benedict! I rejoice in thy glory, and I give thanks to our Lord for all the benefits which he has showered upon thee; I praise Him, and glorify Him, and offer thee, for an increase of thy joy and honor, the most gentle Heart of Jesus. Deign therefore, O beloved Father, to pray for us that we may become according to the Heart of God. Amen.

BOOK THREE

LIFE OF SAINT BENEDICT

THE GREAT PATRON OF WESTERN CIVILIZATION

SAINT GREGORY THE GREAT

LIFE OF ST. BENEDICT

PATRIARCH OF THE WESTERN MONKS

The life of St. Benedict was written in Latin by St. Gregory the Great. The text of the English translation is taken with very few changes, from an old manuscript dated 1638.

∾

INTRODUCTION*

The life of St. Benedict is related to us by Pope Gregory the Great, who, being a relative of the great Patriarch, and a member of his Order, was particularly qualified for this task. Pope Gregory was not personally acquainted with St. Benedict, as the latter died when Gregory (540–604) was but three years old. But he lived and associated with St. Benedict's disciples, and was informed by them, as faithful eye-witnesses, of the life and deeds of this great man. Those who contributed to the facts recorded by Pope Gregory are the following: Abbot Constantine, first successor of St. Benedict in the monastery of Monte Cassino; Abbot Valentinian who directed the monastery of the Lateran; Simplicius, third Abbot of Monte Cassino; and finally Honoratus, who was Abbot of Subiaco at the time of St. Gregory. These are the commanding authorities to which he refers in portraying to us the life of the Patriarch of monks.

The Downfall of the Roman Empire.

With regard to Church and state, never was the condition of Europe, so sad and deplorable as at the time when St. Benedict was born. A total downfall of existing conditions had taken place; all

---

* In this third book the Introduction, Conclusion, and the visions of Bl. Anne Catherine Emmerich, are taken from the 1914 edition of *The Very Rev. Father Paul of Moll.*

bonds of order seemed dissolved, and civil laws and authorities done away with. More than ever was the Church infected with heresy and schism. The greater number of the European nations adopted the heresies of Arius, Nestorius and Eutyches. Some countries such as Germany and England, were still in the darkness of paganism. The Roman empire, that gigantic union of two hundred millions of people under Emperor Augustus, was overthrown amid the invasions of the barbarous hordes from the North, who, penetrating into the heart of Europe, devastated the entire country, and spreading to the South and West, brought about that immense movement known in history, as the migration of nations. In Italy alone, the Ostrogoths had founded a kingdom which was effectually governed by several kings, such as Theodoric the Great, Totila, and others.

A Prey to Heresy and Barbarism.

These unsteady conditions and ever changing circumstances were most detrimental to the Church. The new barbarous tribes, it is true, embraced Christianity, nevertheless, they were to a great extent given to the Arian heresy, and thus the countries in which the first disciples of Christ had preached the Gospel, became a prey to heresy and barbarism. It was, therefore, necessary that the world should be reconquered for Christ. And this enormous work of conversion was in great measure effected by St. Benedict, through the organization of his renowned Order of monks in the West. This holy Order God had chosen for His Church, in establishing the Christian world upon the ruins of the dilapidated Roman empire, and in instructing and civilizing the new tribes unto Christ and Christian society. "It is wonderful," says a historian, "how Divine Providence has manifested its care for the Church, by calling St. Benedict for this great work. Because at the very time when all Italy, France, Spain, and the northern coast of Africa were in the possession of the Goths and Vandals, and almost the entire East was infected with heresy—in this frightful darkness, so bright a light shone forth from St. Benedict and his Order, that the whole world was thereby illumined."

St. Benedict of Noble Family.

St. Benedict was born in the year 480, at Nursia, a city in southern Italy. He was descended from the Anicians, a noble Roman family, which numbered among its members most renowned men: senators, generals and even saints. His father's name was Eupropius, his mother's Abundantia, his pious and holy twin sister whom he cherished with tender affection his life long, was called Scholastica. Regarding the early years of St. Benedict and St. Scholastica little is known; but we rejoice in the possession of a beautiful "vision" of Anna Catherine Emmerich, which contains a very touching description of the childhood years of the twin brother and sister. For the edification and instruction of the reader, it is here inserted.

The Vision of Anna Catherine Emmerich.

"Through the relics of St. Scholastica, I saw many scenes in her life and that of St. Benedict. I saw their paternal home in a great city, not far from Rome. It was not built entirely in the Roman style. Before it was a paved courtyard whose low wall was surmounted by a red latticework, and behind lay another court with a garden and a fountain. In the garden was a beautiful summer-house overrun with vines, and here I saw Benedict and his little sister Scholastica, playing as loving, innocent children are wont to amuse themselves. The flat ceiling of the summer-house was painted all over with figures, which at first I thought sculptured, so clearly were their outlines defined.

"The brother and sister were very fond of each other and so nearly of the same age that I thought them twins. The birds flew in familiarly at the windows, with flowers and twigs in their beaks and sat looking intently at the children who were playing with flowers and leaves, planting sticks and making gardens. I saw them writing and cutting all sorts of figures out of colored stuffs. Occasionally their nurse came to look after them.

"Their parents seemed to be people of wealth, who had much business on hand, for I saw about twenty persons employed in the house; but they did not seem to trouble themselves about their children. The father was a large, powerful man, dressed in the Roman style; he took his meals with his wife and some other members of the family in the lower part of the house, whilst the children lived entirely upstairs in separate apartments. Benedict had for preceptor an old ecclesiastic with whom he stayed almost all the time; and Scholastica had a nurse near whom she slept. The brother and sister were not often allowed to be alone together; but whenever they could steal off for a while, they were very gleeful and happy. I saw Scholastica by her nurse's side, learning some kind of work. In the room adjoining that in which she slept stood a table on which lay in baskets the material for her work, a variety of colored stuff, from which she cut figures of birds, flowers, etc., to be sewed on other larger pieces. When finished they looked as if carved on the groundwork.

"The ceilings of the rooms, like that of the summer-house, were covered with different colored pictures. The windows were not glass: they were of some kind of stuff on which were embroidered all sorts of figures, trees, lines, and pointed ornaments. Scholastica slept on a low bed behind a curtain. I saw her in the morning when her nurse left the room, spring out of bed and prostrate in prayer before a crucifix on the wall. When she heard the nurse returning she used to slip quickly behind the curtain and be in bed again before the nurse entered the room. I saw Benedict and Scholastica separately learning from the former's tutor. They read from great rolls of parchment, and they painted letters in red, gold, and an extraordinarily fine blue; as they wrote they rolled the parchment. They made use of an instrument about as long as one's finger. The older the children grew, the less were they allowed to be together.

"I saw Benedict at Rome, when about fourteen years old, in a large building in which there was a corridor with many rooms. It looked like a school or a monastery. There were many young men and some old ecclesiastics in a large hall, as if at a holiday feast. The ceilings were adorned with the same kind of paintings as those in Benedict's home. The guests did not eat reclining. They sat on round seats so low that they were obliged to stretch out their feet; some sat on one side, back to back, at a very low table. There were holes hollowed in the massive table to receive the yellow plates and dishes; but I did not see much food, only three large plates of flat, yellow cakes in the center of the table.

"When all had finished, I saw six females of different ages, relatives of the youths, enter the hall, carrying something like sweetmeats and little flasks in baskets on their arms. The young men arose and conversed with their friends at one end of the hall, eating the dainties and drinking from the flasks. There was one woman about thirty years of age, whom I had once before seen at Benedict's home. She approached the young man with an enticing mien; but he, perfectly innocent, suspected nothing bad in her. I saw that she hated his purity and entertained a sinful love for him. She gave him a poisoned, an enchanted drink from a flask. Benedict suspected nothing, but I saw him that evening in his cell restless and tormented. He went, at last, to a man and asked permission to go down into the courtyard, for he never went out without leave. There he knelt in a corner of the yard, disciplining himself with long thorn branches and nettles. I saw him later on, when a hermit, helping this his would-be seducer who had fallen into deep distress precisely because she had sought to tempt him. Benedict had been interiorly warned of her guilt.

"Afterwards I saw Benedict on a high, rocky mountain when, perhaps in his twentieth year. He had hollowed out a cell for himself in the rock. To this he added a passage and another cell, and then several cells all cut in the rock; but only the first opened outside. Before it he had planted an avenue of trees. He arched them and ornamented the vaulted roof with pictures which seemed to be made of many small stones put together. In one cell I saw three such pictures; heaven in the center, the nativity of Christ on one side, the last judgment on the other. In the last our Lord was represented sitting on an arch, a sword issuing from His mouth; below, between the elect and the reprobate, stood an angel with a pair of scales. Benedict had besides made a representation of a monastery with its abbot, and crowds of monks in the background. He seemed to have had a foresight of his own monastery.

"More than once I saw Benedict's sister, who lived at home, going on foot to visit her brother. He never allowed her to stay with him over night. Sometimes she brought him a roll of parchment which she had written. Then he showed her what he had done, and they conversed together on divine things. Benedict was always very grave in his sister's presence whilst she, in her innocence, was mirthful and joyous. When she found him too serious, she turned to God in prayer, and he instantly became like herself, bright and gay.

"Later on I saw her under her brother's direction, establishing a convent on a neighboring mountain, distant only a short day's journey. To it flocked numbers of religious women. I saw her teaching them to chant: they had no organs. Organs have been very prejudical to singing. They make of it only a secondary affair. The nuns prepared all the church ornaments themselves in the same kind of needlework that Scholastica had learned when a child at home. On the refectory table was a large cloth on which were all sorts of figures, pictures, and sentences, so that each religious always had before her that to which she was especially obliged. Scholastica spoke to me of the sweets and consolations of spiritual labor and the labor of ecclesiastics.

"I always saw Scholastica and Benedict surrounded by tame birds. Whilst the former was yet in her father's house, I used to see doves flying from her to Benedict in the desert; and in the convent I saw around her doves and larks bringing her red, white, yellow and violet-blue flowers. Once I saw a dove bringing her a rose with a leaf. I cannot repeat all the scenes of her life that were shown me, for I am so sick and miserable! Scholastica was purity itself. I see her in heaven as white as snow. With the exception of Mary and Magdalen, I know of no saint so loving." Thus far the "vision" of Anna Catherine Emmerich.

THE LIFE AND MIRACLES OF SAINT BENEDICT
BY ST. GREGORY THE GREAT.

There was a man of venerable life, Benedict by name and grace, who from the time of his very childhood carried the heart of an old man. His demeanour indeed surpassing his age, he gave himself no disport or pleasure, but living here upon earth he despised the world with all the glory thereof, at such time as he might have most freely enjoyed it. He was born in the province of Nursia of honourable parentage and sent to Rome to study the liberal sciences. But when he saw there many through the uneven paths of vice run headlong to their own ruin, he drew back his foot, but new-set in the world, lest, in the search of human knowledge, he might also fall into the same dangerous precipice. Contemning therefore learning and studies and abandoning his father's house and goods, he desired only to please God in a virtuous life. Therefore he departed skilfully ignorant and wisely unlearned. I have not attained unto all this man did, but the few things which I here set down, were related to me by four of his disciples; namely, Constantine, a very reverend man, who succeeded him in the government of the Monastery; Valentinian, who for many years bore rule in the Monastery of Lateran; Simplicius, who was the third superior of that congregation after him; and Honoratus who yet governeth the Monastery which he first inhabited.

Chapter I.

Benedict having now left the schools resolved to betake himself to the desert, accompanied only by his nurse who most tenderly loved him. Coming therefore to a place called Affile, and remaining for some time in the Church of St. Peter by the charitable invitement of many virtuous people who lived there for devotion, so it chanced that his nurse borrowed of a neighbour a sieve to cleanse wheat, which being left carelessly upon the table was found broken in two pieces. Therefore on her return finding it broke, she began to weep bitterly because it was only lent her. But the religious and pious boy, Benedict, seeing his nurse lament was moved with compassion, and taking with him the two pieces of the broken sieve, with tears he gave himself to prayer, which no sooner ended, but he found the sieve whole, and found not any sign that it had been broken. Then presently he restored the sieve which had been broken, whole to his nurse, to her exceeding comfort. This matter was divulged unto all that lived thereabout, and so much admired by all, that the inhabitants of that place caused the sieve to be hanged up in the Church porch, that not only those present, but all posterity might know with how great gifts of grace Benedict had been endowed from the beginning of his conversion. The sieve remained to be seen for many years after, and hung over the Church door even until the times of the Longobards.

But Benedict more desirous to suffer afflictions than covetous of praise; and rather willing to undergo labours for the honour of God, than to be extolled with the favours of this world, fled secretly from his nurse to a remote place in the desert called Subiaco, distant about forty miles from Rome, in which a fountain springing with cool and crystal waters, extendeth itself at first into a broad lake, and running farther with increase of waters becometh at the last a river. As he was travelling to this place, a certain monk called Romanus met him and asked whither he was going. Having understood his intention, he both kept it secret and afforded him help, moreover he gave him a religious habit and assisted him in all things. The man of God being come to this place lived for the space of three years in an obscure cave, unknown to any man except Romanus the Monk, who lived not far off in a Monastery governed by Father Deodatus. But he would piously steal forth, and on certain days bring to Benedict a loaf of bread which he had spared from his own allowance. But there being no way to the cave from Romanus his cell by reason of a steep and high rock which hung over it, Romanus used to let down the loaf by a long cord to which also he fastened a little bell, that by the sound of it, the man of God might know when Romanus brought him the bread, and going out may receive it. But the old enemy, envying the charity of the one and the refection of the other, when on a certain day he beheld the bread let down in this manner, threw a stone and brake the bell. Notwithstanding, Romanus afterwards failed not to assist him in the best manner he was able. Now when it pleased Almighty God that Romanus should rest from his labours, and that the life of Benedict should be manifest to the world for an example to all men, that the candle set upon a candlestick might shine and give light to the whole Church of God, our Lord vouchsafed to appear to a certain Priest living far off, who had make ready his dinner for Easter Day, saying to him: "Thou hast prepared good cheer for thyself, and My servant in such a place is famished for hunger." Who presently rose up, and on the solemn day of Easter went towards the place with such meat as he had provided for himself, where seeking the man of God, amongst craggy rocks, winding valleys and hollow pits he found him hid in a cave. Then after prayers, and blessing the Almighty Lord, they sat down, and after some spiritual discourse the Priest said: "Rise, and let us take our refection, for this is Easter Day." To whom the man of God answered: "I know it is Easter, because I have found so much favour as to see thee." (For not having a long time conversed with men, he did not know it was Easter Day.) The good Priest did therefore again affirm it, saying: "Truly this is the day of our Lord's Resurrection, and therefore it is not fit that you should keep abstinence, and for this cause I am sent that we may eat together that which Almighty God hath bestowed on us." Whereupon blessing God, they fell to their meat. Their discourse and dinner ended, the Priest returned to his Church. About the same time certain shepherds found him hid in a cave; who, at the first, spying him among the bushes, clothed in the skins of beasts, took him for some wild beast, but afterwards knowing him to be a servant of God, many of them were converted from their savage life to virtue. By this means his name began to be famous in the country, and many did resort unto him, bringing with them necessaries for his body, while they received from his lips the food of life.

CHAPTER II

How he overcame a temptation of the flesh.

The holy man being on a certain day alone, the tempter was at hand; for a little black bird, commonly called an ousel, began to fly about his face, and that so near as the holy man, if he would. might have taken it with his hand; but no sooner had he made the sign of the cross than the bird vanished. When presently so great a carnal temptation assailed him, that before the holy man had never felt the like. For the remembrance of a woman which some time he had seen, was so lively represented to his fancy by the wicked spirit, and so vehemently did her image inflame his breast with lustful desires, that almost overcome by pleasure, he was determining to leave the wilderness. But suddenly assisted with divine grace he came to himself, and, seeing near him a thicket full of nettles and briars, he threw off his garments and cast himself naked into the midst of those sharp thorns and nettles, where he rolled himself so long, that, when he rose up, all his body was pitifully rent; thus by the wounds of his flesh he cured those of his soul, by turning pleasure into pain; and by the vehemence of outward torments he extinguished the unlawful flame which burnt within overcoming sin by changing the fire. After which time, as he himself related to his disciples, he was so free from the like temptation, that he never felt any such motion.

Many after this began to forsake the world and to hasten to put themselves under his government. Being now altogether free from vice, he worthily deserved to be made a master of virtue. As it is commanded by Moses that the Levites should serve from five and twenty years and upward, and after fifty years they should be appointed to keep the holy vessels.

PETER.

I have already understood something of this testimony alleged, yet I pray make it more plain unto me.

GREGORY.

It is manifest, Peter, that in youth the temptations of the flesh are great, but after fifty natural heat waxeth cold: now the souls of good men are the holy vessels. Therefore while the elect are in temptation, it is necessary that they live under obedience, and be wearied with labours, but when, by reason of their age, the fervour of temptations is assuaged, they are ordained keepers of holy vessels, that is become instructors of souls.

PETER.

I confess what you say has given me full satisfaction, and therefore this place of Scripture being clearly expounded, I pray you hasten on with the holy man's life which you have begun.

CHAPTER III.

How St. Benedict brake a glass by the sign of the cross.

Having thus vanquished this temptation, the man of God like a good soil well manured and weeded, brought forth abundant fruit of the seed of virtue, so that his fame began to spread itself more largely. Not far off was a Monastery, whose Abbot being dead, the whole Convent repaired to the venerable man Benedict, and with earnest persuasions requested him for their Abbot, which he refused for a long time, forewarning them that his manner of life and theirs were not agreeable; yet at length overcome with importunity he gave consent. But when in the same Monastery he began to observe regular discipline, so that none of the Monks (as in former time) were permitted by their disorder to swerve any way form the path of virtue, which receiving they fell into a great rage, and began accusing themselves of their choice in receiving him for a Superior, whose integrity of life was disproportionate to their perverseness.

And therefore, when they perceived themselves restrained from unlawful acts, it grieved them to leave their desires, and hard it was to relinquish old customs and begin a new life, besides the conversation of good men is always odious to the wicked, they began therefore to plot his death, and after consultation had together, they poisoned his wine. So when the glass which contained the empoisoned drink was, according to the custom of the Monastery, presented at table to be blessed by the Abbot, Benedict putting forth his hand and making the sign of the Cross, the glass which was held far off brake in pieces, as if instead of blessing the vase of death, he had thrown a stone against it. By this the man of God perceived that the glass had in it the drink of death which could not endure the sign of life. So presently rising up with a mild countenance and tranquil mind, having called the Brethren together, he thus spake unto them: "Almighty God of His mercy forgive you, Brethren, why have you dealt thus with me? Did not I foretell you that my manner of life and yours would not agree? Go, and seek a Superior to your liking; for you can have me no longer with you." This said, he forthwith returned to the solitude he loved so well, and lived there with himself, in the sight of Him who seeth all things.

PETER.

I do not well understand what you mean: "He lived with himself."

GREGORY.

If the holy man had been longer constrained to govern those who had unanimously conspired against him, and were so contrary to him in life and manners, it might, peradventure, have diminished his own vigour and fervour of devotion, withdrawing his mind from the light of contemplation. So that over much busied in correcting the faults of others, he might have neglected his own; and so perhaps lost himself, and yet not gained others. For as often as by contagious motions we are transported out of ourselves we remain the same, but not with ourselves, because not looking into our own actions, we are wandering about other things. For do we think that he was with himself who went into a far country, consumed the portion allotted to him, and, after he had put himself into the service of a citizen of that country, kept his hogs, and was glad to eat the husks which they are: notwithstanding, when he began to consider what he had lost, as the Scripture testifieth: "Being come to himself, he said: how many hirelings in my father's house have plenty of bread." If, therefore, he were before with himself, how was it true that he returned to himself?

I may well say, therefore, that his holy man lived with himself, because he never turned the eye of his soul from himself, but standing always on his guard with great circumspection, he kept himself continually in the all-seeing eye of his Creator.

PETER.

How is it then to be understood, which is written of the Apostle Peter, when he was led by the Angel out of the prison? Who returning to himself said: "Now I know assuredly that the Lord hath sent his Angel, and hath delivered me out of the hands of Herod, and from all the expectation of the people of the Jews."

GREGORY.

Two ways, Peter, we are carried out of ourselves: for either by sinfulness of thought we fall beneath ourselves, or by the grace of contemplation we are raised above ourselves. He therefore, that kept the hogs, by his inconstancy of mind and uncleanness, fell beneath himself: but he, whom the Angel loosed and ravished into an ecstasy, was indeed out of himself, but yet above himself. But both of them returned to themselves, the one when, reclaiming his lewd life, he was converted at heart, the other when from the height of contemplation, he returned to his natural and ordinary understanding. Thus venerable Benedict in that solitude dwelt with himself, for as much as he kept himself within his thoughts: for as often as by the fervour of contemplation he was elevated, without doubt he left himself as it were beneath himself.

PETER.

I like well this you say but resolve me, I pray you, should he have left those Monks of whom he had once taken charge?

GREGORY.

In my opinion, Peter, a bad community may be tolerated where there are found at least some good which may be helped. But where there is no benefit to be expected of any good, labour is many times lost upon the bad. Especially if there be any present occasions wherein we may do God better service. Now whom was there whom the holy man should have stayed to govern, when they had all conspired against him? And many things are considered by the soul of the perfect which ought not to be passed in silence, for they, perceiving their endeavours to be without effect, depart to some other place, there to employ themselves more profitably. Wherefore that famous preacher who desired to be dissolved and to be with Christ, unto whom to live is Christ, and to die is gain, did not only desire himself to suffer, but did also animate others to do the like. He being persecuted at Damascus, caused himself to be let down from the wall by a cord and basket whereby he escaped privately. Shall we say then that Paul feared death which he earnestly desired for the love of Christ, as appeareth by his own testimony? But as he foresaw that his endeavours there would profit little, with much difficulty he reserved himself to labour in another place with better success. For this valiant champion of God would not be confined to so narrow limits, but sought battles in the open field. So you may observe that the venerable Benedict, left not so many incorrigible in that place as he converted to a spiritual life elsewhere.

PETER.

You say true, as both reason and the example alleged prove, but I pray return to prosecute the life of this holy Father.

GREGORY.

The holy man for many years in that desert increased wonderfully in virtues and miracles, whereby a great number in those parts were gathered together in the service of Almighty God: so that, by the assistance of our Lord Jesus Christ, he built there twelve monasteries, in each of which he put twelve Monks with their superiors, and retained a few with himself whom he thought to instruct further.

Now began divers noble and devout personages from Rome to resort to him, and commended their children to be brought up by him in the service of Almighty God. At the same time, Equitius brought unto him Maurus, and Tertullus a Senator his son Placidus, both very hopeful children, of which two, Maurus, although young, yet by reason of his forwardness in the school of virtue, began to assist his master, but Placidus was as yet a child of tender years.

Chapter IV.

How he reclaimed an indevout Monk.

In one of those Monasteries which he had built thereabout, was a certain Monk that could not stay at his prayers, but, so soon as he saw his brethren kneel and dispose themselves for their mental prayer, he would go out, and there spend his wandering thoughts upon worldly and transitory things. For which, having been often admonished by his Abbot, he was brought before the man of God, who also sharply reprehended him for his folly; but, returning to his Monastery, he scarce remembered two days what the man of God had said to him, for the third day he fell to his old custom, and at the time of prayer went out again: whereof when the servant of God was informed by the Abbot the second time, he said: "I will come myself and reform him." And when he was come to the same Monastery, and the Brethren after the Psalms ended, at the accustomed time betook themselves to prayer, he perceived a little black boy, who pulled this Monk (who could not remain at his prayers) out by the hem of his garment. This he insinuated secretly to Pompeianus Abbot of the Monastery, and to Maurus: "See you not there who it is that draweth this Monk out?" Who answered, "No." "Let us pray", replied he, "that you may likewise see whom this Monk followeth." After prayer continued for two days, Maurus the monk saw, but Pompeianus the Abbot of the Monastery could not perceive anything. The next day when the man of God had finished his prayer he went out of the Oratory, and found the Monk standing without, whom he forthwith strake with a wand, and from that time ever after the Monk was free form the wicked suggestion of the black boy, and remained constant at his prayers. For the old enemy, as if himself had been beaten with the whip, dared no more to take command of his thoughts.

CHAPTER V.

How by the prayer of the man of God a spring issued from the top of a mountain.

Three of the Monasteries, which he founded in that place, were built upon the cliffs of a mountain, which was very troublesome to the Monks always to be forced to descend to the lake to fetch up their water, for, on account of the steepness of the mountain side, it was very difficult and dangerous to descend. Hereupon the Brethren of these three Monasteries came together to the servant of God Benedict saying: "It is very troublesome to us to have daily to go down for water as far as the lake, and therefore the Monasteries must of necessity be removed to some more commodious place." He dismissed them with comfortable words, and at night with little

Placidus, whom we mentioned before, went up to the rock and there prayed a long time. Having ended his prayers, he put three stones for a mark in the same place, and so unknown to all he returned to his Monastery. Next day, when the Brethren came again to him for want of water he said: "Go, and on the rock where you shall find three stones one upon another, dig a little, for Almighty God is able to make water spring from the top of that mountain, that you may be eased of this labour." When they had made a hollow in that place, it was immediately filled with water, which issueth forth so plentifully that to this day it continueth running down to the floor of the mountain.

Chapter VI.

How the iron head of a bill from the bottom of the water returned to the handle again.

At another time, a certain Goth poor of spirit, desirous to lead a religious life, repaired to the man of God, Benedict, who most willingly received him. One day he ordered a bill to be given to him to cut up brambles in a place which he intended for a garden. This place, which the Goth had undertaken to accommodate, was over the lake's side. While the Goth laboured amain in the cutting up the thick briars, the iron, slipping out of the handle, fell into the lake in a place so deep, that there was no hope to recover it. The Goth, having lost his bill, ran trembling to the Monk Maurus, and told him the mischance, confessing his fault penitently, who presently advertised Benedict the servant of God thereof. Immediately the man of God came himself to the lake, took the haft out of the Goth's hand, and cast it into the lake, when, behold, the iron rose up from the bottom and entered into the haft as before. Which he there rendered to the Goth saying: "Behold! work on and be not discomforted."

Chapter VII.

How his disciple Maurus walked on the water.

One day as venerable Benedict was in his cell, the aforesaid young Placidus, a Monk of the holy man, went out to the lake to fetch water, and letting down the bucket to take up water, by chance fell in himself after it, and was presently carried away by the stream, a bow's shoot from the side. This accident was at the same time revealed to the man of God in his cell, who quickly called Maurus, saying: "Run, brother Maurus, for the child who went to fetch water is fallen into the lake, and the stream hath carried him a great way." A wonderful thing and not heard of since the time of Peter the Apostle! Maurus having asked and received his benediction, upon the command of his Superior went forth in haste, and, being come to the place to which the child was driven by the stream, thinking still he went upon the dry land, he ran upon the water, took him by the hair of the head, and returned speedily back. No sooner had he set foot upon firm ground but he came to himself, and perceiving that he had gone upon the water, much astonished, he wondered how he had done that which wittingly he durst not adventure. So, returning to his Superior, he related what had happened, which the venerable man Benedict ascribed to Maurus his prompt obedience, and not to his own merits; but contrariwise Maurus attributed it wholly to his command, not imputing any virtue to himself in that which he had done unwittingly. This humble and charitable contention, the child who was saved, was to decide, for he said: "When I was drawn out of the water, methought I saw my Abbot's garments over my head and imagined that he had drawn me out."

PETER.

These are wonderful things you report, and may be to the edification of many: for my own part, the more I drink of this good man's miracles, the more I thirst.

Chapter VIII.

Of the poisoned loaf which the crow carried away.

When, as now, the places far and wide were very zealous in the love of our Lord God Jesus Christ, many abandoning the vanities of the world and putting themselves under the sweet yoke of our Redeemer; as it is the custom of the wicked to repine at the virtues of others, which themselves desire not to follow, one Florentius, the Priest of a Church hard by, and grandfather to Florentius our subdeacon, began by the instigation of the devil to be envious of the virtuous proceedings of the holy man, to derogate from his course of living hindering also as many as he could from resorting to him. But seeing that he could not stop his progress, the fame of his virtues still more increasing, and many upon the report of his sanctity reforming their lives daily, he became more and more envious, and constantly grew worse, for he desired himself the commendations of Benedict's life, but would not live commendably. Thus, blinded with envy, he sent to the servant of Almighty God a poisoned loaf for an offering, which the man of God received thankfully, although he was not ignorant of the poison in it. There used to come to him at the time of dinner a crow from the next forest, which took bread from his hand. Coming therefore, as she was wont, the man of God case before her the bread that the Priest had sent him, saying: "In the name of the Lord Jesus Christ take this bread and cast it in some place where no man may find it." The crow, gaping and spreading her wings, run croaking about it, as though she would have said, I would willingly fulfil thy command, but I am not able. The man of God commanded again saying: "Take it up, take it up, and cast it where no man may find it." So at length the crow took it up in her beak and flew away with it and three hours after returned again to receive from his hand her ordinary allowance. But the venerable Father, seeing the Priest so perversely bent to seek his life, was more sorry for him than grieved for himself. When the aforesaid Florentius saw that he could not kill the body of his master, he attempted what he could against the souls of his disciples, in so much that he sent seven naked girls into the garden of the Cloister where Benedict lived, that so playing for a long time hand in hand, they might entice their souls to naughtiness, which when the holy man espied out of his cell, to prevent the fall of his younger disciples, and considering that all this was done only for the persecuting of himself, he gave place to envy, and after he had disposed of the Oratories and other buildings, leaving in them a competent number of Brethren with Superiors, he took with him a few monks and removed to another place. Thus the man of God with humility avoided his hatred, whom Almighty God struck with a terrible judgment: for when the aforesaid Priest, standing in his summer house, heard to his great joy, that Benedict was gone, the room wherein he was fell down and crushed and killed the enemy of Benedict, all the rest of the house remaining immovable. This Maurus, the disciple of the man of God, thought fit to signify forthwith to the venerable Father Benedict, who was yet scarce gone ten miles saying: "Return for the Priest that did persecute you is slain." Which the man of God hearing took very heavily, both because his enemy was dead and because his disciple rejoiced thereat. Whereupon he enjoined him a penance for presuming in a joyful manner to bring such news to him.

PETER.

These are wonderful strange things which thou sayest. For in the drawing water out of a rock methinks I behold in him Moses; in raising the iron from the bottom of the water he representeth Eliseus; in walking on the water Peter; in the obedience of the crow I conceive him another Elias; in bewailing his enemy's death I see David. In my opinion, this man was filled with the spirit of all the just.

GREGORY.

The man of God, Benedict, had in him, Peter, the spirit of God alone, which by the grace of free redemption replenished the hearts of all the elect, of which St. John saith: "There was true light which illuminateth every man that cometh into this world." Of which again it is written: "Of his plentitude and fulness we have all received." For the holy ones of God could indeed receive graces from God, but they could not impart them to others. He then gave signs of power to the lowly, who promised that He would shew the miracle of Jonas to His enemies, deigning in their sight to die, and in the sight of the humble to arise. So that the one should have what they would contemn, and the other what reverence and love. By which mystery it came to pass, that while the proud were spectators of His ignominious death, the humble contrariwise, against death, lay hold of the power of His glory.

PETER.

But declare, I pray, whither the holy man removed or if he wrought miracles in any other place?

GREGORY.

The holy man by removing changed his habitation, but not his adversary. For afterwards he endured so much the more grievous battles, by how much he had now the master of wickedness fighting openly against him. The castle called Cassino is situated upon the side of a high mountain, which containeth as it were, in the lap thereof, the same castle, and riseth into the air three miles high so that the top seemeth to touch the very heavens: on this stood an old temple where Apollo was worshipped by the foolish country people, according to the custom of the ancient heathens. Round about it, likewise, grew groves, in which even until that time, the mad multitude of infidels offered their idolatrous sacrifices. The man of God coming to that place brake down the idol, overthrew the altar, burnt the groves, and, of the temple of Apollo, made a chapel to St. Martin, and, where the profane altar had stood, he built a chapel of St. John; and, by continual preaching, converted many of the people thereabout. But the old enemy not bearing this silently, did present himself, not covertly or in a dream but openly and visibly in the sight of the Father, and with great cries complained of the violence he suffered, in so much that the brethren heard him though they could see nothing. For, as the venerable Father told his disciples, the wicked fiend represented himself to his sight all on fire, and, with flaming mouth and flashing eyes, seemed to rage against him. And, then, they all heard what he said, for, first, he called him by his name, and, when the man of God would make him no answer, he fell to reviling him. And whereas before he cried: "Benedict, Benedict," and saw he could get no answer, then he cried: "Maledict, not Benedict, what hast thou to do with me, and why dost thou persecute me?" But now we shall behold new assaults of the old enemy against the servant of God, against whom willingly did he make war, but against his will did he give him occasions of many victories.

Chapter IX.

How the man of God by his prayer, removed a huge stone.

One day, as the brethren were building the cells of the Cloister, there lay a stone in the midst which they determined to lift up and put into the building. When two or three were not able to move it, they set more to it, but it remained as immoveable as if it had been held by roots to the ground, so that it was easy to conceive that the old enemy sat upon it, since that so many men were not able to lift it. After much labour in vain, they sent to the man of God to help them with his prayers to drive away the enemy, who presently came, and having first prayed, he gave his blessing, when behold the stone was as easily lifted as if it had not weight at all.

Chapter X.

Of the fantastical fire which burned the kitchen.

Then the man of God thought good that they should dig in that place. When they had entered a good deepness, the Brethren found a brazen idol, which happening for the present to be cast in the kitchen, suddenly there seemed a flame to rise out of it, and, to the sight of all the Monks it appeared that all the kitchen was on fire. As they were casting on water to quench this fire, the man of God, hearing the tumult, came, and perceiving that there appeared fire in the eyes of the Brethren and not in his, he forthwith bowed his head in prayer, and calling upon those whom he saw deluded with an imaginary fire, he bade them sign their eyes that they might behold the kitchen entire, and not those fantastical flames which the enemy had counterfeited.

Chapter XI.

How a boy crushed by the fall of a wall was healed by the servant of God.

Again, when the Brethren were raising the wall a little higher for more convenience, the man of God was at his devotions in his cell, to whom the old enemy appeared in an insulting manner and told him he was going to his Brethren at work; the man of God straightway by a messenger advertized the Brethren thereof saying: "Brethren, have a care of yourselves, for the wicked spirit at this hour is coming to molest you." Scarce had the messenger told his errand when the malignant spirit overthrew the wall that was abuilding, and with the fall thereof crushed a young monk, son to a certain Senator. Hereat all of them much grieved and discomforted, not for the loss of the wall but for the harm to their brother, brought the heavy tidings to their venerable Father Benedict, who bid them bring the boy to him, who could not be carried but in a sheet, by reason that not only his body was bruised but also his bones crushed with the fall. Then the man of God willed them to lay him in his cell upon his mat where he used to pray; so causing the Brethren to go out he shut the door, and with more than ordinary devotion fell to his prayers. A wonder to hear, the very same hour he sent him to his work again, whole and sound as ever he was before, to help his Brethren in making up the wall; whereas the old enemy hoped to have had occasion to insult over Benedict for his death.

Chapter XII.

Of Monks who had eaten out of their monastery.

Now began the man of God, by the spirit of prophecy, to foretell things to come, and to certify those that were present with him of things that passed far off. It was the custom of the Monastery that the Brethren, sent abroad about any business, should neither eat nor drink anything outside their Cloister. This in the practice of the Rule being carefully observed, one day some Brethren upon occasion went abroad, and were forced to stay later than usual, so they rested and refreshed themselves in the house of a certain devout woman of their acquaintance. Returning late to the Monastery, they asked, as was the custom, the Abbot's blessing, of whom he straightway demanded, saying: "Where dined you?" they answered: "Nowhere." To whom he said: "Why do you lie? Did you not go into such a woman's house? Eat you not there such and such meats? Drank you not so many cups?" When the venerable Father had told them both the woman's lodging, the several sorts of meats, with the number of their draughts, they, in great terror fell down at his feet, and with acknowledgment of all that they had done confessed their fault. But he straightway pardoned them, persuading himself they would never afterwards attempt the like in his absence knowing he was always present with them in spirit.

CHAPTER XIII.

How he reproved the brother of Valentinian the Monk for eating by the way.

Moreover, the brother of Valentinian, the Monk, whom we mentioned in the beginning, was very devout although but a secular; and he used to go to the Monastery from his dwelling once every year and that fasting, that he might partake of the prayers of the servant of God, and see his brother. As he was on his way to the Monastery, another traveller, who carried meat with him, put himself into his company After they had travelled a good while, he said to him: "Come, Brother, let us refresh ourselves, lest we faint by the way." "God forbid!" answered the other, "by no means, Brother, for my custom is always to go to the venerable Father Benedict fasting." At which answer, his fellow-traveller, for the present, said no more; but, when they had gone a little further, he moved him again to ear, but he would not consent because he resolved to keep his fast. So the other was awhile silent, and went forward with him without taking any thing himself. After they had gone a great way, wearied with long travel, in their way they came to a meadow and a spring, with what else might delight them, there to take their repast. Then said his fellow-traveller: "So! Here is water, here is a meadow, here is a pleasant place for us to refresh and rest us awhile, that we may safely make an end of our journey." So, at the third motion, these words pleasing his ear and the place his eye, he was overcome, consented and ate. In the evening he came to the Monastery, where, conducted to the venerable Father Benedict, he craved his prayers, but soon the holy man reproved him for what he had done in the way, saying: "What was it, Brother, the malignant enemy suggested to thee by they fellow traveller? The first time he could not persuade nor yet the second, but the third time he prevailed and obtained his desire." Then the man acknowledging his fault fell at his feet, and began all the more to weep and to be ashamed, by reason that he perceived he had offended, although absent, in the sight of Father Benedict.

PETER.

I discover in the breast of the holy man the spirit of Eliseus, who was present with his disciple though far from him.

Chapter XIV.

How he discovered the dissimulation of King Totila.

GREGORY.

You must, Peter, for a little while be silent, that you may know matters far more important. For, in the time of the Goths, their king, informed that the holy man had the gift of prophecy, went towards his Monastery and made some stay a little way off, and gave notice of his coming. To whom answer was made from the Monastery that he might come at his pleasure. The king, being of a treacherous nature, attempted to try whether the man of God had the spirit of prophecy. There was one of his guards called Riggo, upon whom he caused his own buskins to be put and so commanded him taking on him the king's person to go forward to the man of God, three of his chief pages attending upon him, to wit Vulderic, Ruderic and

Blindin, to the end they should wait upon him in the presence of the servant of God, that so, by reason of his attendants and purple robes, he might be taken for the king. When the said Riggo, with his brave apparel and attendance, entered the cloister the man of God sat a little distance off, and seeing him come so nigh as he might hear him, he cried to him, saying: "Put off, son, put off that which thou carriest, for it is not thine." Riggo straightway fell to the ground and was much afraid, for having presumed to delude so holy a man; all his followers likewise fell down astonished, and rising, they durst not approach unto him, but returned to their king, and trembling related unto him how soon they were discovered.

CHAPTER XV.

How he prophesied to King Totila and to the Bishop of Canosa.

Then Totila came himself to the man of God, whom as soon as he saw sitting afar off, he durst not come nigh, but fell prostrate to the ground. The holy man twice of three bade him rise, but he durst not get up, then Benedict, the servant of Jesus Christ our Lord, deigned himself to come to the prostrate king, whom, raising from the ground, he rebuked for his deeds, and foretold in a few words all that should befall him saying: "Much evil dost thou do, and much wickedness hast thou done, as least now give over thy iniquity. Into Rome shalt thou enter, thou wilt cross over the sea, nine years shalt thou reign, and die the tenth." At the hearing whereof, the king sore appalled, craved his prayers and departed, but from that time he was less cruel. Not long after he went to Rome, sailed thence to Sicily, and in the tenth year of his reign, by the judgment of Almighty God, lost both crown and life.

Moreover, the Bishop of the Church of Canosa used to come to the servant of God, who much loved him for his virtuous life. He, therefore, conferring with him concerning the coming of king Totila and the taking of the City of Rome, said: "The city doubtless will be destroyed by this king, so that it will never more be inhabited." To whom the man of God replied: "Rome shall never be destroyed by the Pagans, but shall be so shaken by tempests, lightnings and earthquakes that it will decay of itself." The mysteries of which prophecy we now behold as clear as day, for, in this city, we see the walls ruined, houses overturned, churches destroyed by tempestuous winds, and buildings rotten with old age, decay and falling into ruins. Although Honoratus, his disciple, from whose relation I had it, told me heard it not himself from his own mouth but was told it by the Brethren.

Chapter XVI.

How venerable Benedict dispossessed a certain clerk from the Devil.

At that time one of the clergy of the church of Aquin was molested with an evil spirit, whom the venerable man, Constantius, Bishop of that Diocese, had sent to divers martyrs' shrines to be cured; but the holy martyrs would not cure him, that the gifts of grace in Benedict might be made manifest. He was therefore brought to the servant of Almighty God, Benedict, who, by pouring forth prayers to our Lord Jesus Christ, presently drove out the enemy. Having cured him, he commanded him, saying: "Go! And hereafter never eat flesh, and presume not to take Holy Orders, for what time soever you shall presume to take Holy Orders, you shall again become a slave to the devil." The Clerk therefore went his way healed, and as present punishments make deep impressions, he carefully for a while observed the man of God's command. But when, after many years, all his seniors were dead and he saw his juniors preferred before him in Holy Orders, he neglected the words of the man of God, as though forgotten through length of time, and took upon him Holy Orders; whereupon, presently, the devil, who before had left him, took power of him, and never ceased to torment him till he severed his soul from his body.

PETER.

This holy man, I perceive, understood the secret decrees of God, in that he knew this Clerk to be delivered to the power of the devil, lest he should presume to receive Holy Orders.

GREGORY.

Why should not he know the secret decrees of Divine Providence, who kept the commandments of God, whence it is written that "he who adhereth to God is one spirit with Him."

PETER.

If he who adhereth to our Lord become one spirit with Him, how comes the same excellent Preacher to say: "Who hath known the mind of the Lord, or who has been His counsellor?" For it seems altogether unlikely that he, who is made one with another, should not know his mind.

GREGORY.

Holy men, so far as they are united with God, are not ignorant of His meaning, for the same Apostle saith; "For what man knoweth the things of a man, but the spirit of a man that is in him? So the things also, that are of God, no man knoweth but the spirit of God."

And to shew that he knew things of God, he addeth: "But we have not received the spirit of this world, but the spirit which is of God." And again: "That eye hath not seen, nor ear heard, neither hath it ascended into the heart of man, what things God hath prepared for those that love Him, but to us God hath revealed by His spirit."

PETER.

If then those things which appertained to God were revealed to the said Apostle by the spirit of God, what meaneth he to make this preamble, saying: "O the depth of the riches of the wisdom and knowledge of God; how incomprehensible are His judgments and His ways unsearchable." But as I am saying this, another question arises: for the Prophet David says to our Lord: "With my lips I have uttered all the judgments of Thy mouth." And, whereas, it is less to comprehend or know than to pronounce, what is the reason that St. Paul should affirm the judgments of God to be incomprehensible, while David professeth not only to know them but also to pronounce them with his lips?

GREGORY.

To both these difficulties — I briefly answered before, when I said: that holy men, as far as they are one with God, are not ignorant of the mind of our Lord, for all such as do devoutly follow the Lord are also by devotion one with God; and yet, in that they are laden with the burden of this corruptible flesh, they are not with God. Therefore, for as much as they are united with God they know His secret judgments, of which likewise they are ignorant for as much as in respect separated from Him: and so they pronounce His judgments incomprehensible which they cannot as yet thoroughly understand. But they who in spirit adhere to Him, in this adhesion know His judgments, either by the sacred words of Scripture, or by hidden revelations, as far as they are capable; these therefore they know and declare, but they are ignorant of those which God concealeth. Whereupon the prophet David when he had said: "In my lips I will pronounce all Thy judgments," as if he had said plainly: "Those judgments I could both know and pronounce which Thou didst tell me, for those which Thou speakest not, without doubt Thou concealest from our knowledge. Thus, the saying of the Prophet agreeth with that of the Apostle, for the judgments of God are both incomprehensible, and yet those which proceed from His mouth are uttered with the lips of men, for being so manifested by God they may be conceived by men, nor can they be concealed.

PETER.

By occasion of the difficulty I propounded, I have obtained a clear solution. But if there remain aught concerning the virtue of this man, I pray you declare it.

Chapter XVII.

How he prophecied the destruction of his Monastery.

A certain nobleman, named Theoprobus, was by the admonition of Father Benedict converted, and for the merit of his life was very familiar and intimate with him. He one day entered into the cell of the man of God, found him weeping bitterly; when he had waited a good while and saw he did not give over, (though it was his custom in prayer mildly to weep and not to use any doleful lamentations) he boldly demanded of him the cause of so great grief. To whom the man of God presently replied: "All this Monastery which I have built, with whatsoever I have prepared for my Brethren, are, by the judgment of Almighty God, delivered over to the heathen: and I could scarce obtain to save the lives of those in this place. His words Theoprobus heard, but we see them verified in the destruction of his Monastery by the Longobards. For of late these Lombards, by night, when the Brethren were at rest, entered the Monastery and ransacked all, yet had not the power to lay hand on any man. But Almighty God fulfilled what he had promised to His faithful servant, Benedict, that although he gave their goods into the hands of the Paynims, yet he preserved their lives. In this Benedict did most clearly resemble St. Paul, whose ship with all its goods being lost, yet, for his comfort, he had the lives of all that were in his company bestowed upon him.

CHAPTER XVIII.

How St. Benedict discovered the hiding of a flagon of wine.

Our monk Exhilaratus, whom you know well, on a time was sent by his master with two wooden vessels (which we call flagons) full of wine, to the man of God in his Monastery. He brought one but hid the other in the way, notwithstanding, the man of God, although he was not ignorant of anything done in his absence, received it thankfully, and advised the boy as he was returning back, in this manner: "Take care, son, thou drink not of that flagon which thou hast hid, but turn the mouth of it downward and then thou wilt perceive what is in it." He departed from the holy man much ashamed, and desirous to make further trial of what he had heard, held the flagon downwards, and presently there came forth a snake, at which the boy was sore affrighted and terrified for the evil he had committed.

Chapter XIX.

How the man of God reproved a Monk
for receiving certain napkins.

Not far distant from the monastery was a certain town in which no small number of people, by the exhortations of Benedict, were converted from the worship of idols to the faith of God. In that place were certain religious women, and the servant of God, Benedict, used to send often some of his Brethren thither to instruct and edify their souls. One day, as his custom was, he appointed one to go; but the Monk who was sent, after his exhortation, by the entreaty of the Nuns, took some small napkins and hid them in his bosom. As soon as he came back, the man of God began very sharply to rebuke him, saying: "How hath iniquity entered thy breast?" The Monk was amazed, and because he had forgotten what he had done, he wondered why he was so reprehended. To whom the holy Father said: "What! Was not I present when thou tookest the napkins of the handmaids of God and didst put them in thy bosom?" Whereupon he presently fell at his feet, and repenting of his folly threw away the napkins which he had hid in his bosom.

Chapter XX.

How the man of God understood the proud
thought of one of his Monks.

One day as the venerable Father late in the evening was at his repast, it happened that one of his Monks, the son of a lawyer, held the candle to him; and whilst the man of God was eating, he standing in that manner, began by the suggestion of pride to say within himself, "Who is he whom I should wait upon at table, or hold the candle unto with such attendance? Who am I who should serve him?" To whom the man of God presently turning, checked him sharply saying: "Sign thy breast, Brother, what is this you say? Sign thy breast." Then he forthwith called upon the Brethren and willed them to take the candle out of his hand, and bade him for that time to leave his attendance and sit down quietly by him. The Monk being asked afterward of the Brethren concerning his thoughts at that time, told them how he was puffed up with a spirit of pride, and what he spake against the man of God secretly in his own heart. By this it was easily to be perceived that nothing could be kept from the knowledge of venerable Benedict, in whose ears the words of unspoken thoughts resounded.

Chapter XXI.

Of two hundred measures of meal found before the man of God's cell.

At another time also in the country of Campania began a great famine, and all people suffered from great scarcity of food, so that all the wheat in Benedict's Monastery was spent, and likewise almost all the bread, so that but five loaves remained for the Brethren's refection. When the venerable Father perceived them sad, he endeavoured by a mild and gentle reproach to reprehend their pusillanimity, and with fair promises to comfort them, saying: "Why is your soul sad for want of bread? To day you are in want but to-morrow you shall have plenty." The next day there were found two hundred sacks of meal before the Monastery gates, by whom God Almighty sent it as yet no man knoweth. Which when the Monks beheld, they gave thanks to God, and by this were taught in their greatest want to hope for plenty.

PETER.

Tell me, I pray you, is it to be thought that this servant of God had continually the spirit of prophecy, when himself pleased, or only at certain times with some discontinuance.

GREGORY.

The spirit of prophecy, Peter, doth not always cast his beams upon the understanding of the Prophets, for as it is written of the Holy Ghost: "He breatheth where He will." So likewise must we conceive, also, when He pleaseth. And, therefore, Nathan being asked by the king if he might build the Temple, first allowed him to do it, and afterwards forbade him. This was the reason that Eliseus knew not the cause why the woman wept but said to his servant who did oppose her: "Let her alone for her soul is in anguish, and the Lord hath concealed it from me and hath not made it known." Thus Almighty God of His great mercy so disposeth in His providence, for the end that by giving the spirit of prophecy sometimes, and at other times withdrawing it, the minds of the Prophets be both elevated above themselves, and also be kept in humility, for by receiving the spirit they may know they are inspired by God, and again they receive it not, they may consider what they are of themselves.

PETER.

It standeth with good reason what you have said. But, I beseech you, prosecute what else you remember of the venerable Father Benedict.

Chapter XXII.

How by a vision, he gave order to construct the Monastery of Terracina.

At another time, he was requested by a certain devout man to send some of his disciples to build a Monastery on his estate near the city of Terracina. To which request he consented, and sent some Monks, appointing an Abbot and Prior over them. As they were setting forward, he promised, saying: "Go, and upon such a day I will come and shew you where to build the Oratory, where the Refectory and lodging for the guests, or what else shall be necessary." So they received his blessing and departed, in hope to see him at the appointed day, for which they prepared all things they thought fit and necessary for their Father and his company. The night before the appointed day the man of God appeared in sleep to him whom he had constituted Abbot and to his Prior, and described to them most exactly how he would have the building ordered. When they awaked, they related to each other what they had seen, yet not altogether relying upon that vision, they expected the man of God according to his promise, but seeing he came not at his appointed time, they returned to him very pensive, saying: "We have expected, Father, your coming, as you promised, but you came not to shew us where and what we should build." To whom he said: "Why, Brethren, why do you say so? Did not I come according to my promise?" And when they said: "When came you?" he replied: "Did I not appear to each of you in your sleep and describe every place? Go, and according to the direction given you in that vision construct the Monastery." Hearing this they were much astonished, and so, returning to the manor, they erected the whole building according to the revelation.

PETER.

I would gladly be informed how and in what manner he could express his mind to them so far off, so they should both hear and understand by an apparition.

GREGORY.

What is the reason, Peter, thou dost so curiously search out the manner how it was done? It is evident that the spirit is of more mobile nature than the body. And we are taught by Scripture how the Prophet was taken up in Judea and set down, with the dinner he carried, in Chaldea, and, after he had refreshed another Prophet with his dinner, found himself again in Judea. If then Habacuc in a moment could corporally go so far and carry his dinner, what wonder if Father Benedict obtained to go in spirit and intimate to the spirits of his Brethren what was necessary; that as the other went corporally to convey corporal food, so he might go in spirit to inform them of things concerning a spiritual life?

PETER.

I confess that by this your discourse you have given full satisfaction to my doubtful mind; but I would gladly know what kind of man he was in his common conversation.

Chapter XXIII.

How certain Religious women were absolved after their death.

GREGORY.

Even his ordinary discourse, Peter, had a certain efficacious virtue, for his heart being elevated in contemplation, he would not allow a word to pass from his mouth in vain. If at any time he spake aught, yet not as one that determined what was best to be done, but by way of threatening, his words had the same force as if he had absolutely decreed it. For, not far from his Monastery, two Nuns of noble race and parentage lived in a place of their own: and a certain Religious man provided them with all things for their exterior. But as in some, nobility of birth causeth baseness in mind, so those, who bear in mind their own greatness do less humble themselves in this world. There aforesaid Nuns had not, as yet, refrained their tongues by a Religious habit, but, by their unadvised speeches, oftentimes provoked to anger the Religious man who had care over them. Wherefore, after he had for a long time endured their contumelious language, he complained to the man of God of the injuries he suffered. Which as soon as he heard he commanded them forthwith, saying: "Have a care of your tongues, for if you do not amend I excommunicate you." Which sentence of excommunication notwithstanding, he did not pronounce but threaten. Yet for all this, they nothing changed in their former conditions. Within a few days after they departed this life, and were buried in the Church. At such time as a Solemn Mass was sung, and the Deacon, as the custom is, cried aloud: "If there be any that communicateth not, let him go forth," then their nurse, who used to make offerings to our Lord for them, saw them rise out of their graves and go forth. This she often observed, that, when the Deacon cried in that manner, they went out, not able to remain in the Church, and, calling to mind what the man of God had said to them whilst they were living, (for he excluded them from communion unless they amended their language and manners) she, with great sorrow, informed the servant of God what she had seen. He presently with his own hands gave the offering saying: "Go and cause this oblation to be offered to our Lord, and they shall be no longer excommunicated." When therefore, this offering was made, and the Deacon, according to custom, cried out that such as did not communicate should go out of the Church, they were not seen to go forth any more. Whereby it was apparent that, whereas they went not forth with the excommunicated, they were admitted by our Lord to communion.

PETER.

It is marvellous strange that this man, although venerable and most holy, as yet living in the mortal body, should be able to release those who were standing at the invisible tribunal.

GREGORY.

And was not he, Peter, yet in this flesh who heard; "Whatsoever thou shalt bind upon earth shall be bound also in Heave, and whatsoever thou shalt loose on earth shall be loosed also in Heaven." Whose place and authority in binding and loosing they possess, who, by faith and virtuous life, obtain the dignity of holy government. And that man, an earthly creature, might receive this power, the Creator of Heaven and earth came down from Heaven to earth and that flesh might judge of spiritual things He became man for the redemption of mankind. For God thus condescending beneath Himself raised our weakness above itself.

PETER.

For the virtue of his miracles your words do yield a very good reason.

CHAPTER XXIV.

Of a boy who was cast out of his grave.

GREGORY.

Upon a certain day, a young Monk of his, who was over-much affected towards his parents, went from the Monastery to their abode without his benediction, and the very same day, as soon as he was come to them he died. The day following his burial they found his body cast up, which they interred the second time, and the next day after it was found in like manner lying above ground as before. Hereupon they ran straight way and fell at the feet of the most mild Father Benedict imploring his aid, to whom the man of God with his own hand gave the communion of the Lord's Body saying: "Go, and lay the Body of the Lord upon his breast and so bury him." This done, the earth kept his body, and never after cast it up. You perceive, Peter, of what merit this man was with our Lord Jesus Christ, seeing that the very earth cast forth the body of him who had not received the blessing of Benedict.

PETER.

I do plainly perceive it, and am much astonished thereat.

Chapter XXV.

Of the Monk, who leaving his Monastery met a dragon in the way.

One of his Monks of a wandering and inconstant disposition, would by no means abide in the Monastery. Although the man of God had often reproved and admonished him of it, he would in no wise consent to remain in the congregation, and often entreated earnestly to be released. So the venerable Father, overcome with his importunity in anger bade him begone. Scarce was he got out of the Monastery, when he met in the way a dragon who, with open mouth made towards him. Seeing it ready to devour him, he began to quake and tremble, crying out aloud: "Help, help, for this dragon will devour me." The Brethren upon this ran out, yet saw no dragon, but took the panting and afrighted Monk back again to the Monastery, who forthwith promised never to depart and from that time he remained always constant in his promise. He, by the prayers of the holy man, was made to see the dragon ready to devour him, which before he had followed unperceived.

Chapter XXVI.

Of the boy cured of the Leprosy.

But I must not pass over in silence what I heard of a very honourable man named Anthony, who affirmed that a servant of his father fell into a leprosy, insomuch that his hair fell off, and his skin was swollen so that he could no longer hide the increase of his disease. Who being sent by the gentleman's father to the man of God, he was by him quickly restored to his former health.

Chapter XXVII.

How St. Benedict miraculously procured money for a poor man to discharge his debt.

Nor will I conceal that which his disciple Peregrine was wont to relate: how, on a certain day, an honest man, constrained by the necessity of a debt, thought his only remedy was to have recourse to the man of God, and acquaint him with his necessity. So he came to the Monastery, where finding the servant of Almighty God, told him how he was extremely urged by his creditor for the payment of twelve shillings. The venerable father answered him that, in very deed, he had not twelve shillings, but yet he comforted his want with good words, saying: "Go, and after two days return hither again for today I have it not to give thee." These two days, as his custom was, he spent in prayer, and, on the third day, when the poor debtor came again, thirteen shillings were found upon a chest of the Monastery that was full of corn. These the man of God caused to be brought to him, and gave them to the distressed man, saying that he might pay twelve, and have one to defray his charges.

But to return to those things which I learned of his disciples of whom I spoke in the beginning of this book, there was a certain man had an adversary who bore him deadly hatred, and so great was his malice that he gave him poison in his drink; which potion, although it procured not his death, yet so altered his colour that his body became all speckled like a leper. This man was brought to the man of God and was quickly restored to his former health; for as soon as he touched him, the diversity of colours vanished from his skin.

Chapter XXVIII.

How a bottle was cast down upon the Stones and not broken.

At such time as the great famine was in Campania, the man of God gave all he had in his Monastery to those in want, insomuch as there was almost nothing left in the cellar save only a little oil in a glass vessel. When one Agapitus, a Subdeacon, came earnestly entreating to have a little oil given him, the man of God (who had resolved to give all upon earth that he might have all in Heaven) commanded this little oil that was left to be given him. The Monk, who was Cellarer, heard his command but was loath to fulfill it. And the holy man a little while after demanded whether he had done what he willed him, and the Monk answered that he had not given it, because if he had given it, there would be nothing left for the Brothers. Hereat, much displeased, the good father bade some other take the glass bottle in which there remained a little oil, and cast it out of the window, to the end that nothing of the fruits of disobedience might remain in the Monastery. This was accordingly done; under the window was a steep fall, full of huge rough stones, upon which the glass fell, yet it remained as whole and entire as if it had not been thrown down, so that neither was the glass broke nor the oil spilt. Then the man of God commanded it to be taken up and given to him that asked it. Then calling the Brothers together, he rebuked the disobedient Monk before them all for his pride and unfaithfulness.

Chapter XXIX.

How an empty barrel was filled with oil.

Having ended the Chapter, he and all the Brethren fell to their prayers. In the place where they prayed was an empty oil-barrel close covered. As the holy man continued his prayer, the cover of the said tun began to be heaved up by the oil increasing under it, which ran over the brim of the vessel upon the floor in great abundance. Which so soon as the servant of God, Benedict, beheld, he forthwith ended his prayer, and the oil ceased to run over. Then he admonished the distrustful and disobedient brother to have confidence and learn humility. So the brother thus reprehended was much ashamed, because the venerable Father had by his admonition and by his miracle shewn the power of Almighty God, nor could anyone afterwards doubt of what he promised, since, as it were in a moment, for a glass bottle almost empty, he had restored a tun full of oil.

CHAPTER XXX.

How he delivered a monk from the devil.

One day as he was going to St. John's Oratory, which stands upon the very top of the mountain, he met the old enemy upon a mule, in the habit and comportment of a physician, carrying a horn and a mortar; who, being demanded whither he went, answered he was going to the monks to minister a potion. So the venerable Father Benedict went forward to the chapel to pray, and, having finished, returned back in great haste, for the wicked spirit found one of the ancient Monks drawing water, and presently he entered into him, threw him on to the ground and tortured him pitifully. As soon as the man of God, returning from prayer, found him thus cruelly tormented, he only gave him a blow on the cheek with his hand, and immediately drave the wicked spirit out of him, so that he durst never after return.

PETER.

I would know whether he obtained these great miracles always by prayer, or did them some times only by the intimation of his will?

GREGORY.

They who are perfectly united with God, when necessity requireth, work miracles both ways, sometimes they do wonders by prayer, sometimes by power. For since St. John saith: "As many as received Him, to them He gave power to become sons of God." What wonder is it if they have the privilege and power to work miracles who are exalted to the dignity of children of God. And that they work miracles in both ways is manifest in St. Peter, who by prayer, raised

Tabitha from death, and punished with death Ananias and Sapphira for their falsehood. For we do not read that he prayed when they fell down dead, but only that he rebuked them for their fault committed. It is evident therefore that these things are done sometimes by power, sometimes by petition: since that by reproof he deprived these of their life, and by prayer revived the other.

But now I will produce two other acts of the faithful servant of God, Benedict, in which it shall clearly appear that some things he could do by power received from Heaven, and others by prayer.

Chapter XXXI.

How a country man was loosed by only the sight of the man of God.

A certain Goth named Galla was of the impious sect of the Arians, and he, in the time of their king Totila did, with such monstrous cruelty, persecute religious men of the Catholic Church, insomuch that if any cleric or monk came in his sight, he was sure not to escape from his hands alive. This man enraged with an insatiable covetousness of spoil and pillage, lighted one day upon a husbandman whom he tortured with cruel torments. The rustic, overcome with pain, professed that he had committed his goods to the custody of the servant of God, Benedict. This he feigned that he might free himself from torments and prolong his life for some time. Then this Galla gave over tormenting him, and tying his arms together with a strong cord, made him run before his horse to shew him who this Benedict was, that had received his goods. Thus the man went in front, having his arms bound, and brought him to the holy man's Monastery, whom he found sitting alone at the Monastery gate reading. Then the countryman said to Galla, who followed furiously after him: "See! This is Father Benedict whom I told you of." The barbarous ruffian, looking upon him with enraged fury, thought to affright him with his usual threats, and began to cry out with a loud voice, saying: "Rise, rise and deliver up this rustic's goods which thou hast received." At whose voice the man of God suddenly lifted up his eyes from reading, and saw him and also the countryman whom he kept bound: thus, as he cast his eyes upon his arms, in a wonderful manner the cords began to fall off so quickly, that no man could possibly have so soon untied them.

When Galla perceived the man whom he brought bound, so suddenly loosened and at liberty, struck into fear at the sight of so great power, he fell prostrate, and bowing his stiff and cruel neck at the holy man's feet, begged his prayers. But the holy man rose not from his reading but called upon the Brethren to bring him to receive his benediction. When he was brought to him, he exhorted him to leave his barbarous and inhuman cruelty. So, vanquished, he departed, never after presuming to ask anything of the countryman, whom the man of God unloosed not by touching but by casting his eye upon. Thus you see, Peter, as I said, that those who are the true servants of Almighty God, sometimes do work miracles by a commanding power, for he who sitting still abated the fury of that terrible Goth and with his only look unloosed the cords wherewith the innocent man's arms were fast pinioned, sheweth, evidently, by the swiftness of the miracle, that he wrought it by a power received. Now I will also shew you how great and strange a miracle he obtained by prayer.

Chapter XXXII.

How he raised a child from the dead.

As he was one day in the field labouring with his Brethren, a certain peasant came to the Monastery, carrying in his arms the dead body of his son, and pitifully lamenting his loss, asked for the holy Father Benedict. When they said that he was in the field, he presently laid down the dead body of his son at the Monastery gate, and, as one distracted with grief, began running to find out the venerable father. At the same time the man of God was coming home with his Brethren from labouring in the field, whom, when the distressed countryman espied, he began to cry out: "Restore me my son, restore me my son." But the man of God amazed at this voice said: "What! have I taken your son from you?" To whom the man replied: "He is dead, come and raise him." When the servant of God heard this he was much grieved, and said: "Go, Brethren, go! This is not a work for us, but such as were the holy Apostles. Why will you impose burdens upon us which we cannot bear?" Notwithstanding, the man enforced with excessive grief, persisted in his petition, swearing that he would not depart unless he raised his son to life. Then the servant of God enquired, saying: "Where is he?" He answered: "Lo! his body lieth at the Monastery Gate." Whither, when the man of God with his Brethren was come, he knelt down and laid himself on the body of the child; then, raising himself and with his hands held up towards Heaven, he prayed: "O Lord, regard not my sins, but the faith of this man who craveth to have his son restored to life, and restore again to this body the soul which thou hast taken from it." Scarce had he finished these words, but all the body of the boy began to tremble at the re-entry of the soul, so that in the sight of all who were present he was seen with wonderful quaking to pant and breathe. Whom he presently took by the hand and delivered alive and sound to his father.

It seemeth to me, Peter, he had not this miracle actually in his power, which he prostrated himself to obtain by prayer.

PETER.

What you have said is undoubtedly true, because you prove by deeds what was said in words. But I pray, certify me, whether holy men can effect and obtain whatsoever they will or desire?

Chapter XXXIII.

Of the miracle wrought by his sister Scholastica.

GREGORY.

Who was ever, Peter, in this life more sublime than St. Paul, who, notwithstanding, three times craved of our Lord to be free from the pricks of the flesh, yet could not obtain it? To this purpose, I must tell you a passage concerning the venerable Father Benedict, that there was something he desired and was not able to accomplish.

His sister Scholastica, who was consecrated to God from her very childhood, used to come once a year to see him; unto whom the man of God was wont to go to a house not far from the gate, within the possession of the Monastery. Thither she came one day according to her custom, and her venerable brother likewise with his disciples: where, after they had spent the whole day in the praise of God and pious discourses, the night drawing on, they took their refection together. As they were yet sitting at table, and protracting the time with holy conference, the religious woman, his sister, entreated him saying: "I beseech you, leave me not this night, that we may talk until morning of the joys of the heavenly life." To whom he answered: "What is this you say, sister? By no means can I stay out of my Monastery." At this time the sky was serene, and not a cloud was to be seen in the air. The holy woman, therefore, hearing her brother's refusal, clasped her hands together upon the table, and bowing her head upon them she prayed to Almighty God. As she raised up her head from the table, there began such vehement lightning and thunder, with such abundance of rain, that neither venerable Benedict nor his Brethren were able to put foot out of doors. For the holy woman when she leaned her head upon her hands, poured forth a flood of tears upon the table by which she changed the fair weather into foul and rainy. For, immediately after her prayers, followed the inundation, and the two did so concur that, as she lifted up her head, the crack of thunder was heard, so that in one and the same instant she lifted up her head and brought down the rain. Then the man of God perceiving that, by reason of thunder and lightening with continual showers of rain, he could not possibly return to his monastery, was sad and began to complain, saying: "God Almighty forgive you, sister, what is this you have done?" To whom she made answer: "I prayed you to stay and you would not hear me; I prayed to Almighty God and He heard me! Now, therefore, if you can, go forth to the Monastery and leave me." But he not able to go forth, was forced to stay against his will.

Thus it fell out that they spent the night in watching, and received full content in spiritual discourse of heavenly matters. By this it appears, as I said before, that he desired something which he could not obtain; for if we consider the mind of the venerable man, he would, without doubt, have had the fair weather to continue in which he set out. But, contrary to what he willed, he found a miracle worked by the courage of a woman in the strength of

Almighty God. And no wonder if at that time a woman were more powerful than he, considering she had long desired to see her brother. For according to the saying of St. John: "God is charity," and with good reason she was more powerful who loved more.

PETER.

I confess that I am wonderfully pleased with that which you tell me.

CHAPTER XXXIV.

In what manner St. Benedict saw the soul of his sister go forth from her body.

GREGORY.

The next day, the venerable woman returned to her Cloister and the man of God to his Monastery. When, behold, three days after, while standing in his cell, he saw the soul of his sister depart out of her body, and, in the form of a dove, ascend and enter into the celestial mansions. Who rejoicing much to see her great glory, gave thanks to God Almighty in hymns and praises, and announced her death to the Brethren. Whom he forthwith sent to bring her body to the Monastery, and caused it to be buried in the same tomb that he had prepared for himself. By means of which it fell out, that as their minds were always one in God, so also their bodies were not separated in their burial.

CHAPTER XXXV.

How the whole world was repesented before his eyes: and the soul of Germanus, Bishop of Capua.

Another time, Servandus, Deacon and Abbot of that Monastery which was built by Liberius, sometime a senator, in the Campania, used often to visit him, for being also illuminated with grace and heavenly doctrine, he repaired divers times to the Monastery that they might mutually communicate one to another, and, at least with sighs and longing desires, taste of that sweet food of the celestial country whose perfect fruition they were not as yet permitted to enjoy. When it was time to go to rest, venerable Benedict went up to the top of the tower in the lower part of which Servandus the Deacon had his lodging, and from which there was an open passage to ascend to the higher. Over against the said tower was a large building in which the disciples of both reposed. While as yet the Monks were at rest, the man of God, Benedict, being diligent in watching, rose up before the night office and stood at the window making his prayer to Almighty God about midnight, when suddenly, looking forth, he saw a light glancing from above, so bright and resplendent that it not only dispersed the darkness of the night, but shined more clear than the day itself. Upon this sight a marvellous strange thing followed, for, as he afterwards related, the whole world, compacted as it were together, was represented to his eyes in one ray of light. As the venerable Father had his eyes fixed upon this glorious lustre, he beheld the soul of Germanus, Bishop of Capua, carried by angels to Heaven in a fiery globe. Then, for the testimony of so great a miracle, with a loud voice he called upon Servandus the Deacon, twice or thrice by his name, who, troubled at such an unusual crying out of the man of God, came up, looked forth, and saw a little stream of light then disappearing, and wondered greatly at this miracle. Whereupon the man of God told him in order all that he had seen, and sent presently to Theoprobus, a Religious man in the town of Cassino, ordering him to go the same night to Capua, and learn what had happened to Germanus the Bishop. It fell out so, that he who was sent found the most reverend Bishop Germanus dead, and on enquiring more exactly, he learned that his departure was the very same moment in which the man of God had seen him ascend.

PETER.

A wonderful thing and much to be admired, but, whereas you said that the whole world, as it were, under one sunbeam, was represented to his sight, as I never experienced the like, so I cannot imagine how or in what manner this was possible that the whole world should be seen of any one man.

GREGORY.

Assure yourself, Peter, of that which I speak: that in a soul that beholdeth the Creator, all creatures appear but narrow; for, should we partake never so little of the light of the Creator, whatsoever is created would seem very little; because the soul is enlarged by this Beatific vision, and so dilated in the Divine perfections, that it far transcends the world and itself also. The soul thus rapt in the light of God is in her interior lifted up, and enabled above itself, and while thus elevated it contemplates itself, and it easily comprehendeth how little that is which before it was not able to conceive. So the blessed man who saw the globe of fire with the Angels returning to Heaven could not possibly have beheld those things but only in the light of God. What wonder then if he saw the world at one view who was in mind exalted above the world? But whereas I said that the whole world compacted as it were together was represented before his eyes, it is not meant that heaven and earth were straitened by contraction, but that the mind of the beholder was dilated, which, rapt in the sight of God might, without difficulty, see all that is under God. Therefore, in that light which appeared to his outward eyes, the inward light which was in his soul ravished the mind of the beholder with higher things, and shewed how mean are all inferior things.

PETER.

I perceive that it was to my profit that I understood you not before, for my slowness has been the occasion of so long and profitable a discourse. But, since you have clearly explained these things to me, I beseech you continue your former narration.

Chapter XXXVI.

How he wrote a Rule for Monks.

I would willingly, Peter, relate many things concerning this venerable Father, but some of purpose I omit, because I hasten to speak of the acts of others. Only this I would not have you to be ignorant of, that the man of God, among so many miracles wherewith he shined to the world, was also eminent for his doctrine, for he wrote a Rule for Monks both excellent for discretion and eloquent in style. Of whose life and conversation if any wish to know further, he may in the institution of that Rule understand all his manner of life and discipline, for the holy man could not possibly teach otherwise than he lived.

Chapter XXXVII.

How he prophetically foretold his death to his brethren.

The same year in which he departed out of this life, he foretold the day of his most holy death to some of his disciples who conversed with him, and to others who were far off; giving strict charge to those who were present to keep in silence what they had heard, and declaring to the absent by what sign they should know when his soul departed out of his body. Six days before his departure he caused his grave to be opened, and immediately after he fell into a fever, by the violence whereof his strength began to wax faint, and the infirmity daily increasing, the sixth day he caused his disciples to carry him into the Oratory, where he did arm himself for his going forth by receiving the Body and Blood of the Lord; then, supporting his weak limbs by the hands of his disciples, he stood up, his hands lifted towards Heaven, and with words of prayer at last breathed forth his soul. The same day two of his Brethren, the one living in the Monastery and the other in a place far remote, had a revelation in one and the self-same manner. For they beheld a way, spread with garments and shining with innumerable lamps, stretching directly eastwards from his cell up to Heaven; a man of venerable aspect stood above and asked them whose way that was. But they professing they knew not, he said to them: "This is the way by which the beloved of the Lord, Benedict, ascended." Thus the disciples who were present knew of the death of the holy man, and so also those who were absent understood it by the sign foretold them. He was buried in the Oratory of St. John the Baptist which he himself had built upon the ruins of Apollo's altar.

Chapter XXXVIII.

How a mad woman was cured in his cave.

In the cave also in which he formerly lived in Subiaco, even to this day, miracles are wrought upon such as repair thither with true faith. For very lately happened that which I now relate. A certain woman bereft of reason, and altogether distracted in her senses, roamed over mountains and valleys, through woods and fields by day and night, never resting, except when forced from weariness to lie down. One day, as she raged thus madly up and down, she lighted upon the cave of blessed Benedict, and by chance entered and remained there. The next morning she came out as sound and perfect in her senses as if she had never been out of them, and from that time remained all her life in the health which she had there recovered.

PETER.

What should be the reason that we experience, even in the patronage of martyrs, that they do not bestow so great favours by their bodies as by their relics: yea, and do greater miracles where themselves be not?

GREGORY.

Where the bodies of holy martyrs lie, no doubt, Peter, but there they are able to shew many miracles, as they do; for to such as have recourse unto them, with pure mind, they shew many marvellous favours. But forasmuch as weak souls might doubt whether they be present to hear them or no in those places where their bodies be not, it is necessary to shew more miracles where weak souls may doubt of their presence. For they whose minds are fixed in God have so much the greater merit of faith, that though their bodies lie not there, yet they be there present to hear our prayers. Wherefore Truth Itself to increase the faith of His disciples said: "If I go not away the Paraclete will not come unto you." For whereas it is certain, that the Holy Ghost, the Comforter, always proceedeth from the Father and the Son: why doth the Son say that He will go from them that the Paraclete may come, who never departeth from the Son? But because the Disciples beholding our Lord in the flesh, did desire always to behold Him with their corporeal eyes, it was rightly said unto them: "Unless I go away the Paraclete will not come." As if He had said plainly: If I withdraw not My bodily presence, I do not shew you the love of the Spirit: and, unless you cease to see Me carnally, you will never learn to love spiritually.

PETER.
What you say pleaseth me.

GREGORY.
Let us now for a while cease our discourse, that by silence we may be the better enabled to prosecute the miracles of other saints.

END of Gregory's treatise.

CONCLUSION.

St. Benedict, the great patriarch of the Western monks, died March 21, 543, on the Saturday preceding Passion Sunday. His edifying and victorious death, was indeed suited to so great a champion of Christ. In his last hour, he assumed a standing position, and thus manifested the power and authority his soul had attained over his body; even to the last moment, while a burning fever was consuming his life and strength, he held himself erect. He died in the church, in that sanctified place, where daily with his brethren he had sung the praises of the Triune God and assisted in the celebration of the Sacred Mystery, the life-giving sacrifice of the Mass. Even to this day, his sacred remains are resting beside those of his sister Scholastica, in the church of St. John the Baptist, at Monte Cassino.

In course of years, numberless miracles have glorified his tomb. Gregory the Great mentions that at his time, miracles were wrought through the intercession of St. Benedict, whenever the petitioner was penetrated with lively faith.

The Rule of St. Benedict.

St. Gregory says, "Not only on account of his numerous miracles, was St. Benedict a shining light to the world, but also by reason of his precepts and his teachings. He wrote a rule for monks which is distinguished for its wonderful discretion and clearness of thought."

In this rule, the Saint laid down laws and precepts necessary for conventual life. In seventy-three chapters he regulates the entire monastic life, by combining the principles of the Gospel into a clear, concise rule for the life in a monastery. It is true that many holy men, as Basilius, Pachomius and the Irish Abbot Columban, had written monastic rules previous to this, but these were soon replaced by the rule of St. Benedict, and within a hundred years, it was introduced into nearly all the convents of Europe. When at the Council of Aachen, in 817, this rule was exclusively elevated as the code of laws for the monastic life, it became a source of blessing to the holy Church, throughout the Middle Ages, and up to the time of the suppression of monasteries. In the meantime it was faithfully and punctually observed in about 37,000 convents, and became a powerful factor in laying the foundation and fostering civilization and morality, science and art, among the people of Europe.

It had been assumed of old, and popes and councils had clearly expressed, that the holy rule was written through the enlightenment of the Holy Ghost. For this reason it is so perfect and complete, that it remained unaltered during fourteen centuries, and no one had ever thought of changing or improving it. In the general and essential precepts for the monastic life, for example, the teachings regarding obedience, silence, charity, poverty, etc., this rule was the standard not only for the Order of St. Benedict, but for the monastic and religious life in general, and for all later forms and branches thereof.

As St. Gregory mentions, the holy rule is characterized by prudent regulation, and by a wonderful discretion, the mother of all virtues, and therefore, we behold a truly admirable combination of severity and mildness, of prudence and love. St. Fulgentius says that the rule of St. Benedict contains everything that is required, and is lacking in nothing; the followers thereof will attain to eternal glory.

The truth of this statement is confirmed by the fourteen centuries of its existence, and by the thousands of saints it has produced. The Benedictine Order numbers about 60,000 saints recognized by the Church, all of whom are indebted to the holy rule for their place upon its altars.

St. Benedict's Glory in Heaven.

At the time when St. Benedict entered the realms of eternal bliss, it was not yet customary for the Church to make investigations into the lives of those who had died in the odor of sanctity, for the purpose of bringing about their canonization. It was sufficient whenever the voice of the people and clergy agreed with that of the bishop. This was the case with the servant of God, St. Benedict. Already during his life he was universally believed to be a saint, and his sanctity and miracles proved this beyond all doubt. After his death no one doubted for a moment that he was permitted to take possession of the glory of heaven, as a recompense for his exceedingly meritorious life. God himself confirmed this pious belief in his sanctity, by the miracles which glorified his tomb and by granting the numerous petitions of those who invoked him. Popes and learned men vied with one another in praising and exalting the glories of the Saint. The greatest reward of heaven is the vision of God, and this constitutes the actual and essential bliss, which is imparted to a soul according to the degree of grace it has merited. Let us consider the abundance of graces that St. Benedict possessed even as a youth, and how by faithful cooperation he constantly increased therein to the end of his life. How glorious must his soul now be and how near God's throne! He was also endowed with the special prerogatives and adornments of the virgins, martyrs, and doctors of the Church; for he distinguished himself in virginal purity, was a martyr of love by unceasingly crucifying his flesh and performing frequent and fervent acts of love, he was a teacher and father to millions by word and example.

The immense number of his followers, who, under his leadership, attained to eternal life and now surround him at the throne of God, are to him a source of most extraordinary joy and glory. St. Gertrude, one of the most renowned of his spiritual daughters, once on the feast of St. Benedict saw this, her glorious Father, before the throne of the Blessed Trinity all radiant and resplendent. His garments were brilliant, his countenance full of majesty and beauty, while magnificent roses seemed to spring forth from all the members of his body. From each of these roses there sprouted forth another, and from this again another, the last of which always surpassed the others in beauty and fragrance. The holy Father, thus adorned, was a wonderful spectacle of bliss and joy, to the adorable Trinity and the whole heavenly host. From this vision, St. Gertrude understood that the roses signified the pious exercises whereby he subjected his flesh to the spirit, and all the holy actions which he himself had performed during his life, as also the acts of virtue of those who through his example and teaching were induced to renounce the world, and following him on the royal road of monastic discipline, had already entered, or would still enter the heavenly kingdom. Each of these is a particular glory to this great Patriarch, and while the entire heavenly host rejoices at his glory and happiness, they praise God for it unceasingly.

The love and confidence with which the faithful at Subiaco and Monte Cassino were devoted to St. Benedict increased still more after his death. The resting-place of his sacred remains were frequently visited by great numbers. They prayed to him in their homes and everywhere, with the confidence that his power had not been lessened in heaven, and that his love would be as active and charitable as during life. Thus within a very short time the veneration of the Saint had spread throughout Italy, and later on with the extension of his order, over the entire West. Two hundred years later in every village and city of Europe, his name was honored and his intercession invoked; and every country had erected monasteries in his honor. Princes and people, clergy and laity, the learned and the ignorant, all were intent on honoring him.

St. Benedict has ever been considered patron of a happy death, and a most powerful intercessor at the last hour. His own death was most happy and precious. Standing praying before the Most Blessed Sacrament he died like a champion, conquering flesh and hell. St. Benedict appeared once to St. Gertrude saying, "Whosoever reminds me of the extraordinary prerogative with which the Lord deigned to glorify my death, shall be assisted by me at his death, and I will be his faithful protector against the assaults of the wicked enemy. Fortified by my presence, he will escape the snares of the evil one, and safely attain to eternal glory." This accounts for the confidence which animates the faithful in those countries where St. Benedict is specially venerated, that he would give them some sign of their approaching death and induce them to prepare themselves.

Promises

made to the holy Father regarding the destiny of his Order, and that of its friends and enemies.*

1. His Order will continue to exist to the end of the world.

2. It will, at the end of the world in the final battle, render great services to the holy Church and confirm many in the faith.

3. No one shall die in the Order, whose salvation would not be assured. And if a monk begins to lead a bad life and does not amend, he will fall into disgrace, or be expelled from the Order, or will leave it of his own accord.

4. Everyone who persecutes his Order, and does not repent, will see his days shortened, or meet with an unfortunate end.

5. All, however, who love his Order, will obtain a happy death.

---

* See Arnoldus Visiones: Lignum vitae, Rome 1595.

Hymn to St. Benedict

Father of many children! in the gloom
  Of the long past, how beautiful thou art!
And still, dear Saint! the weary nations come
  To drink from out thine unexhausted heart.

There are sweet waters in thy fountains still,
  In every changeful age they have been flowing;
While faithful sons thy destinies fulfil
  Through the wide world, like rivers in their going.

Kings with thy wisdom in their hearts, dear Saint!
  Have grown more royal 'neath thy Christlike rule;
And when the earth with ignorance was faint,
  Learning found shelter in thy tranquil school.

Deserts have blossomed where thy feet have trod;
  Thy homes have been safe shelters for the weary;
And in dark times the glory of our God
  Fled to thy houses to find sanctuary.

O Benedict! thy special gifts are peace,
  Freedom of heart and sweet simplicity;
They fail not with the ages, but increase,
  As thine own graces grew of old in thee.

Give us great hearts, dear Father! hearts as wide
  As thine, that was far wider than the world—
Hearts by incessant labour sanctified,
  Yet with the peace of prayer within them furled.

Thou art the Christian Abraham—to thee,
  Saint of insatiate love! thy God hath given,
For thy grand faith, a sainted family,
  Countless as are the crowded stars in heaven.

Kind Shepherd ! tend us with thy pastoral love
  Across the mountains to our heavenly rest!
Father! we see thee beckoning from above—
  We come! we come! to bless thee, and be blest!

—*Faber*

APPENDIX

Novena in Honor of Father Paul of Moll*

OPENING PRAYER
To be recited each day.

O God, I adore you with all my heart. I thank you for the life and holiness of your servant, Father Paul. In imitation of your Son and filled with His gifts, he poured himself out in devotion, proclaiming the blazing charity of your ardent love for man, in your saving Gospel and wondrous works. Through his union with you in powerful intercession, grant the favor I beseech you, (*name intention*) so that your glory may be manifested and we shall praise you forever, through Christ Our Lord. Amen.

FIRST DAY

Opening prayer on this first page of novena…

For God so loved the world that he gave his only Son, so that everyone who believes in him might not perish but might have eternal life. For God did not send his Son into the world to condemn the world, but that the world might be saved through him. ~Jn 3:16-18

O love of God! Love so little known! so little loved! Who can describe the love of God for us? No, the love of all the mothers united to the love of all the angels and saints is only an atom compared to His divine love!... One may say that a drop of water is a portion of the ocean; but all of the love we can imagine cannot give us an idea of the least part of the love of God for man. ~Fr. Paul

Our Father… Hail Mary… Glory be…
Jesus, I trust in you. For love of you I forgive everyone who has ever harmed me.

---

* Novena for private devotion.

Father Paul, pray for my intention.

Closing prayer on last page of novena...

SECOND DAY

Opening prayer...

Jesus said, Whatever you ask in my name, I will do, so that the Father may be glorified in the Son. If you ask anything of me in my name, I will do it. ~Jn 14:13-14

If it were given you to see one little ray of his great love, you would never be able to say anything else but, "Love! O infinite, or beautiful love of God!"... When the most beautiful angels contemplate the sanctity of God, they sing with one voice and with the greatest astonishment, Holy! Holy! Holy! is the God of all eternity! And, at sight of that astonishing love, they cry out in the same manner three times, O infinite and eternal love of God! ~Fr. Paul

Our Father... Hail Mary... Glory be...
Jesus, I trust in you. For love of you I forgive everyone who has ever harmed me.
Father Paul, pray for my intention.

Closing prayer...

THIRD DAY

Opening prayer...

Jesus said, Ask and it will be given to you; seek and you will find; knock and the door will be opened to you. For everyone who asks, receives; and the one who seeks, finds; and to the one who knocks, the door will be opened. Which one of you would hand his son a stone when he asks for a loaf of bread, or a snake when he asks for a fish? If you then, who are wicked, know how to give good gifts to your children, how much more will your heavenly Father give good things to those who ask him. ~Mt 7:7-11

Does not a son enjoy the riches of a good father? How agreeable it is for a child to enjoy with his father his great riches! Which are the riches of God? They are His infinite perfections, and the ability to be loved by an infinite love, and to be able to love. ~Fr. Paul

Our Father… Hail Mary… Glory be…
Jesus, I trust in you. For love of you I forgive everyone who has ever harmed me.
Father Paul, pray for my intention.

Closing prayer …

FOURTH DAY

Opening prayer…

Since we have "a great priest over the house of God," let us approach with a sincere heart and in absolute trust, with our hearts sprinkled clean from an evil conscience and our bodies washed in pure water. Let us hold unwaveringly to our confession that gives us hope, for he who made the promise is trustworthy. ~Heb 10:21-23

God does not demand of you, in order to be a child of love, that you should do more than you are able to do, but all He says to you is, "My child give me your heart!" ~Fr. Paul

Our Father… Hail Mary… Glory be…
Jesus, I trust in you. For love of you I forgive everyone who has ever harmed me.
Father Paul, pray for my intention.

Closing prayer …

FIFTH DAY

Opening prayer…

A woman suffering hemorrhages for twelve years came up behind Jesus and touched the tassel on his cloak. She said to herself, "If only I can touch his cloak, I shall be cured." Jesus turned around and saw her, and said, "Courage, daughter! Your faith has saved you." And from that hour the woman was cured. ~Mt 9:20-22

I wish you ardent love for God, it is the richest and most beautiful treasure you can wish or desire. All other treasures will disappear like smoke; but the treasure of love shall remain forever in heaven. Ask God for this beautiful treasure, for it must come from him... Love surpasses incomparably, both in value and in beauty, all satisfaction... If Adam had not sinned, love would be the sole desire of man; but sins have diminished and obscured in man his desire for the love of God. We may revive that desire by prayer, by ardent and earnest prayer, by detachment, by a perfect life, and thus arrive at ardent love for God. ~Fr. Paul

Our Father... Hail Mary... Glory be...
Jesus, I trust in you. For love of you I forgive everyone who has ever harmed me.
Father Paul, pray for my intention.

Closing prayer ...

Sixth Day

Opening prayer...

Now as Jesus approached Jericho a blind man was sitting by the roadside begging, and hearing a crowd going by, he inquired what was happening. They told him, "Jesus of Nazareth is passing by." He shouted, "Jesus, Son of David, have pity on me!" The people walking in front rebuked him, telling him to be silent, but he kept calling out all the more, "Son of David, have pity on me!" Then Jesus stopped and ordered that he be brought to him; and when he came near, Jesus asked him, "What do you want me to do for you?" He replied, "Lord, please let me see." Jesus told him, "Have sight; your faith has saved you." He immediately received his sight and followed him, giving glory to God. ~Lk 18:35-43

What is the Holy Sacrament of love if not a union of the love of God with man?... We shall never understand the love that God bears towards his children of love, and how much he desires to unite himself with them by love. It is on account of this love for man that

Jesus had the will to suffer, with great patience, all outrages, contempt, and pain. ~Fr. Paul

Our Father... Hail Mary... Glory be...
Jesus, I trust in you. For love of you I forgive everyone who has ever harmed me.
Father Paul, pray for my intention.

Closing prayer ...

SEVENTH DAY

Opening prayer...

Jesus said, Suppose one of you has a friend to whom he goes at midnight and says, "Friend, lend me three loaves of bread, for a friend of mine has arrived at my house from a journey and I have nothing to offer him," and he says in reply from within, "Do not bother me; the door has already been locked and my children and I are already in bed. I cannot get up to give you anything." I tell you, if he does not get up to give him the loaves because of their friendship, he will get up to give him whatever he needs because of his persistence. ~Lk 11:5-8

Always recalled to yourself the presence of God, burning with a love greater than ocean; be convinced that he desires ceaselessly to communicate to you his love, his burning love... Before eating, sleeping, opening or closing a door, or any other action, always have the intention of doing all for the love of Jesus. In this way you will continually reap a rich harvest for heaven... God will not ask, "Have you done much?" but, "Have you worked for the love of God?" Quantity is not sufficient, it is quality that is necessary... never cease saying, 'O love! O great love! O infinite love of God!' If men knew how pleasing this is to God, they would repeat it without ceasing; several persons have become saints in this way. ~Fr. Paul

Our Father... Hail Mary... Glory be...
Jesus, I trust in you. For love of you I forgive everyone who has ever harmed me.

Father Paul, pray for my intention.

Closing prayer ...

EIGHTH DAY

Opening prayer...

As Jesus passed by he saw a man blind from birth. His disciples asked him, "Rabbi, who sinned, this man or his parents, that he was born blind?" Jesus answered, "Neither he nor his parents sinned; it is so that the works of God might be made visible through him. We have to do the works of the one who sent me while it is day. Night is coming when no one can work. While I am in the world, I am the light of the world." When he had said this, he spat on the ground and made clay with the saliva, and smeared the clay on his eyes, and said to him, "Go wash in the Pool of Siloam" (which means Sent). So he went and washed, and came back able to see." ~Jn 9:1-7

God imparts his love sometimes and peace, and sometimes also in misfortunes or sufferings; we must praise and thank God for all he does, whether it be pleasing to us or not... If it were permitted to one of the elect to live again in this world, he would submit with joy to all the sufferings that men have ever endured here below, in order to add to his merits that which he would acquire the recital of one *Ave* Maria... An act of love for God in suffering causes the astonishment of the angels; an act of love for God in suffering is formidable to the demon; an act of love for God in suffering will shine in heaven for all eternity. ~Fr. Paul

Our Father... Hail Mary... Glory be...
Jesus, I trust in you. For love of you I forgive everyone who has ever harmed me.
Father Paul, pray for my intention.

Closing prayer ...

NINTH DAY

Opening prayer...

Jesus said, Heaven and earth will pass away, but my words will not pass away. ~Lk 21:33

When you enter the church in the morning it will be like a burning furnace; fire everywhere, the fire of the love of God to welcome you. You will not see this fire, but the whole church will be full of it... O love! O infinite love of Jesus! O excess of love! When shall I be able to love Thee enough, when shall my will be inflamed with love for Thee, O boundless ocean of love? When shall all my desires be desires of love, so that I may be able to love Thee and to love nothing else but Thee and Thee alone, O my God, O infinite love? I shall seek until I shall find Thee, I shall knock until Thou shalt open for me, I shall pray until Thou shalt give me an ardent love and shalt suppress in me all other sentiments. ~Fr. Paul

Our Father... Hail Mary... Glory be...
Jesus, I trust in you. For love of you I forgive everyone who has ever harmed me.
Father Paul, pray for my intention.

Closing prayer ...

CLOSING PRAYER
To be recited each day.

Lord, I thank you for all the graces received through the intercession of Father Paul by this novena. You are the Almighty Lord, who knows all things and who "does whatever he wills, in heaven, on earth, in the seas" (Ps 135:6). I trust in your care, ever solicitous and full of loving-kindness, and so I commend my petition and myself to you, body, soul, and spirit, without reserve and with boundless confidence, to do with as you will. Amen.

ROSARY OF THE SEVEN SORROWS OF THE BLESSED VIRGIN MARY

This Chaplet consists of seven divisions, in memory of our Lady's seven sorrows, on which we are to meditate, saying the *Pater noster* once and the *Ave Maria* seven times at each of the seven sorrows, then ending with *Ave* thrice in honour of our Lady's tears.

Act of Contrition.

O MY LORD, Thou who alone art most worthy of my love, behold me standing-before thy Divine Presence utterly overwhelmed by the thought of the many grievous injuries I have done Thee. I ask thy pardon for them with my whole heart, repenting of them purely for love of Thee, and at the thought of thy great goodness hating and loathing them above every evil of this life. As I would rather have died a thousand times than have offended Thee, so now I am most firmly resolved to die a thousand deaths rather than offend Thee again. My crucified Jesus, I firmly purpose to cleanse my soul as soon as possible by thy most Precious Blood in the Sacrament of Penance. And thou, most tender Virgin, Mother of mercy and Refuge of sinners, do thou obtain for me by virtue of thy bitter pains, the pardon of sin which I desire; whilst, praying according to the mind of so many holy Pontiffs in order to obtain the Indulgences granted to this the holy Rosary, I hope thereby to obtain remission of all pains due to my sins.

With this confidence in my heart, I meditate on the **First Sorrow**, when Mary, Virgin Mother of my God, presented Jesus her only Son in the Temple, laid Him in the arms of holy and aged Simeon, and heard his prophetic word, "The sword of grief shall pierce thy soul," foretelling thereby the Passion and Death of her Son Jesus. *Pater* once, *Ave* seven times.

The **Second Sorrow** of the Blessed Virgin was when she was obliged to fly into Egypt by reason of the persecution of cruel Herod, who impiously sought to slay her well beloved Son. *Pater* once, *Ave* seven times.

The **Third Sorrow** of the Blessed Virgin was when, after having gone up to Jerusalem at the Paschal Feast with Joseph her spouse and Jesus her beloved Son, she lost Him on the way back to her poor house, and for three days bewailed the loss of her only Love. *Pater* once, *Ave* seven times.

The **Fourth Sorrow** of the Blessed Virgin was when she met her dear Son JESUS carrying to Mount Calvary on his tender shoulders the heavy Cross whereon He was to be crucified for our salvation. *Pater* once, *Ave* seven times.

The **Fifth Sorrow** of the Blessed Virgin was when she saw her Son Jesus raised upon the hard tree of the Cross, and blood flowing from every part of his sacred Body, and then beheld Him die after three hours' agony. *Pater* once, *Ave* seven times.

The **Sixth Sorrow** of the Blessed Virgin was when she saw the lance pierce the sacred Side of Jesus, her beloved Son, the nails withdrawn, and his holy Body laid in her purest bosom. *Pater* once, *Ave* seven times.

The **Seventh** and last Sorrow of the Blessed Virgin, Queen and Advocate of us, her servants, miserable sinners, was when she saw the hply Body of her Son buried in the grave. *Pater* once, *Ave* seven times.

Then say *Ave* thrice in veneration of the tears which Mary shed in her sorrows, to obtain thereby true sorrow for sins and the holy Indulgences attached to this pious exercise.

V. Pray for us, Virgin most sorrowful.

R. That we may be made worthy of the promises of Christ.

Let us pray.

GRANT, we beseech Thee, O Lord Jesus Christ, that the most blessed Virgin Mary, thy Mother, may intercede for us before the throne of thy mercy, now and at the hour of our death, whose most holy soul was transfixed with the sword of sorrow in the hour of thine own Passion. Through Thee, Jesus Christ, Saviour of the world, who livest and reignest, etc. Amen.

Rosary in Honor of the Nine Choirs of Angels*

V. O God, come to my assistance.
R. O Lord, make haste to help me.
Glory be to the Father, etc.

First Salutation. *Pater* once, *Ave* thrice, to the First Angelic Choir. At the intercession of St Michael and the heavenly choir of the Seraphim, may it please God to make us worthy to receive into our hearts the fire of his perfect charity. Amen.

Second Salutation. *Pater* once, *Ave* thrice, to the Second Angelic Choir.

At the intercession of St Michael and the heavenly choir of the Cherubim, may God grant us grace to abandon the ways of sin, and follow the path of Christian perfection. Amen.

Third Salutation. *Pater* once, *Ave* thrice, to the Third Angelic Choir.

At the intercession of St Michael and the sacred choir of the Thrones, may it please God to infuse into our hearts a true and earnest spirit of humility. Amen.

Fourth Salutation. *Pater* once, *Ave* thrice, to the Fourth Angelic Choir.

At the intercession of St Michael and the heavenly choir of the Dominations, may it please God to grant us grace to have dominion over our senses, and to correct our depraved passions. Amen.

Fifth Salutation. *Pater* once, *Ave* thrice, to the Fifth Angelic Choir. At the intercession of St Michael and the heavenly choir of the Powers, may God vouchsafe to keep our souls from the wiles and temptations of the devil. Amen.

Sixth Salutation. *Pater* once, *Ave* thrice, to the Sixth Angelic Choir. At the intercession of St Michael and the choir of the admirable celestial Virtues, may our Lord keep us from falling into temptations and deliver us from evil. Amen.

---

* The rosary referred to was likely this one also known as the Chaplet of St. Michael.

Seventh Salutation. *Pater* once, *Ave* thrice, to the Seventh Angelic Choir.

At the intercession of St Michael and the heavenly choir of the Principalities, may it please God to fill our souls with the spirit of true and hearty obedience. Amen.

Eighth Salutation. *Pater* once, *Ave* thrice, to the Eighth Angelic Choir.

At the intercession of St Michael and the heavenly choir of Archangels, may it please God to grant us the gift of perseverance in the faith and in all good works, that we may thereby be enabled to attain unto the glory of Paradise. Amen,

Ninth Salutation. *Pater* once, *Ave* thrice, to the Ninth Angelic Choir.

At the intercession of St Michael and the heavenly choir of Angels, may God vouchsafe to grant that the Holy Angels may protect us during life, and after death may lead us into the everlasting glory of heaven. Amen.

Then say *Pater noster* four times in conclusion, the first to St Michael, the second to St Gabriel, the third to St Raphael, the fourth to our Angel Guardian. Then end with the following Antiphon:

Michael, glorious Prince, chief and champion of the heavenly host, guardian of the souls of men, conqueror of the rebel angels, who art set over the palace of God, our worthy captain under Jesus Christ, endowed with superhuman excellence and virtue; vouchsafe to free us from every evil, who with full confidence have recourse to thee; and by thy powerful protection enable us to make progress every day in the faithful service of our God.

V. Pray for us, most blessed Michael, Prince of the Church of Jesus Christ.

R. That we may be made worthy of his promises.

Let us pray.

Almighty and eternal God, who in thy own marvellous goodness and pity didst, for the common salvation of man, choose the glorious Archangel Michael to be the Prince of thy Church; make us worthy, we pray Thee, to be delivered by his beneficent protection from all our enemies, that at the hour of our death no one of them may approach to harm us, and that by the same Archangel Michael we may be introduced into the presence of thy high and heavenly Majesty. Through the merits of Jesus Christ our Lord, Amen.

THE BLUE SCAPULAR AND THE HOLY SOULS IN PURGATORY

The 433 Plenary Indulgences

"And let it be particularly made known that, besides many particular indulgences, there are annexed to the scapular of the Immaculate Conception, which is blessed by the Theatine Fathers, all the indulgences which are granted to any religious order, pious place, or person. And particularly by reciting *Our Father, Hail Mary,* and *Glory be to the Father,* six times, in honor of the most holy Trinity, and of the Immaculate Mary, are gained each time all the indulgences of Rome, Portiuncula, Jerusalem, Galicia, which reach the number of four hundred and thirty-three plenary indulgences, besides the temporal, which are innumerable."

~ St. Alphonsus Maria de Liguori, *The Glories of Mary*

A Wonderworker in the Nineteenth Century

Written by Marquis A. de Segur.*

"Truth on this side of the Pyrenees, error on the other," remarked Pascal, and never did he speak more truthfully. Famous on one side of the Belgian frontier, unknown on the other—such too is the language I would use, when speaking of a poor monk, whose renown has filled all Flanders, and who had become known to me through the present reverent tribute to his memory.

Never before had I heard of the Rev. Father Paul, a Benedictine of the abbey of Termonde, founder of the monastery of Steenbrugge and restorer of the abbey of Afflighem, who in 1896 crowned by a saintly death a long life, adorned with heroic virtues and works, as authentic as they are extraordinary.

Everything in this book is new, original, sometimes eccentric, and is naught else than a collection of edifying anecdotes, marvelous works, wholesome advice, which at times are astounding and always soul-inspiring. It is an unpretentious book devoid of ornament, claiming no apparent plan or order; yet it exhales an odor of truth, a profound faith, an unfeigned sanctity, and a simplicity that often provokes a smile or calls forth a tear. It is in a word, a publication of a class rarely seen, a class which we should like to have better represented and more and more extensively circulated in the reading world.

I Made Inquiries.

Before discussing the merits of the work, I wished to be in a position to satisfy myself and to assure my readers of its authenticity. To this end I made inquiries through the venerable pastor of Lorraine, a subscriber to "L'Univers," as to the position of the author, the names of the witnesses, and also of those who were cured.

---

* This account of the Author's first edition of "Father Paul of Moll," which was published in 1898, appeared in the *L'Univers* of Paris, March 20, 1899.

The letters and the information I received from France and Belgium leave no doubt as to the trustworthiness of the author and the truthfulness of this book. It is without hesitation and with much pleasure I exert my efforts to increase the circulation of an edifying book, and also to give forcible expression to my admiration of a contemporary monk, who in this second half of the nineteenth century, has revived some characteristics in the history of a St. Francis of Assisi, a St. Vincent de Paul, and a Curé of Ars.

From the very first lines of this brief and interesting biography of Father Paul, which form the preface of the book, appear its originality, its characteristic simplicity, and the author's familiarity with the facts he relates. So truly descriptive is it, that it would seem as if the model, who posed before the author for twenty years, had imbued him with his childlike and lovable spirit.

The Childhood of Father Paul.

Father Paul was born at Moll, in the province of Antwerp, January 15, 1824. Before entering the religious life he was known as Francis Luyckx. He began his primary studies under the tutorship of a master, unique in his method of imparting instruction.

As the greater part of the pupils lived at a distance from the school, during the pleasant days in spring and summer this kind-hearted teacher met his scholars half ways, in a meadow surrounded by mighty shade trees. The joyous and grateful pupils were well content with nature's green sod for benches, and the branches of the luxuriant oak for a roof. Here, amid the gentle rustling of the leaves and the sweet music of the birds' song, they attentively listened to their beloved master's words.

They loved their lessons, which were consequently well learned and tenaciously retained. Happy the inspiration of the devoted master in thus harmoniously combining instruction with the beauties of nature's God, as manifested in the pure, fresh air, the clear, blue sky, and the fragrant perfume of the meadow's newly cultivated soil—a class room admirably suited to inspire youthful minds with heavenly knowledge and saintly maxims.

Doubtless the cherished oaks of Moll, beneath whose shade the future Apostle of Flanders so often studied and meditated, must be akin to those grand, old oaks beneath which St. Vincent de Paul watched and guarded his father's flocks.

Francis made his classical studies at the college in Ghent, situated about four miles from his native village. A change has come over the scene. The teacher no longer meets him half way; but he is obliged to walk a long distance, rehearsing his lessons as he journeys along a road where rich nature proclaims the glory of God as revealed in His works.

Enters the Benedictine Monastery.

Although religiously inclined, and never for a moment abandoning his desire to embrace the monastic life, yet it was only in his twenty-fourth year that he became an inmate of the abbey at Termonde. Having finished his novitiate September 30, 1849, he pronounced his vows of chastity, poverty, and obedience, which made him a monk, but not a priest. Ten years of study, prayer, and self-sacrifice were required before he attained this sublime dignity, and so it was not until he had completed his two years post-graduate course of Theology at the celebrated Benedictine College in Parma, Italy, that, November 21, 1858, he offered with angelic piety the adorable Sacrifice for the first time. He had therefore attained his thirty-fourth year when he entered upon his priestly and apostolic career—a life of prayer, sacrifice and miracles, which he pursued without interruption for nigh forty years.

Receives Extraordinary Power.

The circumstances which attended the conferring of the extraordinary power of a wonderworker upon him, are thus described by Father Paul himself: —

"At the commencement of my religious career, I was so critically ill that my life was despaired of. Our Lord appeared to me, accompanied by the Blessed Virgin, St. Joseph, and St. Benedict. While Mary held my hand, our Savior placed His hand upon my head and said to me, 'Be cured. Henceforth thou shalt live for the consolation of a great number of persons; I grant thee all that thou shalt demand of Me for others.' Suddenly I was cured."

From this mission so divinely entrusted to Father Paul proceeded his familiar simplicity, his impersonal attitude, his seeming unconsciousness of the miracles he wrought, considering himself rather a witness, than a chosen instrument in the hands of God.

To the same cause may likewise be attributed the use of haughty terms, especially when he answered unbelievers, and which sounded so incompatible with his profound humility. Thus he would say, "This will be accomplished because *I* tell you so," that *I* signifying *God through me*. Just as the Curé of Ars ascribed his miracles to St. Philomena, so did Father Paul frequently screen himself behind St. Benedict.

Be this as it may, one thing is certain—our Benedictine Monk took the Lord at His word, and began without delay his wonder-working mission.

His Fame Heralded Through Flanders.

After his return to the abbey of Termonde, which became the central scene of his activity, and whence his fame was heralded throughout Flanders and Belgium, the people of those Catholic regions were deeply impressed with his sanctity which daily increased until his death. So successfully did Father Paul, in his humility, conceal the marvelous power which he possessed, and which he so unremittingly exercised, from his brother monks, that although they could not fail to perceive his popularity from the crowds that had recourse to him, yet they were ignorant of the cause of his attractive influence.

It is estimated that a million persons had recourse to him, the majority of whom were benefited by him spiritually or temporally; and hence his history is but a recital of the wondrous works he performed. It would seem as if the superhuman power imparted to Father Paul depended solely upon his own discretion, so generously did he distribute favors along his path of life.

A witness of his works remarked: "Truly did it appear that he wrought miracles by habit, and as a matter of pastime. None can come in contact with him and not feel better in themselves, and better disposed toward others."

The city of Antwerp, which he frequented, fondly cherishes the memory of his benevolence and amiability. Hundreds of visitors, anxious to see him, lined the street conducting to the house. Sadness, unrest, and discouragement were depicted upon their countenances. But as they came forth, their faces radiant with happiness, bespoke the fullness of joy that pervaded their hearts.

Helps in Manifold Needs.

Manifold, various and singular were the needs exposed, the counsels sought, and the blessings which radiated from Father Paul, even as the light and heat that come forth from the sun. Those enrolled for military service were guided by him in the selection of a fortunate number; the young consulted him in their choice of a vocation; those about to enter the married state sought his advice and implored his prayers; and weighty was the burden of human misery, suffering and affliction, that appealed to his sympathetic heart. And in all cases, Father Paul proved himself the far-sighted prophet, the wise counselor, the powerful intercessor and the generous distributor of spiritual and temporal gifts and favors.

Kindness, compassion, and tenderness were the peculiarly attractive characteristics of Father Paul; he made himself all to all: he wept, he smiled, he was even jovial at times, in the exercise of his extraordinary power. Even as St. Ignatius restored life to a chicken in order to console a little farm girl, so likewise did Father Paul cure beasts as well as men. Thus at one time it was a sick horse, a workman's sole wealth; again a dying calf would jump up, and frolic about, much to the amusement and mirth of the children of the farm.

When necessary he knew well how to season kindness with rebuke, and to administer a severe but salutary lesson; and opportunely he refused his help to scoffers, to the unworthy, and the unrepentant.

Such are the tone, circumstances, and variety of the wonderful examples cited, that God's action always appears joined with the charity of the man. Wonder follows wonder with such interesting diversity throughout his strange life, that the book never becomes irksome or monotonous to the reader.

This man of God fearlessly opposed the counsel of physicians, or the calculations of parents who objected to a large offspring, and he procured for many a mother the blessing of God through her children.

His Penitential Austerities.

The facts we have related are certainly sufficient to justify Father Paul's reputation as a wonderworker. I will now refer briefly to his penitential austerities.

"A man's value is his prayers, and the value of his prayers, is that of his self-denial"—such is the standard set up by St. Vincent de Paul.

A mere glance at Father Paul's biography impresses us with severity of the mortifications he so rigorously practiced. So little time was allotted to rest, that he was ready at any hour of the night to respond to calls for his assistance. His bed was of the poorest, with but a board for a pillow. He not infrequently slept in a standing position with his back leaning against the wall. He carried his mortifications to such an extent, as to wear around his loins an iron chain with a hundred protruding, piercing points. God rewarded his self-inflicted sufferings, as He did those of St. Francis of Assisi, by the generous bestowal of many graces.

As Father Paul had lived, so did he die. His saintly death occurred at the abbey of Termonde, Monday, Febuary 24, 1896.

The funeral solemnities took place in the abbatial church, whither thronged a large concourse of people to testify their veneration for Father Paul. His mortal remains repose in the cemetery of Termonde; his tomb is no less fruitful of wondrous works than his life.

This son of St. Benedict still continues his mission of comforting, consoling, and healing, in the name of our Lord Jesus Christ.

To me has been given the assurance, that if I make know his life I shall participate in his benefits. God grant this promise may be realized.

Father Paul Of Moll
Termonde, Feb. 24, 1896

Recommendations For This Book

Approval of Ecclesiastical Authority.

The author sent copies of his book both to Pope Leo XIII., of happy memory, and to Pope Pius X., and received the following answers.

From Pope Leo XIII.

Dear Sir:

With your letter of october 17th, I received the book which you sent to the Holy Father, to whom I presented it without delay. His Holiness bids me inform you of the pleasure which your work has afforded him, and that he gratefully accepts the sentiments you have expressed.

I am also pleased to assure you that his holiness has deigned to send you a particular blessing.

I am, with sentiments of the most sincere esteem,

Yours etc.

Cardinal Rampolla

Rome, Nov. 1, 1901
Mr. Edward Van Speybrouck, Bruges.

Pope Pius X.

The Vatican, Sept. 28, 1903.

Dear Sir:

I have the pleasure of informing you that His Holiness has deigned to receive with fatherly kindness the expression of your devotedness. The copy of your work, "Father Paul of Moll," which you presented, was also received, and, in return, His Holiness grants you a very special blessing.

Accept, dear Sir, the expression of my esteem.

Jean Bressan,
Chaplain and Secretary to His Holiness.

Feast of St. Paul, 1898.

Father Schurmans, Superior of the Jesuit House in Bruges, thanks Mr. Edward Van Speybrouck for sending his book, "Father Paul of Moll." It is replete with examples of wonderful cures, and with edifying quotations. He hopes the book may be productive of much good.

Brussels, July 4, 1898.

Mr. Edward Van Speybrouck.

The Queen has received the copy of your booklet treating of the late renowned wonderworker, Father Paul, the Benedictine. Her majesty graciously desires me to convey to you her thanks for the presentation of your work.

Receive, dear Sir, the assurance of my great regard.

Bon Goffinet.

Baltimore, July 25, 1898.

Mr. Edward Van Speybrouck.

My dear Sir:

I am in receipt of your letter and book-sketch of the late Very Rev. Father Paul of Moll, O.S.B. It is a most interesting little work and a credit to its author. The more I read of it, the more I am delighted with its contents. Please accept my sincere thanks for same, and for the pleasure it has given me. I think a true translation of this little volume into English would be very acceptable, and command a great sale.

Most respectfully yours,
Brother Alexius, *Provincial.*

Jerusalem, Aug. 16, 1898.

Mr. Edward Van Speybrouck.

I am thankful for the interesting book you have written about the Rev. Father Paul of Moll. I shall not fail to recommend the reading of the same.

✠ F. Ladovic Piavi,
Patriarch of Jerusalem.

Beuron, Dec. 14, 1898.

Mr. Edward Van Speybrouck.

Upon his return from Italy, the Right Rev. Archabbot was much pleased to find your very interesting booklet. He has requested me to express his thanks. As Abbot of Maredsous, he had the happiness of being personally acquainted with the venerated Father Paul.

Please accept, dear Sir, the assurance of my high esteem.

P. Fidelis Von Stotzingen, O.S.B.

Maria-Laach, april 18, 1899.

Mr. Edward Van Speybrouck.

Our Right Rev. Abbot bids me thank you very much for your beautiful book, which he received some time ago. Please accept, dear Sir, his sentiments of respect and gratitude.

Your humble servant in J. C.

P. John Blessing, O.S.B.

Moulins, Oct. 15, 1901.

Mr. Edward Van Speybrouck.

I hasten to thank you for the presentation of your work concerning the renowned Father Paul of Moll. After reading in "L'Univers" the article of the Marquis de Segur, concerning the saintly religious Father Paul, I procured a copy of the first edition of his life, and I read it with a lively interest. I have re-read with still greater satisfaction the copy of the last edition, which you kindly sent me. Many readers in our poor country would derive much advantage from perusing it. I am, with many thanks,

Respectfully,

✠ Augustine,
Bishop of Moulins.

✠ Cardinal Richard, *Archbishop Of Paris,*
has received the work of Mr. Edward Van Speybrouck, and expresses his best thanks.

October 17, 1901.

The Bishop Of Orleans
thanks Mr. Edward Van Speybrouck. He has read, at least in part, the life of Father Paul of Moll, and if the facts related be well established, the author certainly presents the public with a wonderful and saintly life.

October 30, 1901.

Cracow, oct. 30, 1901.

Dear Sir:

Please receive my sincerest thanks for the beautiful and interesting work concerning Father Paul of Moll. I am, dear Sir, with profound respect,

✠ J. Cardinal Puzyna.

Cardinal Perraud, Bishop Of Autun,
Member of the French Academy.

I thank Mr. Edward Van Speybrouck for sending me his edifying account of Father Paul of Moll, and I beg him to accept the expression of my sincere devotedness.

Oct. 30, 1901.

Cardinal Matthieu.

Mr. Edward Van Speybrouck.

Many thanks for your interesting volume.

Rome, Nov. 1, 1901.

———————

Malines, June 30, 1898.

The Redemptorist Sisters thank Mr. Edward Van Speybrouck for the precious book he has sent them, and which will be read with the greatest interest and edification, as they were acquainted with that saintly religious.

———————

Roulers, July 8, 1898.

Mr. Edward Van Speybrouck.

I have received with great satisfaction the marvelous sketch of Father Paul. I hope that the account of his saintly life will be extensively circulated and thereby make better known the life of this true wonderworker. I will recommend the book to the best of my ability, for the honor of God and of the renowned Benedictine Order.

Yours in the Sacred Heart Of Jesus,
P. Hendrickx, C.SS.R.

———————

The first English translation, by the Rev. Patrick Nolan, O.S.B., of Erdinton, published 1907 by the Catholic Union, Port Louis, received from the Right Rev. Bishop of that diocese the following approbation:—

Having read the life of Rev. Paul Of Moll, O.S.B., I do not hesitate to recommend it as a most interesting and edifying work.

It is very surprising and very consoling to find that in this age of worldliness and unbelief, the miraculous gifts of the apostolic age are still to be found in the simple and pure of heart, such as the humble monk, Father Paul of Moll and the devout Catholics who had recourse to him.

✠ P. A. O'Neill, O.S.B.

July 30, 1906.

Nihil obstat   Prelum conceditur
Maucotel   Lizet, vicaire general.

Recommendation of the first American edition published by
The Benedictine Convent, Clyde, Mo.

St. Joseph, Mo., March 2, 1910.

Rev. Dear Mother:

I thank you very much for the copy you kindly sent me of the translation into English of the life of the Very Rev. Father Paul of Moll, and I earnestly recommend this interesting and edifying narrative of his saintly life.

I am, with great regard, very sincerely,

Yours in christ,

✚ M. F. Burke,

Bishop of St. Joseph.

Rite of the Blessing of the Medal of St. Benedict

The Roman Ritual, Rev. Philip Weller, Ed. (1945)

The priest who is to bless the medals of St. Benedict says:

℣. Our help is in the name of the Lord.

℟. Who made heaven and earth.

I PURGE you medals of evil by God ✠ the Father Almighty, Creator of heaven and earth and of the sea and of all that they contain. O every power of the adversary, every cohort of the devil, every attack and appearance of Satan — get thee out of these medals and fly afar! And may they become for all who will use them a help for body and soul, in the name of the Father ✠ Almighty, in the name of Jesus ✠ Christ, His Son, our Lord, in the name of the Holy ✠ Spirit, the Paraclete, and in the love of the selfsame Lord Jesus Christ, Who shall come to judge the living and the dead and the world by fire. ℟. Amen.

Lord, have mercy on us. Christ, have mercy on us. Lord, have mercy on us.

Our Father *inaudibly until*

℣. And lead us not into temptation.

℟. But deliver us from evil.

℣. Preserve thy servants.

℟. Who trust in thee, my God.

℣. Be unto us, O Lord, a tower of strength.

℟. In the face of the enemy.

℣. The Lord will grant strength to His people.

℟. The Lord will bless His people with peace.

℣. Send us, Lord, aid from on high.

℟. And from Sion watch over us.

℣. O Lord, hear my prayer.

℟. And let my cry come unto thee.

℣. The Lord be with you.

℟. And with thy spirit

Let us pray.

ALMIGHTY God, lavish Dispenser of every good, we thy suppliants pray that, by the intercession of St. Benedict, thou wouldst pour out thy ✠ blessing on these sacred medals inscribed with letters and symbols appointed by thee. Let all who will wear them with minds intent on good works deserve to obtain health of body and spirit, the grace of making progress in holiness, as well as the indulgences which have been granted (to us). And may they escape by thy merciful help every onslaught and fraud of the devil, and finally stand before thee sinless and holy. Through Christ our Lord. ℟. Amen.

Let us pray.

O LORD Jesus Christ, thou didst will, in order to redeem the entire world, to be born of a Virgin and to submit to circumcision; to be repudiated by the Jews and betrayed with a kiss by Judas; to be bound in chains, crowned with thorns, thy hands and feet pierced with nails, to be crucified between robbers, thy side pierced with a lance, and to die at last on the Cross! Through this thy sacred Passion, I humbly appeal to thee to drive afar all snares and deceits of the devil from him who devoutly calls upon thy holy name, using these words and symbols appointed by thee, and may it please thee to escort him unto the port of salvation. Who livest and reignest throughout all eternity. ℟. Amen.

May the blessing of almighty God, Father, Son, ✠ and Holy Spirit come upon these medals and all who wear them, and remain for all time. ℟. Amen.

The priest sprinkles the medal with holy water.

Plenary Indulgences for the Jubilee Medal of St. Benedict

A plenary indulgence may be gained on the following feasts of **Our Lord:—**

Christmas,	Epiphany, (Jan. 6.)
Easter,	Ascension,
Pentecost,	Trinity Sunday,

Corpus Christi.

On the following feasts of the **Blessed Virgin:—**

Immaculate Conception, (December 8.)
Nativity of the Blessed Virgin, (September 8.)
Purification, (Candlemas-Day, February 2.)
Annunciation, (March 25.)
Assumption, (August 15.)

Also a plenary indulgence on the principal feasts of our holy Order:

St. Maurus, (January 15.)
St. Scholastica, (sister of St. Benedict, Feb. 10.)
St. Benedict, (March 21.)
Dedication of the Basilica of Monte Cassino, (October 1.)
St. Placidus, (October 5.)
All Saints of our Order, (November 13.)
St. Gertrude, (November 17.)

A plenary indulgence on the feasts of **All Saints**, (November 1.)
Once a year, at choice, and at the hour of death.

For gaining all these plenary indulgences the conditions required are: the wearing of the Jubilee Medal; the usual confession and Communion, visit to a church; prayers for the Pope and for the conversion of sinners.

The "Toties Quoties" Indulgence.

A great privilege connected with the Jubilee medal by the decree of the Sacred Congregation of Indulgences, Feb. 27, 1907 deserves special mention; the *toties quoties* plenary indulgence on *All Souls' Day*, Nov. 2d.

By virtue of this decree all who habitually wear the Jubilee Medal can gain a plenary indulgence *as often as (toties quoties)* they visit any church or public oratory and pray according to the intention of the Holy Father and receive the sacraments either on All Saints' or on All Souls' Day. Where there is a Benedictine church within one mile of your own church, the visits must be made to the Benedictine church.

This great indulgence for the poor souls may be gained from twelve o'clock, noon, on All Saints' Day until twelve o'clock midnight on All Souls' Day. For thirty-six hours you may gain as many plenary indulgences as you make visits. What a wonderful help for the poor souls!

Another Privilege.

Those who devoutly wear the Medal of St. Benedict and pray for the propagation of his holy Order, share in all the good works, Masses, Communions, Divine Office, prayers, and fasts of the entire Order.

Made in the USA
Coppell, TX
03 April 2022

75966983R00215